CALIFORNIA

ON-THE-ROAD HISTORIES

CALIFORNIA

Victor Silverman
& Laurie Glover

First published in 2012 by
INTERLINK BOOKS
An imprint of
Interlink Publishing Group, Inc.
46 Crosby Street, Northampton, Massachusetts 01060
www.interlinkbooks.com

Text copyright © Victor Silverman and Laurie Glover, 2012
Design copyright © Interlink Publishing, 2012
Design: LAC Design

Library of Congress Cataloging-in-Publication Data

Silverman, Victor, 1957-
California / by Victor Silverman and Laurie Glover. -- 1st American ed.
    p. cm. -- (On-the-road histories)
Includes bibliographical references and index.
ISBN 978-1-56656-809-8 (pbk.)
1. California--History. 2. California--Social conditions. 3. California--Economic
conditions. I. Glover, Laurie. II. Title.
F861.S49 2010
979.4--dc22
                          2009050070
Printed and bound in China

Image, previous page: *Bar of a Gambling Saloon*
from Frank Maryatt, Mountains and Molehills, or
Recollections of a Burnt Journal (1855).

CONTENTS

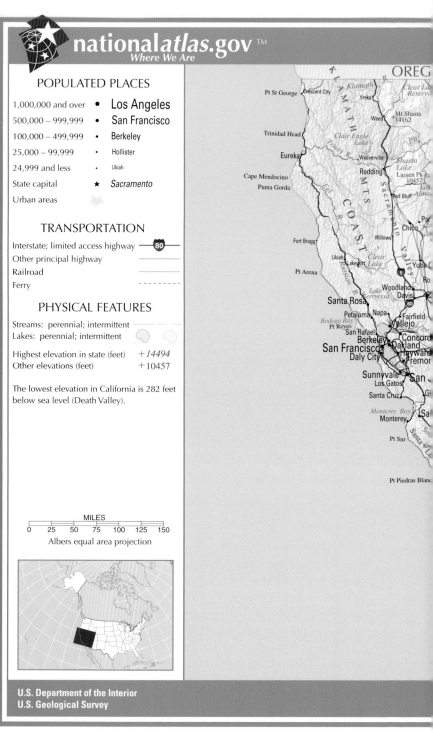

nationalatlas.gov ™
Where We Are

POPULATED PLACES

1,000,000 and over	● Los Angeles
500,000 – 999,999	● San Francisco
100,000 – 499,999	● Berkeley
25,000 – 99,999	· Hollister
24,999 and less	· Ukiah
State capital	★ Sacramento
Urban areas	

TRANSPORTATION

Interstate; limited access highway — 80 —
Other principal highway
Railroad
Ferry

PHYSICAL FEATURES

Streams: perennial; intermittent
Lakes: perennial; intermittent

Highest elevation in state (feet)   +14494
Other elevations (feet)   +10457

The lowest elevation in California is 282 feet
below sea level (Death Valley).

MILES
0   25   50   75   100   125   150
Albers equal area projection

U.S. Department of the Interior
U.S. Geological Survey

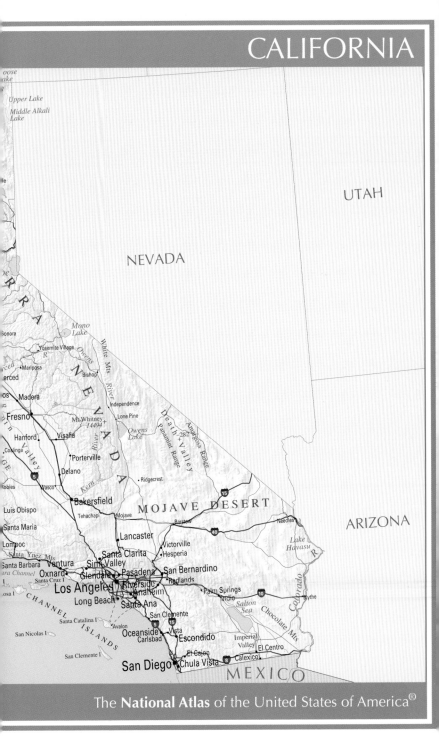

CALIFORNIA

The **National Atlas** of the United States of America®

Acknowledgments

Victor began this book some years ago, thinking it would be a quick and enjoyable project. It turned out to be fun, but hardly quick. Partway through the process, Laurie joined to help Victor tame what had grown into an unwieldy manuscript. Then we developed the idea of nodes—places throughout California where it would be easy to see and travel over some of the many overlapping stories that make up the state's past. Laurie's poetic writing style seemed the perfect way to capture the layers that make up the nodes we chose around the state. She then wrote the node essays and Victor wrote the rest.

Along the way, we have developed many debts to our colleagues, friends, and partners. Vadim Shcherbina conducted reams of research for us. Librarians at the Claremont Colleges, UC Davis, the Bancroft Library, the San Francisco Public Library, Cal Trans and many other places have been an enormous help. Interlink waited patiently for the long overdue manuscript. We hope it is as fun to read as it was to write.

Oakland and Davis, 2011

What is California?

Before 1542 there was no California. Pre-conquest California was far too big and diverse for its people to think of it as a single place. Rather, the towering mountains, vast deserts, and turbulent rivers created many unique regions and ecosystems. In the southeast, hot deserts and rocky peaks supported scattered oases and seasonal rivers. The high deserts of the northeast experienced bitter winter cold and punishing summer heat. Titanic underground forces tumbled enormous granite blocks, building the steep mountains now called the Sierra Nevada, an almost impenetrable barrier between the deserts and the lands to the west and north.

Below the Sierra Nevada lies an enormous flat valley, cut into sections by powerful rivers and dense with life. Smaller mountains farther west create a gentle Mediterranean-like region running for hundreds of miles along the coast. The coast's cool summers and mild winters give way in the north to steeper hills and rainforest canyons filled with the tallest trees in the world. The realm underneath this land is divided too: the west side of the 1,300-mile long San Andreas fault rides north on the Pacific tectonic plate while the east side heads on south with the North American Plate.

Partly because of these great differences, the peoples of the land that came to be known as California did not form any unified whole. California's natives were more varied than any group of people in a similarly sized area anywhere in the world. There were more than 500 tribal groups speaking at least 120 completely distinct languages. Even the "tribe" was a concept later imposed by the European conquerors on a foreign people. There were no "Pomo," for instance, as an organized entity, but rather simply groups of people who lived on the Central Coast and had things in common with others who lived near them. While native Californians did interact and often traded over vast distances, they had no need to imagine their land as any kind of unified area.

California came into existence through cataclysmic social, cultural, military, and political collisions that tumbled one after the other from the mid-16th to the 21st centuries. Like the enormous tectonic plates whose slow grinding against each other produced the very landscape of the place, these series of encounters, transformations, and conflicts continuously made and remade California over hundreds of years.

Those with the most power and wealth usually determined what California became, but even these Spanish, Mexican, and Anglo-American elites could not remake the state easily. The peoples of California—and the land they lived on—resisted this imposition. There was a constant clash between plans and reality, between expectation and actual experience. As the multiple conquests and remakings of California proceeded, the collision of the fantasies, dreams, and visions of its people with powerful physical, social, and economic realities created the state. California was not discovered: it was invented.

The invention of California depended on greed and ambition inspired by romantic images and imagined opportunities. Promoters of the state have manipulated these images in books, journals, advertising, news reports, and Hollywood movies to draw immigrants from every part of the globe. The imagemakers painted a land free of poverty and cold. An imagined California drew hordes of people to the gold rush, to suburban developments in the desert, and to Disneyland. California's image was everything for everyone. It was the land of easy living, of beach boys and girls, of the tanned and blond—and also an economic powerhouse with jobs for all, a Golden Gate to the Orient. It was even the land of alternative living, free from the stifling conformity of New England, the poverty of Mexico and China, the rigid hierarchies of the South, and the lousy weather of the Midwest.

But the California image has not always been positive. To some, it was a barren desert, which required enormous effort to make it lush, fruitful, and habitable. In 1542, Juan Rodríguez Cabrillo and his crew of conscripts became the first Europeans to land on the coast. Instead of seeing a country of gentle climate and plentiful resources, they believed California to be a place of desolation and danger. The Spanish named their new territory "California" after a mythical island in a popular 16th-century epic by García Ordóñez de Montalvo. In the story, violent black Amazons, ruled by the tyrannical yet beautiful Queen Calafía, inhabit the island.

Know then that to the right hand of the Indies, there was an island called California, very near the part of the terrestrial Paradise, and which was inhabited by black women, without there being among them even one man, that their style of living was almost like that of the Amazons. They were of robust bodies and valiant and ardent hearts and of great strength; the island itself was the strongest that could be found in the world through its steep and wild rocks; their arms were all of gold and also the harness of the wild beasts on which they rode after taming them, as there was no other metal in the whole island; ...

On this island, called California, there were a great many griffins... Any man who landed on the island was at once killed and eaten by them; and though they might be glutted, they would not the less take them and lift them up, flying through the air, and when tired of carrying them, they would let them fall, where they would be killed at once.

... there reigned in said Island California a Queen very tall of stature, very handsome for one of them, of blooming age, desiring in her thoughts to do great deeds, valiant in spirit, and in cunning of her fearless heart, more so than any of the others that before her reigned in that land.

—García Ordóñez de Montalvo, *The Exploits of the very valiant Knight Esplandian, son of the excellent King Amadis of Gaul* (1521)

Ordóñez de Montalvo's California is a land rich in gold, yet the Amazons use griffins, vicious beasts with the bodies of lions but the heads and wings of eagles, to defeat—and then eat—men. A white Christian knight eventually captures Calafía and forces her into marriage, but the island remains a barbaric place. The real California was hardly better, the Spanish thought. It had no gold, no wealthy native societies to exploit, no exotic Amazon queens to fight and marry. So the Spanish let it languish as a backwater of their empire. The explorer and conqueror Gaspar de Portolá reportedly told the Spanish viceroy that if the Russians wanted to steal California from Spain, they should be allowed to have it as a punishment for their sins.

Perhaps the Spanish were right: the reality of California often differed profoundly from the idyllic dream of the golden state. The first century of written California history is a story of conquest and war, of genocide and survival. Hardly a romantic story of heroic growth: the poor and the weak repeatedly paid an enormous price for the invention of California. Violent upheavals filled the first hundred years of California's written history as Mexicans, Californios, and then Americans seized the lands once held by the Spanish. By the latter part of the 19th century, however, a new set of processes took center stage in place of revolts, wars, and conquests.

Many earlier histories of the state portray a dramatic break in the narrative when the United States seized possession of California from Mexico in 1846. Indeed, the US conquest and subsequent gold rush not only changed the government but also created a revolutionary upheaval in the society and economy of the state. But the new social hierarchies and ideologies brought by the triumphant Americans were layered and mixed with the existing economies, societies, and cultures of the Californios, the Spanish, and the native peoples. The waves of immigrants and migrants over the next 150 years brought California an astounding diversity, but these changes did not upset the basic structures of power forged by the Spanish, Mexicans, and Americans.

California has always been a multicultural society, but one ruled by people who feared that complexity and sought to control the disorder it brought. This demand for order has led, most recently, to hundreds of thousands of prisoners languishing in the state's extensive jail system. Although a modern innovation, this massive state prison system directly connects to 18th- and 19th-century efforts to control a disorderly world. Anglo elites' efforts to control what they saw as savage Indians, ruthless bandits, and disorderly miners mirrored an earlier Spanish requirement that laboring Indians be servile and "of reason." Conformity to regular work habits and to domesticated sexuality was key to imposing a social hierarchy based on deep inequities of race, gender, class, and sexuality. At the same time, resistance to the ordering power of the elites created countercultures wherever they could survive. Rather than simply an odd byproduct of California's location on the far western edge of the continent, the history of California's countercultures have their roots in beleaguered people finding gaps in elite power to create their own community networks.

People sought more than the remaking of themselves and each other in the far west: they also remade the environment around them both consciously and accidentally. Nothing shows this more than the bitter history of water politics in the state. Indians adapted their lives to the seasonal water flows in the rivers and streams or to oases in the deserts. Spanish and Mexican immigrants to California similarly settled near water, dug shallow wells, and practiced less intensive agriculture, ranching, and logging. These practices sustained the local economies while the trade in Californian hides provided the Californios' main connection to the world economy. Early Anglo immigrants similarly built near sources of water. But quickly the available water seemed far too limited for the Americans. To some, from damper climates, California appeared a desert wasteland. Water wars—along with labor struggles, immigration, and fights over land ownership—rank among the most persistent political conflicts in California history. Water inspired the largest engineering projects in US history, great aqueducts and reservoirs that draw snow-fed water from the rivers of the Sierra Nevada to quench the thirst of enormous farms in the Central Valley and the orchards, suburbs, and industries of the south and west. The water projects drained enormous lakes, pumped rivers over mountains and turned desert valleys into new lakes. These elaborate manipulations of water and similarly large environmental changes in other arenas came with a price. Disasters, floods, droughts, fires, oil spills, earthquakes, smog attacks, and even tornados revealed the limits of human engineering. At the same time the natural world offered more subtle yet equally far-reaching responses: animal extinctions, the disappearance of wetlands, groundwater pollution, alien species invasions, and climate shifts. As in the remaking of the people of California, the story of remaking the landscape involves disaster and devastation, but likewise the environment has hardly been the passive recipient of transformation.

California's past as related here revolves around three interlocking themes. The first is how people interacted with the climate, land, water, and creatures around them—how they remade the face of California. The second is the interactions of and, all too often, bitter conflicts between diverse peoples in this place, people who brought to the contest vastly different resources and power. Finally, the story of California is one of expectations met and disappointed, of dreams clashing with reality. This web of stories makes the history of California both like everywhere else and yet so much its very own story.

The first people to journey to California likely came to the Channel Islands at least 12,000 years ago.

2

FIRST PEOPLES

Creation stories told by the native people of California relate that human beings have been here since they first appeared on the earth. Most of the myths explain that animals and other odder creatures lived here before people arrived. According to the Yokut in the Central Valley, the world started out as nothing but water, just an enormous lake with one stick rising above it. Crow and Hawk kept knocking each other off the stick. One thing led to another, though, and they had sex, then gave birth to the other birds. Like many married couples they kept quarrelling all the while, making mountains out of mud that their daughter, Duck, brought from the depths. Hawk didn't like Crow's decorating choices. He turned the mountains so they ran north/south, draining the water out of the great valley.

Maidu people told of a raft that floated in an infinitely dark ocean with only a turtle and a silent being named Pehe-ipe upon it. Then the Earth Initiate slid down a feather rope onto the raft, without saying a word. Turtle wanted to know to if there would be people in the world and the Earth Initiate, after thinking for a while, said "yes." The Earth Initiate had the ability to make the earth and the animals, but he didn't know when people would appear. Turtle wanted land to lie on, so the Earth Initiate made some out of the dirt under Turtle's fingernails.

The Pomo thought the planet came from armpit wax rolled into a ball by two old brothers, Kuksu and Marumda.

Things weren't always so clear. The Wintu said that "many people came into existence somewhere. They dwelt long and no one knows what they did." The panoply of native stories ranges over the whole human experience of love, betrayal, nobility, laughter, and pain. Coyote, Spider, Raven, and Salmon trick, eat, screw, and harass each other. Out of this confusion came the First People.

Although the first nations' creation legends are as compelling as those of the ancient Hebrews—and much wittier—it is just as unlikely they are true. At least, no evidence exists. There is slightly more evidence of the kind that people who write for academic journals believe supporting the migration of people from elsewhere to North America and California tens of thousands of years ago. Indeed, most Southern California Indians had stories of moving from the north, except for the Kumeyaay people of the San Diego area who remembered coming from the east. Most Indians today appear to be descended from Asians who crossed a land bridge known as Beringia, which appeared in the last Ice Age between 10 and 12,000 years ago. Small groups of families from what was then a dry Alaska followed herds of animals south, down the Great Basin, spreading out over North America. But other people may have already been on the continent—some may have sailed or floated from Australia or Polynesia, others may have paddled from Europe following an uninterrupted coastline of massive glaciers in the north Atlantic.

This confusion about who came first in the ancient past is not just ours. The old stories we have, the names of the peoples, the languages, are things we know about the people who were here when the Spanish arrived—either what they said about themselves or what they had been told about their ancestors. How those people are related to the ones who are thought to have arrived 10–12,000 years ago, we simply don't know.

Native Californians did not leave written documents. Worse, when Europeans did arrive they didn't think the Indians' past mattered much. Anthropologist Alfred L. Kroeber put it in typical early 20th-century fashion: "Nor do the careers of savages afford many incidents of sufficient intrinsic importance to make their chronicling worth while." The result is that we can only know the history of native California before the conquest through a kind of extrapolation. To allow Kroeber to chime in again, we can only "form an estimate of an ancient vanished culture through the medium of its modern and modified representative." This backward extrapolation works for the recent past, but as the years stretch backward into millennia historians can say less and less with any certainty. Bits and pieces of legends, archeological records, relics hidden within forgotten languages and elders' failing memories are all we have for the historical record. Or as Delfina Cuero, a Kumeyaay from near San Diego put it, "There is more to it, but this is all I can remember."

Relying on archeology isn't exactly certain either. Modern travelers to Calico out near Barstow may come across a site run by the Bureau of Land Management that some anthropologists for a time believed held evidence of a truly ancient human presence in California as many as 150,000 years ago—putting the sites in the same league as Eurasian and African sites. The evidence? Many, many pieces of chipped stone. The site drew anthropologist Louis B. Leakey in the 1960s to meet Ruth Simpson who for years ran the excavations. Simpson vigorously advocated the view that the stone chips were indeed tools created by people, but most other anthropologists disagreed, rejecting the idea that people came to Barstow so long ago. Why anyone would go there now is another story.

However they actually came—paddling eastward across vast waters or wandering vast distances southward—the first peoples in what would become California entered a vast rich land, subdivided by great mountains, enormous lakes, vast plains, and powerful rivers. The earliest known settlements were on the Santa Barbara Channel Islands as many as 12,000 years ago. Other early settlement sites were undoubtedly lost underwater as the end of the Ice Age caused rising sea levels. People on the islands ate mostly seafood. They made a variety of stone tools for fishing and milling, even journeying to the mainland to get tools—though if they just took them or traded for them no one knows. Inland, east of the Sierra Nevada, groups

A Cahuila woman on the San Ygnacio Reservation east of San Diego grinds acorns with a metate in the early 20th century.

Grinding rocks at Chaw'se (Grinding Rocks State Park off Hwy 88) in the Gold Country had been used for thousands of years by Miwok people to prepare acorns.

of what anthropologists have named the Clovis people followed the great Mammoths. Some wandered into desert areas of Southern California, leaving their distinctive large arrowheads behind. (Good collections can be found at the Lancaster Indian Museum.) But after mass extinctions of the Mammoths and other large animals about 10,000 years ago, the Clovis people abruptly vanished. What happened to them, no one knows.

It's hard to say which came first: the social organization that made hunting possible or the necessity of hunting that brought about social organization. At least 10,000 years ago many of the first peoples in North America probably hunted in groups of extended families with relatively little gender distinction—all who were able helped to bring down the huge animals. More recently, at least 1,300 years ago, the Chumash had the social organization to build plank canoes large enough to sail along the coast and hunt at sea. They were able to catch dolphins and other large sea mammals by cooperating with each other, which further strengthened their community.

The ancient people who hunted the large game are different than the early Chumash and the many diverse peoples who came to inhabit California in more recent millennia. We don't know how the later people got here or what their connections to the ancients are. On the one hand, the evidence for early hunting is small; we derive our understanding of these ancient people from large spear points only. On the other hand, for the later hunting practices, we have the evidence of entire boats still intact and large sea mammal bones. Inland evidence exists for a number of changes experienced by many of these groups that led to the increased division of labor. Hunting parties pursuing large game animals came to be made up of men only. Women taking care of children stayed closer to camp, gathering food or working at grinding holes, clusters of depressions in broad granite boulders.

The women used these as mortars, crushing acorns with stone pestles, then soaking the mash in four changes of water to remove the bitter tannins.

Even in times when environmental changes or overhunting reduced the numbers of large game, it may be that the hunters still pursued big game as a sign of status. These changes may have given rise to social conflict as the necessity of the food preparation done by women countered the importance of the hunting activity of the men.

When these transitions to greater divisions of labor and broader ethnic and linguistic diversity occurred, we do not know, though some theories posit connections to the vast environmental changes that accompanied climate change.

In any case, grinding hole activity occurred only in the fall. At other times, people moved to other locations near different food sources. For example, coastal people generally migrated from the mountains to the shore and back each year following ripening foods and animal herds. In the spring, Southern Californians moved to camps in the mountains near known stands of mescal agave. They spent the winter in the warmer lowlands, spear fishing in the creeks and gathering shellfish on the shore near their somewhat more permanent homes. In the fall they returned to the foothills for the ripening acorns.

The order of the natural world and the relations between people and animals appeared differently to native people than to the Europeans who conquered them. In early European views, the Indian was "wild," a part of "nature." Such ideas supported the killing or displacing or the enforced acculturation of the people considered "primitives." Later, critics of Anglo society romanticized native ways. Yet the Native Californian relationship to the natural world did not actually fit either of these constructions. They carefully managed their environment, developing such elaborate strategies as selectively harvesting grasses for their seeds or fibers and culling to encourage growth of useful plants. They didn't wander aimlessly in search of plants; they returned, deliberately, to known sites. Fire was an important tool as well, used by people in the foothills and Coast Ranges to reduce the density of shrubs and make gathering and hunting easier. At times the fires got out of control, but deer populations increased in burned-over chaparral areas and dangerous grizzlies didn't like the open country. In this sense the environment of coastal California was not wilderness at all. It gained much of its distinctive combination of grassland, chaparral, and oak from native management. But such practices were not entirely successful: mass extinctions of large animals followed humans into North America. The wooly mammoth vanished, as did the giant sloth, from climate change or perhaps human predation.

The European bifurcation between the "natural" and the "human" appears to have been absent in most indigenous cultures. Similarly, time was not linear—there was a mythic past from which humans and animals originated and a sense of a future time to come, but little of the ideas of millennial apocalypse, progress toward enlightenment, or human evolution that animated the grasping adventurers and spiritual missionar-

Tabuce (Maggie Howard) preparing acorns in 1936, probably in Yosemite Park. Tabuce, which means Nut Grass Tuber in Paiute, performed for visitors in Yosemite and was key to maintaining Paiute history and traditions for her people.

ies from Europe. Daily, seasonal, and yearly cycles, as in most non-market oriented societies, marked the passage of time. These cycles emphasized continuity and connection rather than disjunctions and transitions. Indeed, the commonly held belief that humans and animals were once able to talk with each other and even lived in the same families expressed a sense of human placement quite alien from that of later Europeans who believed humans to be superior to animals and who feared a malevolent nature.

Harvesting, hunting, and production of tools were all organized through rituals common to each region. Sand painting, practiced throughout the south, allowed people to express their vision of the earth and the heavens. Boys took jimson weed during a puberty ceremony and learned a form of the painting and dance. Girls took an herbal sauna at the same age, then dieted without salt or meat for six months. In the south, facial tattoos marked the transition to adulthood—visible and appealing marks that signaled a boy or girl was now part of the adult world. Ceremonies took many hours, often all night, with long song cycles attuned to the time and season and event. Despite regional similarities, no single set of beliefs unified indigenous Californians. Rather, each region and each group, even each community and family, understood their world in ways that fit their circumstances. Ritual, by emphasizing connection to community and family, structured life transitions.

The physical location of people figured deeply in their sense of self. Indians often named themselves and others by geography or by a foodstuff from where they lived. The Coast Yuki called themselves *Ukoht-ontilka*, Ocean people, because they lived next to the ocean. The Hoopa called themselves *Natinno-hoi,* the Trinity River people. In turn they called neighboring groups the "prairie people," or the "people from upstream." The Pitkachi tribe of the Yokuts of the Central Valley lived in stinking alkali marshes called Pitkati along the San Joaquin River near present day Fresno. Yokut itself means simply "people." The Paiute speaker at the Pyramid Lake Paiute Museum and Visitor Center will tell you that his people called themselves *Cui Ui ticutta*, "Eaters of the Cui-ui" (qwui-wui), a fish found only in the lake on which that people made their home. Gathering of *cui-ui* formed a significant part of their communal life. Similarly, Mono Lake Paiute called themselves *Kutzadika'a*, after one of their main foods, the brine fly larvae unique to the Mono basin, which were seasonally gathered, dried, and roasted.

The first Californians undoubtedly had to find ways to identify themselves because of the great ethnic diversity of the region. California was far more densely populated than other regions of the west. Hundreds of villages dotted the coastlines. The large populations meant that territory was clearly defined and village residents defended their land against encroachment and raiding by neighbors. At the same time, trade routes were extensive. The varying groups traded baskets and other handwork across the mountains and up and down the coasts; for example, Coastal Miwok entered the Central Valley to trade with Yosemite Miwok who descended from the foothills, while Shosoenan people—Paiutes—on the eastern side of the Sierra ascended the Mono Trail to Tuolumne Meadows to trade obsidian for shell beads with the Miwok.

Cahuila Indian basket weaver. Some women have preserved these traditional crafts through the present century.

While for the most part native Californians avoided the unstable systems of shifting alliances and wars of other peoples of North America, violence bordering on warfare did occur occasionally. Somewhere between 500 and 1,000 years before the Spanish arrived, Central California Indians removed and buried separately the arms of some young men. Speculation has it that the arms may have been used in ceremonies before being buried along with coyote bones. Native society in the San Francisco Bay Area during that time changed from one that was fairly egalitarian to one with hierarchies of wealth. We know, at least, that some people were buried with possessions while others were not, and material wealth has all too often inspired violence. Some anthropologists have found large numbers of puncture wounds and spear and arrowhead fragments in ancient skeletons. This sampling may be distorted; people who died in war or fighting might have been buried differently than others. Violence between the Pleistocene people in California was common enough that we can still find traces of it.

Whatever the texture of people's daily lives, the nature of their social roles, or their intergroup conflicts, all California's people shared economic, social, and cultural divisions based on gender. Yet for some cultures, these divisions were more fluid than others. The warlike Mojave, who fought people for hundreds of miles around their Colorado River settlements, had a relatively fluid gender system, though one still marked by male-female divisions. Divorce was at will by either men or women. Boys who dreamed that they were *alyha* (transgender) were changed in a ceremony into women. A smaller number of girls, called *kwami*, could without ceremony join the men in hunting or fighting and then marry a woman. Many other peoples in California allowed such transitions; for instance, the Yuki on the North Coast. In contrast, most of the hierarchical and patriarchal northwestern coastal cultures restricted women's independence far more than their neighbors inland or to the south. The Pomo on the Central Coast had one of the societies most favorable to women's independence and authority. Women owned their own property, became initiates in male secret societies, and, on occasion, chiefs. In turn, men made some types of baskets and shared other tasks. Although the Shasta people were as macho as the Yurok and Hoopa, they nonetheless included women in their war parties.

Over thousands of years, successive migrations brought diverse waves of people who kept their own languages, making California a particularly complicated place linguistically. By the time of contact with Europeans, native Californians spoke sixty-four different languages and hundreds of dialects deriving from six distinct root languages, a linguistic diversity unmatched in the world. Most of the languages in California had common roots with native tongues elsewhere on the continent. The relatively densely populated North Coast region had a jumble of languages. The peoples in the far northwest, the Sinkyone and Hoopa, for instance, share language roots with the Athabasacan-speaking peoples that extend all the way up the rugged, river-split northern Pacific Coast to the tail of Alaska and thousands of miles southeast to the canyon and desert lands of the Navajo and Apache. On the other hand, their close neighbors, the Wiyot and Yurok, spoke Algonquian languages similar to those spoken in the Midwest and northeast Atlantic regions. Just south of them, in the areas now called Sonoma and Napa, the Wappo and

The Mojave tattooed themselves elaborately and allowed men and women to take each other's roles.

Yuki spoke a language now extinct but thought to be unrelated to any other. Despite these distinctive languages, the peoples of the North Coast and valleys had extensive interactions, trading regularly and often intermarrying, yet preserving their cultures and languages in a sort of Paleolithic multiculturalism.

The Modoc people found among the lava beds of the far northeast corner of the state share cultural and social practices with other peoples of the inland northwest plateau such as the Spokane and the Nez Perce. The Paiute belong to the Shosonean-speaking peoples whose economy and society derived from living in the water-scarce Mojave basin and rangeland that stretches across Wyoming, Colorado, Nevada, and Utah. They are separated by the long rugged barrier of the transverse ranges from those who live along the Colorado River in the far southeast corner of California. Most of those people are part of a culture area that extends from Arizona and New Mexico deep into what is now Mexico.

Two broadly-defined groups lived west of the mountains: the valley peoples and the coastal peoples. The Wintun, Maidu, Nisenan, Patwin, and Yokuts in the Central Valley as well as those who lived along the delta and out through its estuaries (Ohlone and Miwok), spoke a set of related languages. Some coastal peoples from San Francisco Bay south to Baja, among them the Pomo, Salinan, and Chumash, shared a root language and culture. Yet other southern coastal people had wildly different languages but similar economic and geographically influenced

California's tribal territories at the time of European contact as drawn in 1919 by Berkeley anthropologist Alfred L. Kroeber for the Smithsonian Institution. Native people identified more with their villages and families than with these larger groups.

lives. People of these groups usually lived in thatched huts that they annually burned to fight pervasive flea infestations. They hunted game, gathered acorns, berries, or grass seeds, and dug roots, commuting between the ocean or lake shorelines and the mountains. Voracious and open-minded eaters, they consumed between 100 and 200 different kinds of plants.

Over the centuries, people moved from neighboring regions and back again, sharing cultures, trading, and sometimes fighting. About 500 years ago Numic-speaking people from around Mono Lake moved out of their desert lands to the western

The earliest known drawing of Ohlone people. Their dancing maintained important cultural connections even at Mission San José.

Sierra foothills after a series of volcanic explosions. The Yokuts, who already lived in the foothills, apparently didn't mind the immigrants—no evidence exists of conflict between the peoples. Rather, Yokuts and Mono adopted elements of each other's cultures and economies. This native diversity and adaptability played key roles in the history that unfolded after the arrival of the Europeans. Between the first contact with Europeans in the late 15th century and the creation of the mission system 200 years later, native societies underwent dramatic and painful changes. Epidemics wiped out many and whole societies disappeared. Yet the people of conquered California adapted to new realities, just as they had for millennia.

Throughout California, especially in the deserts of the northeast and southeast, petroglyphs and other ancient art are still to be seen. These are thought to be records of peoples' visions, often had after smoking jimson or tobacco. Many date back as many as 10,000 years, but others were made recently. They are physical evidence of native cultural continuity despite Spanish and Anglo domination.

Round house built in the traditional manner by Miwok people and used for ceremonies every fall at Chaw'se Grinding Rocks State Park.

Obsidian Dating

How do we know about hunting practices from such a long time ago? The answers are hidden in the dark, still-sharp obsidian tools of the inland peoples.

Archaeologists working in the Long Valley, north of Bishop, have found two significantly different kinds of obsidian tool points: large spear points and small arrowheads. These could have been used for different kinds of hunting by the same people or by two different sets of inhabitants, in two different time periods. Carbon dating was of little use in sorting this out because very little carbon-based material survives long in the desert climate. But the obsidian offers many other clues. As a natural glass, obsidian absorbs water molecules from the atmosphere, even in an arid climate, forming a "hydration band." Each time obsidian is worked, each time a toolmaker knocks off a flake, a new band begins. It enlarges over time as more moisture is absorbed. A sample taken from any spear or arrowhead point, sliced very thin, reveals a band that can be used to calculate age. Hydration bands on sections of large spear points are 5/1000 of a millimeter wide, which shows that these implements for hunting large game were made at least 4,000 years ago. On the other hand, the bandwidths of sections taken from smaller arrowheads are a mere 2.3/1000mm wide, which means those points were made only about 300 years ago. The large game hunters lived in a much earlier time than those hunters who used bows and arrows. This difference means that hunting itself probably changed from large groups working cooperatively to single individuals stalking with lightweight weapons.

Every obsidian flow in the Long Valley has its own geochemical fingerprint, visible through the poetically-named process of "x-ray fluorescent spectrometry." Each flake from a flow contains its origin within its glass matrix. By matching a flake's trace element pattern with a flow signature, archeologists can determine where a piece of obsidian was quarried and thus determine the distances the inhabitants of the valley, or their goods, traveled.

The combination of hydration analysis and x-ray spectrometry shows that the oldest obsidian flakes, more than 7,000 years in age, were transported more than 100 miles. Flakes that were knocked from obsidian cores somewhere between 3,000 and 1,500 years ago were transported less far, and the most recent flakes were carried only 25 miles.

So, while we have no written history, those who worked obsidian left a record nonetheless: 7,000 years ago, obsidian was gathered from great distances and was made into spear-sized points big enough to be used to hunt big mammals—bighorn sheep and antelope. But in more recent centuries, obsidian gathering occurred within a much smaller area and the weapons that were made were much smaller, too small to bring down anything larger than a grouse or hare.

Petroglyphs within the territory of the Owens Valley Paiute, north of Bishop. The Bureau of Land Management office in Bishop will give exact directions but prefers that they not be published.

Long Valley Caldera

From the Sierras east, the Great Basin is stretching. It thins like pizza dough, and where it gets too thin, hot, interior earth-stuff rises toward the surface. Driving south of Mammoth (the mountain, the town, the ski resort), the straight line of Highway 395 breaks up, jogs east along the line of the Long Valley Caldera. The curve of the distant, dark brown Glass Mountain marks one side of where a rising dome of gas-infused molten rock pushed up through the surface of the earth and burst like a soap bubble. An eleven-mile-across soap bubble.

Across from Glass Mountain, the Sierra granites are topped with folded, striated rock that was once the coastal edge of a long-gone ocean. How can this statement be true? Beneath the ocean bed, liquid magma "plutons," suspended in heavier liquid rock—like lumps in a lava lamp—cooled slowly, molecules aligning themselves in crystalline grids. Meanwhile, above them, sediments of the ancient ocean sifted down in layers. Pressure from above and heat from below made them into limestones and marbles. When the tectonic plates moved, the cooled plutons heaved up, pushing the sediments above them.

The pluton that we know as the Sierra Nevada is so vast it has been given another name: it is a batholith. So vast, in fact, that is called an "abyssal batholith." To contemplate its size is to contemplate the abyss. But it is young, and the continent it edges is small, only a wandering piece of an earlier, larger, single landmass. When that continent broke up, when the cooled pluton that is the Sierra batholith rose, the seabed of the ancient ocean that surrounded that ancient continent was left on top. The geologist tells us that the green marble "hanging pendants" we see thousands of feet above us were once quiet water sediments, and the white limestones were once shallow reefs.

You could look at all this stuff for days and still not comprehend it. And there's more. We stop at Convict Lake Road to look at glacial moraines: after the granite rose, the Ice Age descended. (I'm skipping a few other eons here.) Solid masses of snow and ice, pulled downward by gravity, dragged pebbles, cobbles, boulders big as cars downward, forming U-shaped canyons, polishing the granite along the way. When the ice melted, piles of this dragged rock, big as hills—moraines—remained. They are like the ridge of sand a child's hand pushes up at the beach. As the ice came and went, successive moraines formed: the child's hand pushing again and again. We drive by these exposed millions of years of geologic history and we are not yet even out of the caldera.

Modern history intrudes. Benton Crossing Road used to run in a straight line east: now it angles north, diverted around Crowley Lake, a reservoir for water diverted by the Los Angeles Department of Water and Power. It lies at the deepest part of the caldera, where glacier water once gathered and rose so high it overtopped the edge of the basin, carving out the Owens River Gorge.

We pull off the highway across from the southernmost curve of the caldera, where the process started. Once the accumulating gas and molten rock broke through in one place, the whole dome unzipped around the edge, the bubble broke, sending out masses of gas/rock foam. Collapsing inward, the land fell a full two miles from its former level. The highway is banked on both sides by the outfall, which ranges from loose gray ash to a pinkish, globby rock called "bishop tuff." Some tuff welded from its own heat.

We pass out of view of the caldera, descending southward with Rock Creek as it passes through carved-out tuff. One ridgeline over, the Owens River Gorge is dry. The LA Aqueduct carries its water now. A solid platform of tuff settled to the east and southeast, its sides convex, like a giant oval pancake cooling on a griddle. We drive around the bottom of the pancake. The southernmost edge of what is called the volcanic tableland is made up of ash white as chalk. Following the curve, we head eastward, turn north again along tuff hardened to a dark red, blackened in places with desert varnish. This is not geological but biological: a bacteria that eats magnesium in the rock excretes a hard, shiny, black crust. Paiute holy people on vision quests carved petroglyphs on it: picked off the black to carve shapes in the deep red. These are revealed as the sun moves across the sky: a changing angle of light reveals shapes on a rock surface that minutes before seemed blank: interconnected circles, circles within circles, eagle claws, bighorn sheep, bear paws.

Mission San Diego de Alcala, the first California Mission, rebuilt after the Kumeyaay Revolt of 1775.

3

Spanish California

When the Spanish missionaries arrived in Acagchemem, now the northwest of San Diego County, to found the Mission of San Luis Rey, the local people "were alarmed, but they didn't flee or take up arms to kill them, but rather sat and watched them." Pablo Tac, the only native writer to chronicle the Spanish conquest, recalled that when the missionaries came near "the chief stood up" and declared "what are you looking for? Leave our country." The Spanish did not leave. Instead, the people of Acagchemem "allowed them to sleep here." That may have been a mistake.

A similar event occurred a hundred miles to the north at the Tongva (Gabrileño) villages of Isanthcag-na and Yang-na. According to Fray Pedro Cambón, "a great multitude of savages appeared and with frightful yells attempted to prevent the founding of the Mission." But the padres had a secret weapon, "a canvas picture of Our Lady of the Sorrows," which caused people of the villages to be "transfixed in wonderment" and to throw "their bows and arrows on the ground." The women of what later became Los Angeles then showered the painting with gifts of jewelry and food. Native people recalled the encounter differently. They turned to their own religious leaders for advice about the whites' guns and strange foods. The wise men "pronounced it white witchcraft."

Even farther north, when Sir Francis Drake landed in the Miwok territory north of modern San Francisco, the people there mistook the English sailors for their long dead ancestors returning from the West. According to Miwok beliefs, the return of the dead meant the end of the world was upon them—in a way they were right.

Few of California's historic sites are more picturesque than its many missions, but few parts of its history are as disturbing as the intertwined tales of conquest, conversion, cultural destruction, and massacre. Often crumbling and run-down, some missions are still used as churches and house active parish lives. Every California school child spends part of the fourth grade studying the missions, making models out of clay or sugar cubes, and otherwise memorializing some of the few buildings left in the state from the 18th century. School children, like so many tourists, imbibe the romanticized history of an institution filled with new converts to Christianity happily raising crops and learning Spanish ways while supervised by kindhearted missionary friars.

But the missions were hardly bucolic places; they were meant to civilize a wilderness and tame a wild people. In every mission graveyard, stones name the Friars whose remains lie below. Nearby, usually unmarked and unmemorialized, are buried thousands of people who died to advance the Spanish religion, civilization, and imperial ambition. Forty percent of the Indians at the missions died each year, mostly from disease, and their often bitter resistance to these genocidal conditions was met by brutal repression and more deaths. Like the rest of the conquered Americas, Europeans brought California into their realm at an incalculable human cost.

California had been relatively unimportant in Spanish eyes since Cabrillo sailed into San Diego Bay in 1542 and claimed an enormous new territory for church and king. The Spanish paid a little more attention to Baja California; Cortéz established an outpost there in the 1530s. Nothing more was done with Alta California, the part that now forms the US state, for another 200 years.

It took a brilliant but tortured politician fearful of other great powers' designs on California to push Spain to colonize its remote frontier in the 1760s. José Bernardo de Gálvez Gallardo, the Marquis of Sonora, Minister of the Indies, believed Mexico's far northwest was potentially valuable and important. He modernized the region's administration by separating Alta California from Baja California in 1768 along the modern border between the Mexican and US states. The following year he launched a "sacred expedition" that brought Captain Gaspar de Portolá as military commander and Franciscan Father Junipero Serra as Padre-Presidente, accompanied by a few skilled troops, Indian laborers, and a handful of craftsmen, to California. The expedition landed at San Diego and then marched up the coast, eventually discovering San Francisco Bay. The Spanish founded a string of settlements, each one a day's ride from the next, and established their capital at Monterey.

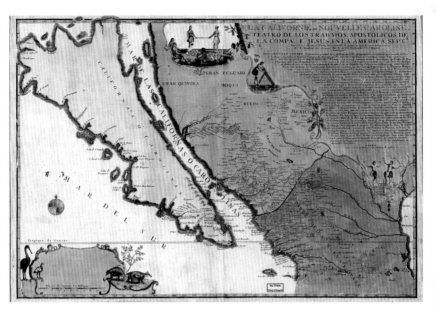

European explorers thought Alta and Baja California were on an island. A map from 1720 by French cartographer Nicolas de Fer.

The Spanish crown attempted to colonize its territory in California, not in response to internal pressures of population growth or market demands, but for geostrategic reasons. Simply put, if the Spanish didn't control California, the British or the Russians would. De Gálvez hoped mining would eventually draw population to the borderlands and make the colony self-financing, but the discovery of precious minerals came decades too late for the Spanish to benefit.

It was a paradox that de Gálvez, who had organized the expulsion of the powerful Catholic Jesuit order from Mexico because of its challenge to colonial authority, would give such a large domain to the Franciscans. Lacking other resources for his colonial enterprise, he reluctantly relied on the Church, replicating the longstanding Spanish strategy in central Mexico and the northern territories. The missions of the Order of Friars Minor, the Franciscans, would provide the economic and social infrastructure to support a Spanish presence on the northern frontier.

The Spanish empire created an efficient system of colonial rule where a few conquerors ruled over a mass of native people. At the end of the Spanish period barely 3,000 settlers lived in a territory larger than Germany. The missions were protected

Fort Ross

The explorations of Russians and British in the Pacific worried the Spanish, who had let their northwestern territories languish. Yet only the Russians managed to establish an actual outpost in California. The Russian America Company started Fort Ross in 1812 to support otter hunting and to grow food for its Alaskan colonies. Russian traders, scientists, trappers, and farmers mixed with Kashaya and Miwok people on the coast, building a small community and a few outlying farms. Although Fort Ross was in territory the Spanish claimed, they lacked the military power to do anything about it. Worse for Spanish territorial claims, the residents of the Yerba Buena (San Francisco) presidio and pueblo liked trading with the Russians. San Franciscans even borrowed gunpowder from Fort Ross to fire a salute from their only working cannon for a visiting Russian ship. Luckily for the Spanish crown, the Russian commitment to settlement and trade on the coast was limited and Fort Ross their only outpost in North America outside of Alaska. The little settlement lasted almost thirty years until the collapse of the otter population made it economically unviable. The Russians tried to preserve the otters by imposing moratoriums on taking skins, but these pioneering population management plans failed to stem the otters' demise. Eventually, Johan Sutter bought the land from the Russian American Company and had the building dismantled and brought to Sacramento. Later the Call family held much of the land, rebuilt some of the fort buildings, and donated them as a park just north of the surprisingly named Russian River.

by military bases, presidios, that were in turn supported by the produce of the missions. These garrisons—many of which still form the core of the state's extensive military bases—had a dual purpose: to dominate the native population and to prevent a foreign takeover of the territory. The missions provided labor, food, and support for the soldiers at the bases while converting the non-Christian natives into a docile Christianized workforce. The Catholic Church—probably Spain's most powerful institution—was satisfied to have new converts, and New Spain was on track to become like the rest of Mexico.

But because of his suspicions of Church power, de Gálvez also wanted to support the formation of pueblos, secular towns, to provide a counterweight to the missions. De Gálvez's plan worked to a certain degree, although he did not live to see its success. He later led reforms of the entire Spanish empire in the Americas but suffered bouts of depression and delusions. He committed suicide in 1787—though not before declaring himself God and proposing using Central American apes as soldiers.

The Franciscans, following the example of holy poverty and service set by St. Francis of Assisi, went to California, in Junipero Serra's words, to answer "the call of so many thousands of pagans who are waiting in California on the threshold of Holy Baptism." Serra had given up a comfortable career as a professor at the University of Majorca to prove his holiness through service and self-mortification on the frontier. His journey, he wrote, was on "a road whose principal end was the greatest honor and glory of God." The mission of the missions was saving the souls of the non-Christianized Californians, referred to as *gentilés*. Most of the padres took this task seriously, from inspirational administrators like Serra, Juan Crespí, and Fermin Lasuén to less well known Franciscans as José María Zalvidea who learned the Tongva language and spent long visits in Southern California native settlements. Serra and Zalvidea, like many of their padres, also practiced brutally painful penances, approaching Indian villages on their knees and flogging themselves. Zalvidea even imitated the crucifixion by driving nails into his feet.

Despite the passionate commitment and ecstatic state of their mortified flesh, not all missionaries were holy men truly following their Christian path. Some broke down under the difficult frontier conditions. Others exploited native people's labor to grow fat on the missions' proceeds. Franciscan superiors regularly complained about the conduct of missionaries who were drunk, having sex with neophytes, or simply incompetent.

Nonetheless, the three-part colonial system worked well enough for the Spanish, producing substantial crops and succeeding in transforming the culture and society of the people of coastal California. The *misionés* renamed the Tongva Gabrileño and the Kumeyaay Diegueño. They and the Chumash were converted from *gentilés* (also at times called *bestias*, beasts) into Christian subjects of the crown. These, called neophytes, also accepted the authority of the padres, though, in the view of the Spanish, only rarely became true *gente de razón* (rational people). The presidios protected the missions from raids by *gentilés* or escaped neophytes and ensured that other imperial powers could not grab the region. The soldiers also captured runaway neophytes who apparently insisted on continuing to be unreasonable. The pueblos provided a place where settlers from central Mexico and transformed *gentilés* would live and work, providing the basis for a larger economy.

The system offered settlers small plots of land in the pueblos and limited economic opportunities for providing services and trade for the presidios. But the conditions were hard and few people were willing to move to the remote frontier for such small reward. Most settlers were illiterate mestizos, some with African ancestry, from Sinaloa and Sonora on Mexico's west coast. They and the soldiers eventually became the *Californios*.

Wealth came to a few soldiers who received large ranchos as rewards for loyal service. While the padres' intention was to save souls and the Spanish crown's intention was to secure California against the Russians and British, the soldiers and other Mexican settlers sought to gain enough land and power to lord it over others. The crown gave the first big land grant, Rancho San Pedro, to a San Juan Capistrano Mission soldier, Juan José Dominguez. Another part of the rancho is now Cal State University, Dominguez Hills. While these enormous gifts made a few wealthy, most of the best land was taken by the missions, limiting the possibilities for land grants. Tension began to develop in the first decade of the 19th century as more and more Californios demanded substantial *haciendas* as the reward for loyal service or the pay off from well-lubricated social connections.

As elsewhere in the empire, California had a dual system of governance. Governors appointed by the crown administered the state from the modest capital in Monterey. At the same time, the Franciscans, who controlled Alta California's only productive institutions, answered solely to the Church hierarchy. Civil society was quite limited and generally functioned poorly. Few competent officials could be convinced to spend their careers in such a remote and unimportant outpost. High turnover reduced the effectiveness of those crown administrators who did come to the far northwest. Soldiers, settlers, and of course padres were almost all men. Few women migrated to the little villages. No doubt homosexual sex occupied some of the men, though there is little historical record. Following Spanish and Mexican tradition, the settlers and soldiers often married native women, a practice that continued into the Mexican era. *Alcades,* who were both more and less than mayors, administered the pueblos and managed their relationship with the presidios and missions.

Father Severin Westhoff at Mission San Juan Capistrano around 1900: The Franciscans continued to minister to congregations long after the collapse of the Mission system.

In 1881, Felipa Yorba, from a wealthy family herself, married into the Dominguez family. Her descendants still run a part of the original 75,000-acre Spanish land grant in southern Los Angeles as a land development company; another part of the rancho is now Cal State University, Dominguez Hills.

Among the few competent officials was Governor Felipe de Neve, who established the system of laws for the province and ordered the founding of the pueblos. Fourteen people from the presidios at Monterey and San Francisco settled the first pueblo, San José de Guadalupe, in 1777. The Spanish liked long names, for instance, *El Pueblo de Nuestra Señora la Reina de los Angeles del Río Porciúncula* (The Town of Our Lady the Queen of the Angels of the Little Portion River). It is little wonder we now shorten the name to LA.

It was not an auspicious beginning for California. Brutal and rapacious soldiers and corrupt local officials worked with fanatical monks to make subjects out of people who died at alarming rates when they didn't run away or kill the missionaries. A paltry few Mexican settlers barely made a living in flea-infested villages. All this was presided over by a revolving cast of incompetent imperial envoys, answerable to a man who thought he was God. Little wonder that a tired Portolá suggested the Russians could have California as punishment for their sins.

Despite the limitations of the Spanish system, the missions grew substantially in just a few years. The Spanish reduced the myriad differences of indigenous groups into a simple bifurcation of *gentilés* and *gente de razón*. The multiracial mestizo settlers from Sonora and elsewhere in Mexico claimed domination over this cultural hierarchy because of their Europeanness, while far above them (and often very far away from them) the truly powerful Spanish fit the place into their ambitious strategies. The term "mission" refers to both the physical institution and the evangelizing activities at that place. The missions were similar to large plantations, providing work for recently converted people. Native workers were trained in Spanish crafts and trades, from weaving, blacksmithing, winemaking, tanning, bootmaking, and cooking to pruning trees, as part of their transformation into people of reason. Setting the pattern for future Californian elites, the mission preeminence grew directly from the land. The missions' enormous land grants, often hundreds of thousands of acres, were supposed to be turned over to the neophytes, and the missions were to be dismantled once their goals were achieved.

Yet the Spanish administrators did not trust the transformation and insisted that padres and mestizos supervise all the neophytes' work. This made sense to the Spanish since they believed the *gentilés* lacked a European tradition of discipline. They had previously only worked according to their own necessity; now they worked because of compulsion by the Spanish, becoming in effect the first California working class. The settlers imposed the basics of European social discipline with the whip, the stock, and other educational tools.

The Spanish believed that the Indians could be made into good Catholics, regular workers, and obedient subjects of the crown if native culture were remade in the image of the patriarchal Spanish family system. To create *gente de razón*, the Spanish sought to control traditional courtship and sexual practices that they saw as demeaning to women and girls and as signs of the devil's control. The role of *llavería* (keeper of the keys) would be given to a matron such as the widow Eulalia Arrila de Pérez, a mestiza who oversaw the kitchens and the domestic life of the San Gabriel Mission in the 1820s. She made sure the girls were safely locked up at night with the help of a blind Gabrieleño Indian who called out the names of each girl as she entered the room. In Spanish culture, parents had a profound responsibility to protect the virginity of girls and to maintain patriarchal domination. Locking in female children at night or severely restricting their movement made sense when a girl's "innocence" insured her marriageability. Control of a girl's sexuality allowed her safe passage to adulthood and fulfillment of her proper role, the perpetuation of the family in subordination to her father or husband. The seeming anarchy of *gentilés'* sexuality, the padres reasoned, required similar control. Elite control of the apparently outlandish sexuality of subservient groups became a way of establishing the Spanish order as much as the presidio, the workshop, and the Church.

In Southern California, "the women who went to the mission," historian Douglas Monroy writes, were "trading one patriarch for another." But while the south coastal Shoshonean cultures kept most women in subservient positions to their spouses and families, they were not controlled in the same way as women in Spanish or colonial society. The padres' practice of locking women up at night to keep them sexually pure—a practice alien from native traditions—was not necessarily objectionable to many of the women. Native women in the south took to Catholicism and mission life more quickly than men. It is difficult for historians to detail with certainty Indian women's ways of dealing with the conquest since they left all too few records, and much of the information comes from men's words. Nonetheless, the Spanish-Catholic system offered native women something attractive in addition to coercing their labor and devotion.

Captain DeAnza worried that California's people were "fit subjects of the enemy of the human race who has them in his power." But it was not the devil native women needed to watch out for. Because the first Spanish Mexican settlers were almost entirely male, the incidence of rape of Indian women was high—a problem conscientious padres complained of frequently. The dehumanizing attitude of most Spanish toward Indians contributed to the problem. Native women may have agreed that enemies of their race had them in their power. Women who became pregnant because of sexual violence practiced infanticide; few mestizo children survived in the early years. Rape by Spanish soldiers, settlers, and the occasional friar, along with more consensual sex also introduced sexually transmitted diseases among native women. Because many Indian cultures accepted multi-partner sexuality, STDs spread rapidly outside of the settlements. In the days before antibiotics, such diseases caused a slow, painful decline followed by almost certain death. For Indian mothers infected with syphilis, childbirth proved even more dangerous than usual—terribly high rates of infant mortality devastated native families.

At the same time the missionaries tried to defend the neophytes against the worst excesses that the enormous imbalance of power allowed. They campaigned against rape and demanded more respect for native women (while utterly condemning native sexuality and family culture). Unfortunately, while being locked into dormitories may have protected the women from male sexual attention, it also encouraged outbreaks of disease. Epidemics, along with the spread of venereal disease, killed Indian women at alarming rates, far more quickly than it did the native men who lived and worked outside the dormitories.

Native men also benefited by learning Spanish trades. They built the missions and their furnishings, painting and decorating the altars and religious sculptures, santos, within the churches. The mission buildings generally started out as simple wooden structures, but became large adobe and stone structures as they grew and as the neophytes were trained in various crafts.

Because of engineering limitations and a shortage of large lumber at the coastal sites, the missions rarely had large spans of open space. Simple but elegant in design, the mission buildings combined many elements: Moorish arches and patios, Italian campaniles, and North American multi-bell campanarios. As the years passed mission furniture also evolved from the original crude constructions into its own square, heavy style. The neophytes also learned farming—a practice that had deeply impressed many south coast peoples in the first years of Spanish occupation. These skills gave them a place in Spanish-Mexican society, albeit a very low one, while the imposition of Christian morality on marriage and sexual practice deprived them of status in their own communities. The padres enforced the Spanish system of monogamous marriage on native people who previously had plural formal relationships. They solemnized tens of thousands of first and second marriages among the neophytes, but many of the missionaries worried that the natives were still sneaking around behind their backs. While some native women married Mexicans, intermarriage was not available to Indian men. Still a few leaders among Southern Californian tribes retained some prestige in the villages near the mission—Hugo Reid, a Scottish chronicler of old Los Angeles, for instance, legitimized his marriage to an Indian by pointing out that her father

L. Meza repairing santos at Mission San Juan Capistrano, 1908.

was a chief. But most men not only lost their traditional position in their communities, but found themselves at the bottom of a new social hierarchy.

Despite the traumas to California's First Peoples, after a few short years the missions were economically productive, even though the pueblos remained small and poor. The padres introduced European crops and foods, such as citrus, figs, and grapes, as well as items from other parts of the Americas, unknown in California, such as beans and corn. Cows, goats, and sheep thrived on the oak savannahs and grasslands. While the missions may not have succeeded in turning neophytes into *gente de razón*, they did demonstrate the region's fecundity. The mission fathers carefully recorded the mission's products as well as the 24,000 marriages and 88,000 baptisms. Thousands of indigenous Californians had been made to worship in the Catholic way. Even better from the Spanish point of view, this development had been accomplished with only a few thousand soldiers, Franciscan friars, and mestizo migrants from the Mexican center. At the close of the mission period in 1833, 60 friars and 300 soldiers controlled a mission population of 31,000 in an efficient use of scant resources for the Crown that provided the fundamental building blocks for California's society. Unlike later forms of California's economy, the missions' involvement in trade was quite limited. It was mostly a form of subsistence economy where the small amounts of surplus were consumed mostly by neophytes, friars, and soldiers.

As elsewhere in the Americas, the Spanish takeover of California disrupted the balance of intertribal relations. Some natives took advantage of their relationship with the newcomers to gain regional power, while others mounted substantial resistance. Depending on the political system of the surrounding region, the mission fathers and presidio soldiers managed to recruit local leaders to join the missions. Often, however, these same leaders spearheaded the resistance to the Spanish. Native people's violent resistance to the Spanish system imposed on them began within a month of the first mission's founding in San Diego in 1769.

The Mojave and Yuma, most notably, fought the Spanish for decades, making the overland journey from Sonora extremely hazardous. From their inaccessible desert homes, they continued their traditional raiding practices against the coastal peoples, remote ranchos, and mission outposts. The most deadly defeat for the Spanish came in a battle with the Yuma in 1781. These Colorado River residents killed thirty soldiers and four padres (including Padre Francisco Garcés, an intrepid explorer and mission founder in Sonora and Arizona). They took dozens of captives. After this conflict, the Spanish abandoned the overland trail to California, further isolating the region.

Natives living nearer the missions were less successful at keeping the colonizers away, but they also revolted in the early years. Toyipurna, a Gabrileña woman, led an attack in 1785 against the San Gabriel Mission. That a woman organized, directed, and fought in the attack against the friars' power reveals a contrast in the gender order of the two societies. That she was also a shaman further underlines the worlds in conflict. Questioned about her attacks, she supposedly responded: "I hate the padres, and all of you, for living here on my native soil, for trespassing upon the land of my forefathers."

The struggles of native people against the missions often became the stuff of legend, stories that remain with us largely as place names. For instance, Quintin, a runaway from Mission San Rafael, fought off capture at San Quentin point in Marin, the location of a modern institution that also keeps people from running away: San Quentin State Prison.

As the political tide shifted against the missions in the 1820s with the independence of Mexico, larger and more determined revolts broke out. The largest uprising took place in 1824, three years after the creation of the Mexican republic, when Narciso, a neophyte at the Santa Ynes Mission, led an uprising against the brutality of some presidio soldiers. The neophytes burned the mission. Indians in nearby Santa Barbara and La Purísima joined the insurrection when they heard of the conflict. More than 400 Indians barricaded themselves in at Santa Ynes, holding out for a month against troops sent from Monterey. Mexican soldiers killed dozens. Hundreds of the survivors fled through the rugged Santa Barbara mountains into the Central Valley to find shelter with the Yokuts who had not conceded to Spanish or Mexican power.

A few years later, Estanislao, a neophyte from Mission San José, challenged the authorities at the end of the mission period in 1829. Declaring "we are rising in revolt... We have no fear of the soldiers," he led hundreds of neophytes from the mission into the hills. Estanislao's people raided the mission stocks, taking entire herds of cattle and horses. The Mexican governor declared them not rebels but bandits and sent hundreds of troops to capture them. Estanislao and his compatriots, like the Santa Ynes rebels, fled over the coast range into the Central Valley. The pursuing soldiers slaughtered dozens, perhaps hundreds, of Miwok people in the valley, most of whom had nothing to do with the rebels. The soldiers claimed that Estanislao surrendered to them at a creek near what is now Interstate 5 in Stanislaus County. Legend has it, though, that Estanislao escaped at the last minute, disappearing over the hills with hundreds of horses. Stories continued into the middle of the century of Estanislao raiding, a desperado image later inherited by Californio bandit hero Joaquin Murrietta.

More commonly, native people avoided violence, but nonetheless rejected their new overlords. Thousands of recent converts fled the awful conditions in the missions, simply disappearing by running away to nearby free villages. Presidio soldiers' main task was tracking down runaway neophytes and forcing them to return to the ministrations of the padres. Before Narciso's revolt, Santa Barbara area Indians had been fleeing for years into the mountains and then into the Central Valley, a vast region that remained out of Spanish and Mexican control. Trappers and adventurers regularly met with natives who spoke Spanish living with the Central Valley peoples. Ultimately, it was only possible to adapt, flee, or die.

Most of the mountains, the deserts, and the great valley remained Indian territory until the Anglo invasion, but these areas still underwent a profound transformation. Most dramatically, horses, some escaped from mission herds, others stolen, helped transform the society and economy of the Great Valley. These economic and social changes empowered some inland peoples to maintain their independence, though the diverse peoples of the region never created grand war alliances against the conquerors as plains and eastern Indians did.

The complexities of native societies were lost on Spanish, Mexican, and Anglo observers. A Franciscan missionary once described California Indians as "without religion or government, having nothing more than diverse superstitions and a type of democracy similar to ants." Yet frequent border skirmishes, complex inter-group rivalries, and language differences made the diplomacy of the Central Valley and delta region as complicated as any pre-World War I system of European alliances. Miwoks, for instance, resisted the mission and controlled much of the Sacramento delta region, providing sanctuary to runaways and raiding outlying settlements. Yet some natives saw the conquerors as allies. Nisenans distrusted Miwoks and helped European soldiers capture runaway Christianized natives or kill and enslave other "gentile" Indians. Miwoks, Ohlone, Yokuts, and other large groups divided among themselves, with coastal people converted (often by force) and inland villages resisting. North Central Valley people played off trappers from the British-controlled Hudson Bay Company against the Mexicans as well as each other.

The collapse of the mission system occurred in part because of the internal weakness of the missions, their impact on the people whose souls they were supposed to save, and the revolutionary turmoil of the first quarter of the 19th century. Most importantly, the demographic devastation caused by the absorption of native Californians into the Spanish/Mexican realm prevented the missions from developing a larger economy and society in the region. Diseases, always prevalent inside the missions' walls, reached epidemic proportions in the 1820s. "Sickness in general prevails to an incredible extent in all the missions," a British navy officer observed. Thousands of runaways further deprived the missions of a workforce for the Church and of souls for the Christian god. After a decade of struggle, Mexico officially became an independent state in 1821, bringing to power a group of republican reformers who saw the Church as a force perpetuating an old aristocratic system, one that prevented ambitious men from making their own fortunes and success in the world. The Church also just happened to be the largest landowner in the country. What better way to make Mexico into a land of republican opportunity—and to reward loyal friends—than to take the Church's lands and redistribute them, ostensibly to the indigenous people in whose name the new elites ruled the county. The taking of Church lands, however, rarely resulted in the distribution to landless peasants or neophytes. Rather, throughout Mexico the end of Church power enriched and enlarged a class of *hacendados* (huge estate holders). California was no exception. The secularization of the missions, which officially began in 1831, created a new class of California landowners.

The Spanish created a system that devastated native societies, transforming them to the point that even the names of their communities have been lost. This human disaster was not always purposefully caused: European diseases were the main killers. Waves of deadly epidemic repeatedly swept the state—much as they had elsewhere in the Americas after contact. Smallpox was the most common killer, emptying villages often far from the missions, presidios, and pueblos of the Spanish. Other diseases were also rampant, especially in the close confines of the missions and the pueblos. Fleas had been controlled by the Indian system of seasonal migrations and hut burning, which limited outbreaks. But with thousands forced to live in the picturesque and permanent structures of the missions or the adobe huts of the pueblos, the flea populations boomed. Flea-born diseases like bubonic plague repeatedly tore through the missions. Disruption to traditional life—increasingly restricted diets, loss of hunting grounds, the breakdown of family structure, and suppression of culture—proved almost as destructive as the diseases. In a few short years, the Spanish conquest cut California's Indian population in half: 300,000 people lived in the region before the 1780s

Lazy and Difficult

The new Mexican holders of the Mission lands found it difficult to get the former neophytes to stick around and work. The administrator of the former Mission San Luis Rey explained: "These Indians will do absolutely no work nor obey my orders.... I must suffer the pain of being obliged to suspend work for want of hands. The men have mistaken the voice of reason and even of the authority which orders the work, for they declare they are a free nation. In order to enjoy their obstinacy better, they have fled from their house and abandoned their aged parents, who alone are now at this ex-Mission. I have sent various alcaldes to the sierra in order to see if, with sweetness and gentleness, we might succeed in having them return to their homes; but the result was the opposite of my desires. Nothing would suit them, nothing would change their ides, neither the well being which must result for their good behavior, nor the privations which they suffer in their wanderings. All with one voice would shout, "We are free! We do not want to obey! We do not want to work!"

and by the 1820s the native population was 150,000. The mission system especially decimated coastal peoples, who declined from 72,000 in 1780 to 18,000 in the 1830s—a drop of 75 percent. Whole villages disappeared, ways of life vanished, and tens of thousands died to advance the imperial plans of a far-off crown and the Christianizing zeal of the Church.

Spanish colonization of Alta California set the form for the state's overall political structure, social order, and even consciousness. The mission era lasted barely more than 60 years, but was long enough to establish the outlines of California's agricultural economy, despite the missions' lack of market orientation. They created a pattern of vast landholdings—Mission Santa Barbara, for instance, covered 120,000 acres. They established orchards and vineyards and introduced horses, cows, and other livestock. The mission system created a synthetic Indian-Mexican-Spanish society based on the domination of the Church and the presidio over local affairs, the priority of the distant concerns of the Spanish Crown and the interests of a seigniorial landholding system. Most tragically, the Spanish forced the participation of native people, who in turn often resisted this domination.

The missions and pueblos enforced a racially segmented labor system in which a mass of people of one race/nationality provided for the needs of another group, a pattern that has continued to this day. When the region began attracting a larger multiracial population in the mid-19th century, the newcomers entered a society with entrenched social hierarchies and a racial system in which complicated divisions were subsumed under simple binaries imposed by those on the top. Popular images denied the existence of the complexity and depth of the conflicts in the state. Nonetheless, the West Coast, from its first moments in the Euro-American system, was a place of vast ethnic complexity and stunningly huge class divisions. Born of imperial ambitions, the region served the higher strategy of far off powers, its geopolitical importance arising from its well-located ports and productive hinterlands. While the global market was a minor force in the early years of colonization, California's place in the world system was the ultimate payoff.

Environmental transformation, violent control over non-white people, and an expectation that a mass low wage workforce will create the conditions for a bucolic life of leisure for the elite: these are the legacies of the mission system. For those on the bottom, it was a different story. "The brute upshot of missionization, in spite of its kindly flavor and humanitarian roots," anthropologist Alfred Kroeber concluded, "was only one thing: death."

The original caption, "Jose Gracia de Cruz, 1908, 'Old Acu' the last of the Acjachemen Indians, San Juan Capistrano," was wrong. They still exist — though the US government denied them federal tribal status in 2011.

The Environmental Conquest

Europeans conquered California's environment as much as its people. The invaders brought plants and animals, some purposefully, some accidentally. Ice plant, which flowers along the coastal dunes during the early spring, is a European import. Spanish sailors chewed the succulent stems to ward off scurvy. Chewed up stems floated ashore. Spanish explorers spread mustard seed to botanically blaze trails for later settlers. Thriving in California's dry warm climate, the mustard soon displaced other spring flowering annuals, including the California poppy. European grasses, brought as feed and to grow grain, quickly displaced California's indigenous bunch grasses. The European grasses are so successful that the native grasslands that once covered so much of the state and grew as tall as a man in the great valley can only be found in a few remote preserves in the Central Valley and in the remote Carrizzo Plain of the coastal hills east of Paso Robles. Later conquerors followed the same patterns of intentional—and sometimes stupid—plantings and accidental introductions. The fragrant eucalyptus groves of the coast result from the brilliant inspiration of Oakland nursery owners and developers who hoped to use the fast growing Australian trees to replace rapidly disappearing redwoods and oaks. Eucalyptus burn far hotter and more quickly than native trees and have contributed to a number of disastrous fires, including the 1991 Oakland Hills fire that killed 25 people and destroyed thousands of homes. A slower irritant, the snails that pester gardeners around the state, were introduced by a French gold rush immigrant who hoped that the European love of escargot would catch on here. It didn't, but the snails did.

Mission Creek Cemetery

It used to be when you drove into San Francisco from the east, over the Bay Bridge, you avoided the center lane because that's where the repaired seam—the place where the panel of the span that collapsed in the 1989 earthquake—hits the tires hardest. Now the traffic thickens at the S-curve where the old part of the bridge connects to part of its replacement. You still emerge from the tunnel through Yerba Buena Island (which used to be called Alcatraz, and Alcatraz was Yerba Buena), pointed in generally the same direction as a small vessel would have if it were headed into the mouth of Mission Creek. Such a vessel would have passed through China Basin, named for the destination of its ships, now hidden behind the Giants' baseball stadium. A small boat, oared by sailors, could carry goods all the way inland to the Mission, standing on a serpentine rise.

Once over the bridge, a gleaming white monument of a building standing on the north side, high enough to be seen easily from the westbound deck, still carries its carved inscription—Sailors Union of the Pacific, in block capitals—in testament to the union's standing and the improvements it brought to sailors' lives. Used to be, schooners moved lumber and manufactured goods up and down the coast; larger ships plied the oceans to Hawai'i and farther afield. Whalers searched the North Pacific, while bargemen ferried goods to and from the Central Valley. Conditions on board were often horrific, overcrowded, and unsanitary, and floggings were perfectly legal until the 1850s. Twelve-hour shifts and seven-day weeks meant exhausted deckhands often suffered disabling injuries at rate comparable to the most dangerous mines. Mates who brutalized the sailors earned the name "Bucko." Seafarers ran away from ships whenever they docked and were reluctant to sign back on to ship but were "shanghaied," drugged, beaten unconscious, and dragged on board for long voyages to… guess where! But improvements in technology (metal ships, power winches, and pumps, for example) and union organization in the late 19th century eased some of these conditions.

Only a small section of Mission Creek remains, lying along a greenway just south of the ballpark. The men who work on ships and along the shore now work at the Port of Oakland, whose giant cranes gawk over the bay to the southeast. The rest of the creek is underground in concrete conduits. Without a vessel or a creek to row up, we have to take the Mission St. Exit off the freeway. As we approach 16th Street, which would take us to Mission Dolores and her cemetery, we stop-and-go past crowded crosswalks, storefronts selling every size of canvas duffle bags, *quinceñera* dresses, used books. Pupuserias, taquerias. Bohemian coffee shops.

One block over, Valencia Street holds the ghosts of the dot-com boom: hip furniture stores, trendy restaurants. In the alleys between the commercial drags, astronomically priced, meticulously kept condos, 600-700 square feet for as many hundreds of thousands of dollars, house Anglo hipster young-marrieds. We stop for lunch at Ti Couz, the Breton crepe restaurant, because we can. In the 1990s, we would have stood for hours waiting for a table, just to show that we were in the know. On this day it is mostly empty and hot only in the sense that the giant metal convex grill they cook the crepes on overheats a room that lacks air conditioning, of course, in a building made for fog, in a town that now bakes in globally warmed sunshine.

All the gravestones at Mission Dolores are made of granites of various kinds, imported from elsewhere, just like the dead that lie beneath: almost all the individuals memorialized are "native" to Ireland, except one poor lone Scot. And except for De Haro, buried in 1849, and Arguello, in 1832, and several Noes: the young ones dead in 1873; the elders, in 1876. We conjecture a narrative: grandparents bereft of land, children, and grandchildren giving up the ghost a few years after them. Whatever their story, these Noes are the only Californios to be buried here later than 1849. And we know what happened then.

The headstone of Luis Arguello, first Mexican Governor of California, in the Mission Dolores Cemetery.

Fort Ross sometime before 1840 when it was still a Russian outpost.

4

CALIFORNIOS

Vast changes underway in central Mexico in the first decades of the 19th century shook the centuries-old Spanish empire. Incensed by the injustices of Spanish rule and inspired by the French and American Revolutions, beginning in 1810, Mexicans revolted against the Spanish empire. At first the residents of the territory of California hardly noticed, though the independence struggles did disrupt supply ships to California from San Blas. The disorder also encouraged an Argentine privateer to raid Monterey and San Juan Capistrano. Californians, so remote from the center of the revolt, only heard the news of Mexico's independence in 1822, a year after it came about. The post-revolutionary turmoil of Mexican politics only barely affected the territory, but the upheavals encouraged ambitious Californios—Mexican Californians—to grab for land. And not just any land: they wanted the only developed ranches and farms of the region, the land of the missions that were supported by the labor of the neophytes.

The Mexican era ushered in the slow beginning of California's entry into modernity. The arrival of 19th-century liberalism via the Mexican Revolution led to the end of the mission system and the opening of the region to the world market. These changes also just happened to enrich the Californios, a new elite in the territory. Setting a pattern to be repeated in later transformations, the Californios' control of the government and economy drew on a reforming, progressive set of ideas. These ideas, when they thought about them, allowed California's rancheros to justify enormous wealth derived from massive landholdings worked by Indian peons. Hardly imbued with the Protestant ethic of capitalism, California's Dons established a patriarchal culture of hospitality and honor in which men lorded it over their wives, servants, children, and grandchildren yet valued generosity and ranching pastimes—horsemanship, dancing, and gaming. While the Dons' wealth and power derived from enormous ranchos and the hide and tallow trade with the

Americans and British, the Californio world was far removed from the dynamic market societies of the Atlantic world.

On the other end of society, former Indian neophytes and *gentilés* struggled to find their way in the new system. Some simply returned to *gentilé* villages, but others became part of a degraded workforce in the pueblos. New waves of Mexican immigrants, excluded from the circle of the top families, occupied a social rung barely removed from the Indians. Despised as *cholos* (by which the Californios meant a mestizo crook, and which now means gangster or tough guy), poorer Mexican Californians worked as overseers and servants on the ranchos or tried to scrape out an independent existence on marginal lands or by providing services in the pueblos. Early California society was poor in material goods, with little domestic industry—for a time Californians even imported wine from Boston, of all places. The Mexican population was small, little more than 3,000 people in 1821. By 1846, California had barely grown—Los Angeles, the largest town, had 1,200 residents; Yerba Buena (later called San Francisco), less than 1,000; Santa Barbara had just 900 people; and Monterey, the capital, a mere 700. The Mexicans even briefly abandoned the first settlement, San Diego; the newest pueblo, Villa de Branciforte, next to Mission Santa Cruz, disappeared almost entirely. Despite the poverty and small population of Mexicans in California, the region eventually gained a reputation as a wealthy, cultured place. This prosperity, however, depended on the wealth built up by the missions and the continued servitude of thousands of Indians. Control over the rudimentary state apparatus meant control over the spoils—mission lands—and thus wealth, power, and security for those who held it, and their families and friends.

Dominated by a mere 46 families, Mexican California substituted factional rivalry for politics. A series of incompetent governors sent from Mexico City and the regional rivalries of the leading families kept California's nascent government in turmoil. In the five years from 1831 to 1836, for instance, California had eleven governors. *Abajeños* (lower ones/southerners) fought with *Arribeños* (upper ones/northerners) over such life-and-death issues as whether to keep the capital in Monterey or move it to Los Angeles. At times the friction turned into more dramatic confrontations, uprisings, and even the occasional violent set-to. At the Battle of Cahuenga Pass in 1831, Southerners intent on seizing mission lands confronted pro-Church Governor Manuel Victoria. After exchanging insults, José María Avila killed the

Governor's man, Lt. José Antonio Romualdo Pacheco (father of the only Californio to win election as governor after the US takeover). Victoria in turn killed Avila, thus winning the battle, but the violence so offended Californio sensibilities that Victoria had to resign his post.

Victoria's successor, the competent reformer José Figueroa, sincerely believed in the liberal promise of the revolution and hoped to transform the neophyte Indians into landholding Mexican farmers. Figueroa proclaimed the secularization of the missions and called for half of the mission lands to be distributed to the Indians who worked them.

Figueroa's plans didn't quite work out. Two well-connected operators from central Mexico, José María Hijar and José María Padres, hatched the *Compania Cosmopolitania* to grab mission lands and settle Mexico's far north. Their plan involved bringing hundreds of settlers from Sonora to the north, but Figueroa thought it was a conspiracy to unseat him and take lands from the natives. He forced the Cosmopolitanos to settle on the frontier north of San Francisco and sent the two José Marías packing. But Arribeños thought this was a conspiracy against their land ambitions. Crying "Death to Mexico" and "Kill the Mexicans," Arribeños forced most of the Cosmopolitanos, artisans, teachers, and tradesmen, to flee. A few returned to Mexico, but most settled elsewhere in California, including Juan Camarillo, who founded the town with his name, and Agustin Olvera, whose name graces the main tourist street in downtown Los Angeles.

When Governor Figueroa died suddenly in 1835, his plans for turning the missions over to the neophytes went awry. Californios grabbed mission lands, livestock, and workers as quickly as they could. While land grants were supposed to be limited to a paltry 50,000 acres, families thought this wasn't enough and put the property in the names of children and other relatives, thereby accumulating massive haciendas. This result betrayed the liberal dream of creating sturdy yeoman farmers. Lorenzo Asisara, a neophyte from Mission Santa Cruz, recalled that all his people got from the end of the missions were "old mares that were no longer productive and very old rams," along with a small piece of land that "did not do the Indians any good." This result wasn't solely due to Californio greed. Mission fathers, rather than turning over their herds to their Indian charges or to the Californios, had the cattle slaughtered by the tens of thousands, selling their hides to Yankee traders and taking the cash for their Pious Fund. Thousands more head were taken by financially desperate governors to cover government debts. By 1845 the mission herds had collapsed from a peak of 150,000 head of cattle to 50,000. The slaughter depressed hide prices world wide, while stimulating the industrialization of New England's burgeoning shoe industry, the main market for California skins. The devastation of such rapid slaughter and dismantlement of the region's main economic engines was enormous. "Stretched on the parched brown plain" between Los Angeles and Mission San Gabriel, related the Scottish immigrant Hugo Reid, "were the bleaching bones of innumerable cattle and over the Mission buildings... over the whole community hung an indefinable air of desolation and life suspended."

As important to the Californios as the land and herds were the missions' skilled *vaqueros* and other workers. Figueroa's successors dramatically accelerated land grants—mostly as a means of rewarding political loyalty. While the Spanish governors had awarded only 20 private land grants in 50 years, the Mexican governors awarded 500 in half as much time, most of the grants coming in the last 10 years of Mexican rule. In all, the Californios gained 8 million acres from the secularization of the missions.

Juan Bautista Alvarado became the most generous governor after he came to power in a coup d'état that confirmed the pattern of oligarchic rule and interpersonal conflict. With the aid of a group of Anglo adventurers, he took over Monterey in 1836, evicting Mexican officials and declaring California "a free and sovereign state." Alvarado, who had one rancho in Monterey and one by marriage to a Castro in the San Francisco Bay Area, appointed another *Arribeño*, his uncle Mariano Vallejo, military commander. He showered *Abajeños* with land grants and minor offices to appease their disappointment that Los Angeles, recently promoted from pueblo to city, had once again not become the capital. The Mexican government, preoccupied with war against Texan independence, didn't want to bother with a poor outlying territory. Indeed, to most officials in the center, "to speak of California was like mentioning the end of the world." The government caved in to Californio ambitions, appointing Alvarado governor. He in turn convinced American hide dealer and ranchero William Hartnell to oversee the missions. Hartnell, however, fell out with Alvarado's uncle Vallejo because of the latter's raiding of the San Rafael and Sonoma missions. Vallejo, no shrinking violet, arrested Hartnell. To counter Vallejo's power, Alvarado gave an enormous land grant at the junction

Swiss immigrant Johann Sutter played the Mexican system so well that he amassed one of the largest estates in California, located at the site of present day Sacramento.

of the Sacramento and American rivers to Swiss German immigrant Johann Sutter. Sutter built a massive fort there, complete with 3-foot thick walls and cannons mounted at the corners, as much to impress Vallejo as to control the Miwok raiders and Anglo trappers passing through the region.

The heyday of the Californios had arrived—replete with bitter factional politics and increasing involvement with Americans. The Californios' political and social world grew from a massive rancho expansion, which in turn relied on control over former neophyte workers and ongoing defense against raiding by Indians in outlying areas. The Californio political triumph under Alvarado fostered the full development of their culture—what many later observers, smitten with nostalgia for the era, called a golden age.

The Californio culture has alternately inspired derision and romanticization by Anglo observers. The Californios left few written records. Outside descriptions—lazy or noble, stylish or pompous—offered the character of the Californios as an explanation for their brief rule of barely 25 years. Even the otherwise sympathetic historian Leonard Pitt refers to them as "numerically too small and culturally too

> At the time I purchased the Fort Ross property there were around and in the neighborhood of the Fort a large number of Indians. Voluntarily they have become almost a part of the estate and as obedient to my orders as if mind, soul and body. I then raised, a large amount of grain, and had thousands of head of cattle, which gave me ample opportunity to utilize the labor of these untutored aborigines.
>
> —William Bennitz, who bought the Fort Ross rancho from Johann Sutter (1861)

backward to contribute to mankind much that was new or original.... The Yankees beat them badly and all but swept them into the dustbin of history." Believers in Anglo Manifest Destiny viewed the Californios as just another of the "static traditionalist societies" wiped away by the march westward. The combination of incredible natural wealth, the rich legacy appropriated from the missions, and the distance from the ferment of the newly born market capitalism to the east meant there was little reason to work terribly hard—if you owned a rancho. One of the padres displaced by the *hacendados* wrote, "I have good reason to accuse the settlers of laziness, but there is equally good reason to excuse them in large part. Their lack of enthusiasm for their work is not surprising, inasmuch as they regard most of it as fruitless." Richard Henry Dana, an American writer at the time, reassured his readers that "there's no danger of Catholicism spreading in New England. Yankees can't afford the time to be Catholics."

The life of relative abundance and leisure for the Californios, both the wealthy rancheros and poorer *pobladores* in the towns came about because of Indian labor. In the first decades of settlement, Californios employed unbaptized Indians, *gentilés*, though they occasionally paid the friars at the missions for more skilled neophyte labor. After the secularization of the missions, Indians, converted or otherwise, provided labor services on the ranches and in town for a pittance—rather than money, usually they or their village chief received goods, food, beads, blankets, and *aguardiente*, the locally produced hard liquor. Indians built the Californios' houses, dug their irrigation canals, tended their herds, watched their children, harvested and cooked their food. To control this ready workforce, the Californios enacted a series of vagrancy laws in the 1830s and 1840s that allowed punishment

Many Californios were of mixed race, including Pio Pico, the last Governor of Mexican California, whose African and Indian ancestry did not prevent him rising to prominence.

for out-of-work Indians, effectively forcing them into a form of slavery in towns and on ranches. If the local law enforcement proved ineffective, soldiers from the presidios reprised their Spanish roles by chasing runaways and capturing raiders.

Indian labor made the ranchos fruitful while their debased status inflated the rancheros' sense of self. Californios treated the Indians as peons, not only to gain the fruits of their labor but also to insure a culture of Hispanic superiority. The wealthier Californios put on airs of Spanish gentility to emphasize their difference from both the natives and the poorer Mexican settlers. Many of the settler families are familiar today, since their names live on in place names around the state: Olvera Street, Pacheco Pass, Figueroa Street, Vallejo, Avila Beach, and so on. Despite their advantages over the native peoples, they were themselves generally mixed-race except for a few of the elite in government and the military. Anglo visitors in the 1820s and 1830s, far more color conscious than Californios, noticed. The Mexican, wrote one visitor, "resembled a Negro more than a white."

More than 20 percent of the first settlers had African ancestry, including many of the leading families. An even higher

Lola Pacheco, heiress to the largest estate in the Monterey area, entered an arranged marriage to Mariano Malarín. Her mestizo father, Francisco Pacheco, used his wealth to move his family up the racially-charged social hierarchy.

percentage came from Indian backgrounds. Less than 30 percent could claim a "pure" Spanish heritage, yet as the years progressed, families whitewashed themselves, changing their identity on censuses from *coyote* (mixed Indian, African, Spanish), *mulatto*, or mestizo to Spanish. This process increased as Anglo newcomers married the daughters of elite landowners, reinforcing color prejudices and "whiting out" memories of Indian or African forbears. For Mexicans, racial identity derived from social practices—how one behaved and lived determined for the most part one's group identity. Despite this social whitening, hierarchies based on color excluded most dark-skinned people from the top social echelons, where women's complexions could be "even as fair as those of English women" according to Dana.

More important to the Californios themselves, Dana noted, were cultural pretensions, particularly speaking "pure Castillian" as opposed to "the corrupted dialect" spoken "by the lower classes."

Mariano Malarín came from a poorer but whiter family than his wife Lola Pacheco (opposite).

Continued sexual violence and prostitution plagued native women, though marriage between Mexican men and Indian women also occurred frequently. The Mexican racial system tolerated such relationships, though Indian wives themselves had a hard time fitting into elite society and Indian men did not marry Mexican women. Scottish immigrant Hugo Reid married Victoria of the village of Comicrabit, the neophyte daughter of a Gabrieleño chief, in 1837. Reid's friends worried about him marrying Victoria and "living sloppily on the outskirts of town with a thickening, stupid wife, the whole place overrun by unhappy little half-breeds." Yet, according to Reid's 1930s biographer, Susanna Bryant Dakin, Victoria "hardly resembled the squat and humble Indian women" his friends disdained. "Her carriage was proudly erect and her speech the purest Castillian." Dakin, herself descended from the Anglo elite that later took over the Mexican ranchos, relied on this cultural justification of the union to reassure her more race-conscious American readers. Victoria was the protégé of Eulalia Pérez, who had met her

EULALIA PEREZ, 139 YEARS OF AGE.

La Llavera of Mission San Gabriel, Eulalia Perez, was actually closer to a mere 110 when she died in 1878.

while serving as *llavera*, guardian of the girl neophytes' virtue, at Mission San Gabriel. Doña Pérez, herself a mestiza from Baja California, and her second husband, a retired soldier, had received a land grant from the mission fathers, the 15,000 acre Rancho San Pascual. Victoria managed to obtain title to a substantial part of her village's ancestral lands, a rare case of a native gaining more than a tiny plot on a rancheria. The cultural and social distance between Anglo newcomer and Indian daughter was, at least in her case, overcome through property and acculturation.

The Mexican authorities, relatively unconcerned with the social balance on their frontier, used California as dumping ground for petty criminals and political prisoners, sending hundreds of convicts to the remote territory. The Californios excluded the convicts from their society, forcing them to more marginal occupations in the pueblos. A few of these *cholos* were political exiles who apparently preached atheism to the horror of the remaining padres and the shock of the Californio elites, who liked Catholicism as long it didn't stand in the way of taking church lands and cattle.

"In the breast of the old time Californian," recalled Mariano Vallejo, "love of family was stronger than selfish and vile interest." The purpose of the Dons' ambitions, in their view, was to

Although James Walker's 1870s painting is titled Vaquero, *it probably shows the son of a wealthy landowner who was unlikely to actually work as a cowboy wearing such fine clothes.*

provide security and honor for their families outside of market relations. Indeed their economy had only limited contact with markets. The fecundity of the former missions' herds meant that meat was too cheap to sell. If a traveler was hungry, they could simply slaughter anyone's cow for the meat, leaving only the valuable part, the hide, for the rightful owner. Heirs to the Spanish love of horsemanship, the Californios equated a horseman, a *caballero,* with a gentlemen.

"The men of Monterey" appeared to Richard Henry Dana "to be always on horseback. Horses are as abundant here as dogs and chickens." So many horses wandered the coastal regions that, with the exception of a few prize animals, people were free to take any horse they encountered to ride to their destination. This generosity depended on the gentleness of California's environment and the stock built up by the missions, but it also expressed a core value of the Californios. The big rancho owners presided over a complex family life, living with wives, children, grandchildren, in-laws, more distant relatives, poor neighbors, *vaqueros*, and peons. In addition to their generosity, the Dons exercised a dominating authority in the family. In the most conservative families, children would kiss their father's ring before going to bed. A father could legally whip his adult children and beat his wife.

Within the patriarchal, hierarchical world of the ranchos and pueblos, Spanish and Mexican women carved a realm of limited autonomy. Following Catholic doctrine, Mexican law forbade divorce—but women had some recourse from abusive husbands. Wives could bring suits against their husbands to the pueblo's *alcalde* to stop excessive brutality, to end an extramarital affair, or to demand proper support. Daughters, on occasion, refused to marry and even turned to the *alcalde* to prevent such contracts. Indian women formally had recourse to courts, but few were able to take advantage of them. In general, historian Miroslava Chavez writes, "Indian women were seen as lesser beings possessing no honor or esteem that could be insulted" while "assaults by Mexican men on Mexican women were considered to be an affront to the honor of the women and their families."

Close connections to neighboring families, slow transportation, and a leisurely pace of life insured that weddings, funerals, and other social events often lasted days. Frequent dances, fandangos, fiestas, saints' days, and other events brought Californios together for dancing, drinking, horsemanship, and gambling. One American Navy officer wrote of an epic lunchtime party with then Governor Micheltorena: "Dancing commenced immediately, and, in the various combinations of quadrilles, contradances, and waltzes, was kept up until nine o'clock at night." Richard Henry Dana apparently found the ladies at one fandango a bit dull: "on the part of the women" it was a "lifeless affair" but "but the men did better... showing their figures to advantage." The Californios, unlike Dana, loved the events, playing practical jokes on each other, laughing, and drinking heavily into the night. Less gentle pastimes, such as cockfighting and bull baiting, provided more robust entertainment. If Californios caught a grizzly bear they would tie it to a large bull and bet on which animal killed the other first. Bear and bull fighting maintained their popularity even after the US conquest; San Franciscans constructed two bull rings in the 1850s. Such contests served as powerful metaphors for the clash of European with native—cattle and horses were European imports to the Americas, grizzlies indigenous Americans.

Emulation

Since the 1920s, civic buildings and homes, particularly in places such as Santa Barbara and San Diego, are reimaginings of the architecture of the *hacienda*. They refer back to the Californio era, the time when citizens of the Republic of Mexico were accumulating great wealth through the hide and tallow trade and constructing luxury mansions as dynastic families gained control over lands expropriated from the state or religious organizations.

Santa Barbara's annual "Spanish Days" festival notwithstanding, the culture that is being perpetuated is not Spanish, but Mexican. People dress up, play at being veiled ladies, caballeros, and the masked hero Zorro, and they say that they're remembering the Spanish. The vision that the adobe and red-tiled roof buildings evoke is misnamed because of Anglo cultural prejudice against things Mexican. Indeed, for years, descendents of Californios called themselves Spanish for the same reason.

Mexican Americans also used the Spanish tradition to remember their history as shown by the cast of the mission play at San Gabriel in the 1920s.

Elkhorn Slough

A sea kayak is one of your more silent forms of transportation. Two humans on a sea kayak must not look like human beings to a pelican, because none along the bleached fence depart as we float near. Though called "brown," up close these birds are a whole spectrum unto themselves: blues and greens and reds glint among their feathers. They yawp to each other. We explore along the marshy shore where tilting, partial fences mark the efforts of earlier humans to separate grazing land from bog—unsuccessfully. Returning, we get lost in a tule maze, always thinking that one avenue will lead into another, one that will lead us back to the main channel of the slough, which we can see but cannot reach. The lines of reeds, water, hills, and sky are peaceful enough that we don't mind not finding our way out. The wind and incoming tide is against us on the way back, though, because we took so long, and one of us gets grouchy, until we meet sea otters. Twenty or so of them, diving and feeding, lying on their backs and gazing at us, adorable as stuffed animals, mysterious in their absolute otherness. Long, wiry whiskers drooping from pale fur cheeks; unreadable, dark, liquid eyes.

The outlines of this same slough can be traced out on an 1861 map of the ranchos of the area. Low *esteros* lie between *chamisal* hills. On a modern-day map they carry the same names: Tembladero Slough; above it, Mojo Coso Slough. Above that, what is now called Elkhorn. In the whole quadrant, one small square marked *casa*. We decide to spend the next day trying to find the site, using the vague geography of the 1861 map.

That evening, we drive to Monterey, covering in 25 minutes what would have taken the residents of the *casa* one long, hard day. Cannery Row, once a center of the central Californian commercial fishing industry, is now merely a Disney-style destination: the warehouses, preserved in their quaintness, full of shops of beach-shell kitsch, sea otter refrigerator magnets, and lugubrious ceramic fishermen. The restaurant we can get seated in without a wait has these specials: lobster-and-crab encrusted sea bass, crab encrusted salmon. Expensive fish covered with even more expensive shellfish. While we wait at the bar, a man orders a drink for his girlfriend. "She wants something sweet that really packs a punch." The bartender suggests a zombie, which "will really knock her on her—" He leaves the sentence unfinished; everyone laughs. The contemporary fisherman dangles his bait. The drink he serves her is ignited. He assures the boyfriend,

"I promise I'm not burning off the alcohol." The boyfriend cautions the woman, "Don't drink it until the flame goes away."

On the 1861 map, just south of Tembaldero Slough, Mr. John B.D. Cooper, or Don Juan Cooper, had his Rancho Bolsa del Potrero y Moro Cojo. North of Cooper's rancho lay the Rancho de la Bolsa de las Escarpines, owned by Don Salvador Espinosa. We start our search by driving down Cooper Road, through fields of dusty feather-duster-leaved artichokes. The land is deeply ribbed: houses set far back from the road seem to be perched on the edge of the world; chamise-covered canyons drop off behind them, so narrow that we can see the next set of houses on the next ridge, just behind.

The *casa* we are searching for is said to have been known as Rancho Redconada del Sanjón, and was granted to José Eusebio Boronda, the son of a corporal among the Spanish troops who accompanied Portolá on his second expedition on February 1, 1840. The *casa*'s history reflects the movement of lands from Californios to Anglos as his daughter married William Anderson to become Inés Boronda de Anderson. It is recorded that the house they built looked out over a lake, so we try to snatch glimpses behind houses, down the gullies, of standing water.

We find a San Jon Road, but no adobe. We get to the outskirts of Salinas, of modern housing subdivisions that have eradicated any clues that might have been left on the land. We make a series of right turns to head back to the coast, find ourselves on Borondo Road, and then find the adobe. It is closed. It has a wood roof instead of the usual tile and looks isolated within the cyclone fence that protects it as a historic site. But behind it, the ribs of the slough-split hills swoop down toward the sea.

On the way home, driving north on Highway 1, we stop at the state park where San Gregorio Creek wends its way across the sand into the Pacific. We happen to be here on the same day of the year that Portolá and his men paused at this place in their search for Monterey. Veering too far northward, they found San Francisco Bay instead.

The pioneer wagon symbolized the resolve and the vulnerability of the family in westward migration as this 1930s woodcut by Dorothy Smith Sides shows.

5

ANGLO CALIFORNIA

The US conquest of California in 1846 and the subsequent 1849 gold rush brought the most revolutionary period in California history after the Spanish conquest. Like other social and economic revolutions, the upheavals were ground shaking (in California, the default adjective!) but were nonetheless built upon a foundation of existing patterns and relationships. The gold rush dramatically changed the environment of Northern California; made the tiny town of Yerba Buena into San Francisco, then the largest US city west of the Mississippi; brought hundreds of thousands of fortune seekers and adventurers from every corner of the world; and poured millions of dollars of new wealth into the US economy, fueling the country's ongoing industrial revolution and leading to worldwide inflation.

The new populations and the new centers of wealth ended the dominance of the ranching agrarian society of the Californios and devastated surviving Indian societies.

The fortune-seeking adventurers who began to flood the state in 1849 were different than the patriarch-led family groups of Americans who had begun arriving in California well before the US conquest. The 49ers, mostly bachelors, came to get rich quick, whereas the pioneers sought to create a new life for themselves and their families in the West. The image of the hardy miner panning for gold in a rushing stream calls up ideas of rugged independence, but most prospectors came to California in partnerships, even as members of small corporations. These creative financial efforts revolutionized the business of funding and organizing extractive industries and American corporate law in general. The gold rush jumpstarted California's rapid industrialization. The new settlers confirmed it as an anti-slave state, even though some slaves worked the gold country and some capitalists imported thousands of Chinese contract laborers. The gold rush transformation of the new state fit into larger patterns of expansion, sectional division, and ethnic/racial conflict that animated the US in the nineteenth century.

San Francisco, 1849–1850: The Gold Rush transformed San Francisco from a sleepy village into a bustling city, its harbor filled with thousands of ships, many of them abandoned by the men who went off to the gold fields.

Until the 1840s, Americans interested in California were limited to maritime commercial traders, individualist trappers and the odd entrepreneurial adventurer. Massachusetts-based merchant traders, who had already been trading with China and sponsoring whaling in the Pacific, were the first people from English North America to trade with California. New England sailors bought furs and hides from the missions and ranchos to sell to burgeoning shoe manufacturers back home. The appropriately named *Otter* was the first US ship to dock in California, in 1796, and soon the Americans—the citizens of the new nation on the other side of the continent—were the major market for California skins shipped around Cape Horn. The Boston-based maritime trading company, Bryant and Sturgis, set up its regional offices in Santa Barbara, Monterey, and eventually in Macao, the

Portuguese colony in China, connecting California and the China trade during the 1830s. American traders' experiences in Mexican California fed Easterners' dreams of a burgeoning Pacific trade. These enterprising capitalists hoped to capture an imagined China market, a goal that animated American policy in the Pacific for the next 150 years. The key to the trade would be ports on the West Coast and the islands in between Asia and North America. Bryant and Sturgis employees, notably Richard Henry Dana, promoted the bucolic, prosperous image of the California coast back east. California's ties to New England were so great that when a British naval officer arrived at San Francisco Bay in 1845, he complained "D—n it! is there nothing but Yankees here?" New England's demand for high-quality otter skins, along with Russian hunting farther up the coast, decimated that population by the 1820s; by the middle of the century the otter was almost extinct. Instead, the Yankees started buying cow hides, stimulating the growth of the Californio cattle ranches that had taken over the mission herds.

The bountiful game of California's interior attracted American trappers and hunters who traversed the mountain ranges westward in search of pelts for the US fur trade. The trappers, renowned for their individualism, actually worked in groups of ten to forty hardy mountain men. Jedediah Smith, probably the most accomplished western tracker and trapper, became the first Anglo to enter California overland from the east when he and his team left the Santa Fe Trail and crossed the Mojave Desert in 1826. Tough and resolute (he lost an ear in a fight with a grizzly and had a companion stitch it back on "some way or another"), Smith put together the Rocky Mountain Fur Company to try to make more money from the trade. But the independent parties of traders often made little from their furs— the big profits went to those who distributed the furs to eastern manufacturers for hats, gloves, and other clothing. The trapping parties depended on the Indians for cleaning and drying their furs, and for sex. Yet the exploits of Smith earned him the enmity of the natives whose lands he traversed—Mohaves killed ten of his employees in 1826 and Umpqua fighters in southern Oregon killed all but three of his mountain men after one of his party raped a woman. Comanche on the Santa Fe Trail ended Smith's brief life in 1831.

The Mexicans also had their reasons to distrust the trappers and often ordered them out of the territory. Perhaps the least trustworthy was James O. Pattie, another trapper along the Santa Fe Trail, whose atrocities against the Mohaves may have

The Donner Party

George and Jacob Donner, like other Midwestern farmers, chafed at strictures imposed on their lives by an increasingly competitive economic environment and the loss of opportunities to accumulate cheap land for their families. The far West promised an answer in the same way that the Old West of the Mississippi and Ohio River valleys had whispered of opportunities and freedom to their parents and grandparents. By moving west they hoped to occupy cheap land recently saved from its imagined neglect by native peoples and decadent empires. Though such dreams rarely reached the nightmarish depths of the Donner Party's collapse and cannibalism, settlers' hopes for an easier life were rarely fulfilled.

The Donner Party, infamous for the desperate eating of corpses of party members, is memorialized in a park and museum in the Sierra Nevada Mountains and in dozens of books and films. Less well remembered is that the only two people killed for the purpose of cannibalizing their corpses were the Indian cowboys, Luis and Salvador, sent by Johann Sutter to rescue them. The Donner Party survivors thus carried the pattern of pioneer expansion to its most extreme, devouring indigenous people in order to survive. The Donner Party remains a powerful metaphor for the deadly results of pioneering settlement and conquest.

incited them to kill Smith's men. Pattie and his father Sylvester ran afoul of the Mexican authorities in San Diego. Sylvester died in a Mexican jail while his son James continued north. He turned his exploits into *The Personal Narrative of James O. Pattie*, a popular book filled with adventures and tall tales, among them a claim to have saved thousands of lives during a mythical smallpox epidemic in Northern California. The particulars of Pattie's stories may have been false, but his portrayal of the beauty of California, the brutality of Indians, and the venality of the Mexican authorities inspired western fantasies among Americans.

California, however, was not just an empty wilderness, a blank canvas on which the intruding Americans could draw what they pleased. The Spanish and Californios had already established a political and social economy based on ranching and trade. Californio society relied on a racial division of labor in which the lowest caste Indians did the backbreaking menial labor, middle caste mestizos managed the ranches and filled the ranks of soldiers, and an elite claiming to be "white" ruled. The first Anglos who took up residence in California understood this society as their means to accumulate property and wealth beyond the wildest imaginings of their fellows back home. Seeing the huge ranchos favored by Spanish and Mexican land policy, ambitious Americans readily abandoned the Jeffersonian ideal of a democracy of small farmholders and seized upon the Spanish-Californio system as an opportunity to quickly amass wealth.

Early Anglo immigrants settled into the upper two castes of Californio society. Enterprising mercantilist immigrants such as Hugo Reid in Los Angeles moved relatively easily into the elite. Swiss Immigrant Johann Sutter, for instance, ruled over what amounted to a barony at the junction of the Sacramento and San Joaquin Rivers in the Central Valley. He owned over 145,000 acres (226 square miles) of land on which he enslaved hundred of Indians and built a fort, the precursor of the city of Sacramento. He also bought the Russian tracts along Bodega Bay and the Russian river. Sutter's system of enormous landholdings worked by Indians and indentured Hawaiians was duplicated, if on a smaller scale, by many of the other enterprising settlers.

Stories of cheap land in a fertile and easy climate from the likes of Dana and Pattie spread east. Pioneer families with their own vision of life in the west set out walking and riding to California. The more easily reached and more commercially popularized areas of Texas had drawn the first pioneers out of the trans-Appalachian east. The journey overland to California and Oregon was long and dangerous in comparison. Only when the depression of the 1830s and early 1840s disrupted the economy of the Mississippi and the "old West" did significant numbers of pioneers take their chances on the trail to Oregon and California. The first overland pioneers, the Bartelson-Bidwell party, set out in 1841 along the Oregon trail but got lost in the Great Basin region. They stumbled across the Sierra to the Sacramento delta rancho of John Marsh. Marsh had parlayed a fake medical degree into hacienda-scale wealth by charging patients 50 head of cattle for each treatment. Like Sutter, Marsh embraced an earlier form of settlement, but unlike the baron of Sacramento who welcomed pioneers and organized rescue parties if they were lost, Marsh saw the newcomers as a nuisance at worst and an easily exploitable source of money at best. He was probably right on both counts. The same year, other emigrants made the trek from Santa Fe to Los Angeles. By the mid 1840s, Anglo emigrants were pouring into California along trails from the southwest, Utah, and Oregon.

Anglos who entered California formed three main groups. Adventurers and entrepreneurs saw the West Coast as a port by which to reach the fabled markets of China and as the crowning territorial prize in their dreams of a grand continental empire replete with dark-skinned servants. The Free Soil pioneers to California saw it as a non-slave version of Texas, a place of wide open land, fruitful coastal agriculture, and enormous resources. "Free Soil," the rallying cry of one precursor to the Republican Party, meant land that was free to be taken, to be worked by free white people in a place free of competition from unfree or alien racial groups. Soon a massive wave of gold rush immigrants, many of whom shared the same free soil ideology, swelled the ranks of pioneers. The Free Soilers, trappers, and traders supported American expansion. The early American presence in California was a key expression of the welter of causes—

Large boats or launches manned by Indians, and capable of carrying from five to six hundred hides apiece, are attached to the Missions, and sent down to the vessels... [One time,] all the hides... that came down in the boats were soaked with water, and unfit to put below, so that we were obliged to trice them up to dry, in the intervals of sunshine or wind, upon all parts of the vessel.... Between the tops, too and the mast heads, from the fore to the main swifters, and thence to the mizzen rigging, and in all directions, athwartships, tricing lines were run, and strung with hides. The head stays and guys, and the spritsail yard were lined, and, having still more, we got out the swinging-booms, and strung them and the forward and after guys with hides. The rail, fore, and aft, the windlass, capstan, the sides of the ship and every vacant place on the deck, were covered with wet hides, on the least sign of an interval for drying. Out ship was nothing but a mass of hides, from the cat-hairpins to the water's edge, and from the jib-boom-end to the taffrail.

—Richard Henry Dana,
Two Years Before the Mast (1840)

economic, ideological, cultural, and demographic—that led to the Mexican-American War.

In 1846 President Polk, using as a pretext a manufactured border incident, began the war against Mexico. Within two years, US troops had occupied Mexico City and seized most of the mountain west and the west coast—about a third of their southern neighbor's territory. The war fulfilled the wishes of a wide coalition of people in the US: Texans wanting control of the Santa Fe Trail, Eastern merchants interested in controlling Pacific ports, and pioneer settlers hungry for millions of acres of cheap land. In the two-year war, 1,800 US soldiers died in combat, while nearly ten times more Mexicans died. With the signing of the Treaty of Guadalupe Hidalgo in February 1848, California and much of the great basin became part of the US—but this did not occur as easily as it sounds now.

President Andrew Jackson had offered unsuccessfully to buy California from Mexico in 1835 for $3.5 million, but the Panic of 1837 devastated the economy and the US could no longer afford the price tag. With slow economic recovery, adventurous Americans, the "filibusters," began demanding the takeover of former Spanish territories in the West, the Caribbean, and Central America. Fed by these ideas and the false news that the US had started a war with Mexico in 1842, Commodore Thomas ap Catesby Jones and the US Navy's Pacific Squadron briefly seized Monterey. Catesby Jones's apologies notwithstanding, the incident shocked Mexican authorities and ensured that Mexico would never willingly sell its northwestern lands.

But California fit the grand ambitions of US expansionists too well; they did not give up so easily. The US Consul in Monterey, merchant Thomas Oliver Larkin, encouraged the Californios to take the same route taken by the newly formed State of Texas—declare independence and then join the US. Heartened by Governor Alvarado's rebellion, Larkin's quiet diplomacy contrasted with the aggression of the pioneers who simply squatted on Californio lands, claiming them for their own. The more aggressive pioneers soon had a champion. In the spring of 1846, just before the war began, explorer and US Army Captain John C. Frémont arrived in the state with 60 "trappers" (really irregular soldiers) guided by Indian fighter Kit Carson. Confronting the Mexican government just outside Monterey, they raised the US flag on what is now called Fremont Peak in the mountains east of San Juan Bautista. Larkin negotiated a peaceful end to the crisis and Frémont and his men headed back to Oregon. Larkin had secret orders from President Polk to sign an agreement with the Californios and didn't want pioneer aggressiveness spoiling his maneuvers. Under the plan, the Californios would declare an independent republic ruled over by themselves and a few select Anglo friends such as Larkin. The US would then create a military "protectorate" to fend off the British, French, Russians, and any other greedy powers. Larkin thought he had the Californios "eating out of his hand."

Larkin was well suited to this diplomatic approach. He had arrived in California intending to follow the path of Hugo Reid and the other early Anglos: convert to Catholicism, marry the daughter of a ranchero, and become a Don himself. Instead, on board ship in 1832 he met Rachel Holmes, who was on her way to meet her ship-captain husband in Monterey. Somehow, Holmes became pregnant with Larkin's child. "Oh well," Larkin's granddaughter later commented, "it must have been a very long voyage in those days and I suppose there was little else to do." The two were married after Holmes's husband conveniently died. Holmes became the first Anglo woman to live in California, while her husband fit in easily without becoming a Catholic. Larkin's connections to the Californios suited his diplomatic tasks, but his efforts failed to bear fruit before American impatience, a characteristic Larkin apparently shared in other areas, cast diplomacy aside.

Larkin's efforts came to naught. The Mexican government could neither defend California nor give it up. It provided few trained troops to the presidios, leaving the military unable to fend off the Yankees. Yet Mexican *Presidente* Santa Ana, recently humiliated in Texas, refused to sell the territory to the US. The Californios themselves were deeply divided over the prospect of independence held out by Larkin. Caught between his countrymen and his friends among the Californios, he wrote to his wife that defeat for either side "appeared sad and disagreeable to me."

Frémont quietly returned to California, staying with Sutter in New Helvetia. From there he encouraged a group of American settlers in Sonoma and Napa to stage a coup against the Mexicans. In mid June 1846 they seized horses intended for the Mexican military and kidnapped several rancheros, including Mariano Vallejo, who had previously hosted the rebel leaders on his estate. Mexican forces failed to dislodge them in a "battle" at Olompali. (Olompali was a Miwok village in Marin County headed by Camilo Ynitia, the only Indian to have a land grant confirmed by the US.) The fight left one soldier dead and several wounded. On June 14, the rebels declared the independence of the Bear Republic. One man, apparently not much of an artist, created a flag featuring a star and what was supposed to be a grizzly bear (though it looked more like a pig) drawn with berry juice. They named William Ide president of the California Republic. Hundreds of settlers, including quite a few *cholos,* flocked to the Bear Republic banner, however badly drawn. Frémont rode out to Sonoma and took command. "We must be conquerors," Ide warned, or "we are robbers." The Californios, of course, thought them the latter, calling the rebels "exiles from civilization" as bad as "lepers."

In July of 1846, shortly after the start of the Mexican-American War, the new commodore of the Pacific Squadron, John D. Sloat, and his forces took Monterey and Yerba Buena (San Francisco). With the Navy in charge, Frémont cancelled the Republic a bare month after its founding. He placed his California Battalion of 230 frontiersmen under the command of the US forces. In the midst of the war, Robert Stockton, a veteran of the war of 1812 and the first US military actions in Tripoli, succeeded Sloat. Stockton declared himself military governor of California and sent forces to occupy San Diego and Los Angeles. Californio militia resisted, defeating US troops in a skirmish on the San Pedro Rancho in the Dominguez Hills. Nonetheless, Californio forces defeated the Americans at the Battle of San Pascual outside of San Diego in 1846. Angelinos revolted against the rule of the American military and forced out occupying US troops. But the victory was fleeting. José María Amador, a former Presidio soldier, blamed "the bad qualities of the leaders," such as commanders General José Castro and Governor Pío Pico, which "disheartened their subordinates, the troops, and the people."

The Californio forces could not hold out, however, when Frémont's troops arrived from the east and north. Governor Pico surrendered to Frémont at the Cahuenga Pass outside LA in January 1847. The Americans soon retook LA, a victory commemorated today on a boulder monument outside LA's Union Station.

Despite Frémont's military success, squabbling among the American military leaders led to the court martial of the charismatic explorer. Frémont's refusal to obey orders from the new head of the US forces in San Francisco, Brigadier General Stephen Watts Kearny, made him a hero among rebellious Anglo Californians and he was quickly pardoned by President Polk.

John C. Frémont capitalized on his dashing explorer image as his political ambitions grew.

The handsome Frémont, nicknamed "the Pathfinder" for his work finding trails across the mountain west, later grew rich from gold discovered on his land in the Sierra foothills. He controlled an enormous estate gained in the land grab of the early postwar years. He entered national politics, aided by his talented wife, Jessie, daughter of Senator Thomas Hart Benton. The illustrious Benton family distrusted the freewheeling soldier who had eloped with their daughter, referring to him as "Jessie's insanity." But as the well-born Jessie wrote to a friend, "My life from my fifteenth year was the General's." She wrote his speeches, lobbied for his appointments in Washington, and managed his career, often from thousands of miles away. Frémont became one of California's first senators and then ran for President as the first candidate of the Republican Party in 1856. As a general in the Civil War, Frémont continued his independent populist ways. After receiving a promotion to major general, he defied President Lincoln by freeing slaves in Missouri and confiscating slave-owners' property. Frémont paid little attention to his lands, losing them along with most of his wealth. He then worked as a shill promoting a railroad scam in France, bilking French peasants out of close to five million dollars. When the scheme collapsed, he returned to the US, where stealing from French people didn't seem much of an issue. He ended his public service as the first territorial governor of Arizona.

California's rapid ascent from conquered territory to state in three short years played into the bitter politics of pro- and anti-slavery forces that were dividing the USA. The absorption of the enormous territories conquered in the Mexican-American war satisfied ambitious expansionists throughout the country and seemed to fulfill the principles of Manifest Destiny—a belief that the US was ordained to become a great continental and then world power. Yet as Ralph Waldo Emerson pointed out: "The United States will conquer Mexico, but it will be as the man swallows the arsenic; Mexico will poison us." Anti-slavery forces demanded that the new territories be confirmed as free soil, lands where slaves as well as free black people were forbidden to settle. Southern whites deeply resented the geographic constraints on their economic and social system as much as they rejected the moral judgment inherent in the idea of "free soil." Increasingly resentful of the Northerners and fearful for the future of their power over their slaves, the Southerners demanded recognition from the North of their "rights." In the Compromise of 1850, Southerners insisted that the price of California's admission to the union as a state without slavery was the passage of the Fugitive Slave Act, requiring citizens of free states to return runaway slaves to their owners. It was a morally destructive law that forced people to be enforcers for a system they opposed. Northerners worried that the "Slave Power" would continue to dominate US politics and force free white workers and farmers to compete with slaves. The compromises over enslaving African people that had underlain US politics since the revolution continued to rankle. Within a decade the country was plunged into civil war. Ironically, although California played such an important role in hastening the conflict, the Civil War had relatively little impact on California, a Union state.

The American conquest of California brought a new constitutional system to the region. It also added powerful new groups of settlers with views on how society should be organized that differed dramatically from those of the Californios, let alone of the native people. The clashes of the four main groups—the Californios, the Anglo elites, the pioneers, and the Indians—structured the politics of California for decades to come. The arrival of waves of immigrants from the east, south, and overseas during the gold rush swelled the state's population, and complicated but did not fundamentally alter those divisions. The Americans did not like to think they were doing anything wrong in taking over the state and imposing their own ways. The 19th-century chronicler of California history, Hubert Howe Bancroft, observed this blindness: "The idea of conquest in the American mind has never been associated with tyranny. On the contrary, such is the national trust in its own superiority and beneficence, that either as a government or as individuals we have believed ourselves bestowing a precious boon upon whomsoever we confer in brotherly spirit our institutions."

The employment of slaves and peons was not possible or acceptable to most of the pioneers, the 49ers, and later immigrants. Economic competition, especially in the gold fields, was exacerbated when Californio elites tried to bring their Indian peons to work mining claims. While opposed to peonage, the solution the Free Soilers sought, however, was not equality and equal opportunity for all, but rather the exclusion from California of Indians, mestizo Mexicans, and Chinese. The exclusion was often enforced with violence. Indeed the anti-Indian actions of the pioneers led to mass slaughter of California's remaining indigenous people. This conflict was intensified because the areas of the greatest immigration—the gold-filled foothills of the Sierra Nevada and the Coast Ranges of the northwest—had not been effectively colonized by the Mexicans or Spanish. These were the places Indians unwilling to accept mission conversion had fled, where the Central Valley and hill peoples held themselves separate from the decimations of the mission system. While they had continued to live their pre-conquest lives of hunting, gathering, and raiding with only limited involvement in fur trapping for the market, they were no longer able to do so in the face of the onslaught of the American cultural and social conquest.

Elite Anglos, relatively secure in their higher status, tried to preserve the Californio system. But racial conflict flared, sometimes brutally, as Free Soilers sought to insure new forms of white dominance. Lynching, a tool of mobs to enforce frontier justice and establish an Anglo-dominated social order, became all too commonplace. More than 150 Mexicans and Californios were lynched in the decade after the US conquest. The victims were usually Californio *cholos,* Mexicans, or Chinese immigrants. Francisco Torres, for instance, was lynched by a mob in Santa Ana after he killed an Anglo in a fight. The mob caught Torres, a local newspaper reported, in a place "occupied principally by Indian half-breeds, Mexicans and other thieves and outlaws." Another paper sought a larger solution for those on the bottom: "The sooner such savages are exterminated the better for civilization."

The Californio-immigrant conflict might have remained low-key for years had it not been for a keen-eyed carpenter, James Wilson Marshall. Few people took notice when he discovered gold in the winter of 1848 as he built a mill on the American River for Johann Sutter. But when enterprising merchant and excommunicated Mormon Sam Brannan learned of the discovery, he quietly cornered the market on mining supplies, then rode through the sleepy town of San Francisco waving a bottle of gold dust, shouting "Gold! Gold from the American River." Brannan's promotion worked on both counts: gold fever swept the new state, the nation, and the world while Brannan swept in a fortune from sales to the miners. (Brannan also milked naïve Mormon miners who thought they should pay him, as a local church elder, a tithe of their earnings. Brannan did nothing to dissuade them.) Soldiers abandoned their posts for the diggings; newspapers stopped publishing as journalists chased different sorts of leads. Sailors jumped ship in droves, leaving San Francisco's harbor filled with abandoned vessels. Young adventuring men poured into the California foothills where millions of years of metamorphic and fault action had created enormous gold deposits, much of it in river sand "placers." Within a year, hundreds of thousands of people worked the diggings of the Mother Lode country. New cities and towns sprung up throughout the surrounding hills, complete with stores, theaters, bars, and other necessities, such as houses of prostitution.

The gold rush confirmed an American belief in the incredible bounty of nature, the possibility of wresting great wealth with relative ease from the land. At the same time it revolutionized California's society and economy. Along the way, it caused ecological disasters: a moonscape of devastated land that brought massive flooding and poisoned rivers. The runoff flowed into

A bucolic image of mining by printmakers Currier and Ives showing different techniques of gold extraction.

San Francisco Bay, filling it with a deep layer of contaminated silt that still clouds the waters today.

The miners ignored the native people on whose land they worked. The US had not yet established a territorial government, so drawing on a frontier-style democracy, the miners developed their own laws and customs to govern the region, electing record-ers to settle conflicting claims. But the law was limited and order kept as much by gangs' thuggish behavior. Robbery and theft, beatings, murder, and rape threatened everyone. Some mining camps had a murder a day. As one adventurer wrote: "the fallen are trampled into the mud, and are left to the tender mercies of the earth and sky. No longer ago than last night, I saw a man lying on the wet ground, unknown, unconscious, uncared for, and dying... Money, Money, is the all-absorbing object.... There is no government, no law. Whatever depravity there is in man's heart now shows itself without restraint."

Only a few Anglos had any knowledge of mining, instead learning techniques from more experienced men who came from Mexico and Chile, even while racial conflict flared repeatedly in the diggings. To exclude the Mexicans, Chileans, and Chinese, politicians passed a foreign miners tax as soon as California became a state. Less law-abiding American miners simply lynched and beat their competitors, then seized their claims and equipment. Approximately 10,000 Mexicans were forced

The reality of hydraulic mining was hardly bucolic.

out, including quite a few Californios, despite their new US citizenship.

The heady initial moments of the gold rush were followed by a period of consolidation and institutionalization as the dreams and legends of getting rich quick soon came up against mineral reality. Through panning—standing in cold mountain streams while sifting sand—the miners quickly exhausted the easiest placers. Working in teams, miners built more and more elaborate mechanisms, long flues, large arrays of hoses and other hydraulic mining equipment. But even this relatively easy access to chunks of gold in the riverbanks through "hydraulicking" rapidly gave way to more difficult enterprises to extract veins deeper in the ground. Larger mines required much more money and meant the end of the rough-and-ready miner and the small partnerships. Soon, heavily capitalized joint stock corporations dominated the industry and the individualist miners became wage laborers or were replaced by new immigrants from Mexico and China. While a few miners struck it rich, in the end, the people who made the most money were merchants like Sam Brannan and other well-heeled investors who were able to marshal the capital needed to mine over the long term.

Meanwhile, the increasing cost of extracting ores from more remote and more recalcitrant veins after the 1850s meant that only heavily capitalized companies—those with large amounts of money in hand—could manage the costs of equipment and

Floods and Rights

The hydraulic mining and the diggings destroyed the soil of the foothills so it could no longer retain water in the winter rains. Torrential floods inundated Central Valley towns. The worst flood happened in 1862 when Sacramento sank under fifteen feet of water and the governor traveled to his inauguration in a boat. The current downtown is built over the old city. An 1875 flood destroyed the city of Marysville. The devastation led to the first mass environmental movement in the United States as residents of the downstream towns demanded reform. Lawsuits flowed like water. A court ruling, quoted here, banned hydraulic mining and the Central Valley floods subsided—aided by levee construction and a drought that, ironically, threatened the farms in the region as greatly as the floods.

"The Gold Run Ditch and Mining Company... have been for several years last past, in possession of five hundred acres of mineral land, situated adjacent to the North Fork of the American River... The beds of the two rivers have shallowed, and their channels widened, so that the depths of the rivers have greatly lessened, and their liability to overflow has been materially increased, causing the frequent floods to extend their area, and to be more destructive than they otherwise would have been, and covering thousands of acres of good land in the Sacramento valley with mining debris... [T]he main question at issue... is whether the defendant... has the right to dump its hydraulic debris into the river, to the endangerment of habitation and cultivation of large tracts of country.... Undoubtedly, the fact must be recognized, that in the mining regions of the State, the custom of making use of the waters of streams as outlets for mining debris has prevailed for many years...

A legitimate private business, founded upon a local custom, may grow into a force to threaten the safety of the people, and destruction to public and private rights; and when it develops into that condition, the custom upon which it is founded becomes unreasonable, because dangerous to public and private rights... Every business has its laws, and these require of those who are engaged in it to so conduct it as that it shall not violate the rights that belong to others."

—California Supreme Court,
People v. Gold Run Ditch and Mining Company (1884)

Mariano Vallejo's daughter Fannie married the main developer of the city of Vallejo, John B. Frisbie, joining the old elite with the new. She followed him to Mexico City when his financial schemes went sour.

deep mines. Especially with the Silver rush of the 1860s and 1870s, mining became very big business. The only opportunity for adventurous independent young men in the fields was as employees of big companies. Adolph Sutro, later mayor of San Francisco, developed mining techniques needed to get at the deep veins, while the "Silver Kings" of San Francisco came to dominate the desert mines of the eastern Sierra and Nevada. Other fortunes, like that of the Hearst family, depended on mines further afield in the Rockies and Latin America.

The rush of ambitious, adventurous men to the gold fields created a profound gender imbalance in California. More than 70 percent of the new state's population was male. Male cultures—

from many different lands—predominated in the mining camps. Drag entertainment, homosexual relationships, and prostitution created a sexual order that appeared licentious to Victorian sensibilities. The wide open sexual world of the first years of the gold rush was a short-lived phenomenon, as the rough-and-tumble culture was quickly repressed in San Francisco and the gold camps were replaced by mining corporations. Still, those years had established California and San Francisco as places where the normal rules of society about gender, sex, and pleasure could be bent, if not broken.

California's pioneer days, like those in other western states, never were what people imagined them to be—even as they were happening. True, many brave and hardy people had made long and dangerous treks across the continent. True, they worked long and hard to create mines, farms, and ranches throughout the state. True, they created a new society in their new territory. Yet the world they found in California and the way they created their new state did not quite fit the myth. Rather than being complete individualists, the pioneers relied on extensive social networks, often forming communities along the way. Today many ideologues fantasize a mythical western past of freedom to exploit nature and other people unencumbered by federal regulation or taxes. But the federal and state government played an enormous role in making California. The US military established administrative control over the state early on and regulated many aspects of life, from controlling Californios and removing Indians to rescuing stranded pioneers. The government built roads and regulated commerce. Federal policy led to the rapid industrialization of the state and underwrote the creation of the state's network of railroads. Lucrative military and government contracts enriched Anglo Californians. The costs of the ongoing Indian warfare in the conquest of California

The idealized version of the US expansion memorialized in an 1861 US Capitol mural, "Westward the Course of Empire Takes Its Way" by Emanuel Leutze.

far exceeded the state's income. By the 1860s it totaled almost $1 million. (About $21 billion in current dollars.)

While California sided with the Union in the Civil War, it was riven by competing ideologies and labor systems. It was a place with rapidly shifting but still attractive opportunities for enterprising people. Remote settlements, pockets of indigenous cultures, Californio society, and subsistence farmers only marginally involved in the market economy could still survive. But the main thrust of growth and development derived from ever-larger enterprises and continuing concentrations of wealth. Soon the burgeoning market society swept up or swept aside just about everyone in its path. Californians—newcomers and natives, immigrants and Californios alike—had no choice but to adjust to the new reality.

Sacramento Floodplain

Intent on crossing the Sierra, we pass ranked cornfields, dusty almond trees, dolorous, heavy-headed sunflowers. Enclosed-cab tractors trail plumes of dust. A lone patch of tule reeds persists in a ditch, a mound of jimson weed holds up large white toxic flowers against a sumpstone wall. A continuous line of green in the distance delineates the riparian corridor of trees on either side of a creek. Before the valley came under cultivation, dense stands of cottonwoods and willows and tangled understory extended three miles on either side of every creek, and each creek would change its course within these wide bands with yearly rainfall.

The Sacramento River corridor was as wide as its floodplain, which we rumble across for 3.2 miles on a raised causeway over what is now officially called the Yolo Bypass, part of the great Pacific Flyway that birds have been using long before California was a twinkle in anyone's eye.

In the 1930s, a wall was built to divert floodwaters around the city of Sacramento. Land in the floodplain was sold to farmers with the caveat that they not build any protective dams or dikes that would obstruct the movement of waters in wet years. These lands were just profitable enough for the farmers to put up with intermittent flooding for decades. But the inundations were frustrating enough that when, in the 90s, wildlife biologists at the nearby ag school UC Davis launched a plan to change this land use over to wildlife reserves, many farmers were willing to sell. Some have converted to crops amenable to flooding. Now, undulating rice dikes waver together into the distance like marbled endpapers of old history books. On winter mornings, smoky clouds of hundreds of migratory birds agitate above the floodwaters: tundra swans, white-faced ibis, northern shovelers, pintails. Some summers, the whole vista will bake to pale marbled gold; this year, water still stands, and white egrets, greater and lesser, punctuate cursive lines of green.

The river town we drive toward came into being at the junction of the American and the Sacramento rivers, the first now dammed at Folsom, 20 miles upstream, and the second dammed, along with the Pit and the McCloud, at Shasta, 175 miles to the north. Some of Sacramento's streets still trace out the paths of waterways that brought the city into being, the wagon tracks that followed creek beds, the paths of least resistance out of the foothills: Auburn Boulevard leads northward to Old Auburn Road, crossing and recrossing Capple Creek, now over bridges. In the past, each crossing would have been a ford.

Interstate 80 causeway over the Yolo Bypass.

The carriages of wagons would have been suspended high enough to clear the rutted roadbed, cobbled riverbed, to bring passengers and goods safe and dry to their destinations.

Discontinuous, the road picks up again in Miner's Ravine at the Auburn-Folsom Road. We can guess what went on there. These old roads curve and meander according to the topography they follow. Overlain upon them are the street grids. The oldest of these lies within the junction of the two great rivers and follows William Penn's brotherly, democratic city plan: block divisions that are perfectly symmetrical, streets numbered and lettered instead of commemorating important men. On US 50, we pass exits for 15th, 34th, 59th, and 65th Streets. The river was democratic in its flooding, too, so that the houses in this part of town have front doors at the second level, at the top of a full flight of stairs. Residents no longer keep boats in their yards since the river no longer comes in to lift them up.

Between 15th and 34th Streets, a ramp for Interstate 80 veers northward. It will pass to the north of Lake Tahoe, whereas our US 50 will cut below, to the south. While it will still be possible for some time to cut across to 80 as it veers northeast, such a change of plan would mean crossing the rising hips of the foothills.

The decision a driver makes today is between an eight-lane interstate and a six-lane state highway. That choice became possible when Squaw Valley was chosen for the 1960 Winter Olympics, which committed the State of California to widen and improve the development of the route to Lake Tahoe over the Donner Pass. Long before that, at this junction, a traveler would have had to choose between wagon and horseback.

We don't know how far native Californian Ms. Lula Loof and her son traveled to have their portraits taken in an Alturas photography studio.

6

THE END OF THE OLD WAYS

The transition to an American-ordered society proved difficult and deadly in California. Settlers maintained much of the Spanish-Mexican land system, but transformed race relations and reorganized the economy. The result for the Californios was a wrenching change; for native people, it was nothing short of disaster. Indeed, some Yurok people referred to the 1850s as "the time when the stars fell."

Although Californios were legally defined as white, most soon learned that such status was a flexible thing. The 1848 Treaty of Guadalupe Hidalgo gave the Californios US citizenship. It also guaranteed "without restriction" that the Californios "shall be maintained and protected in the free enjoyment of their liberty and property." This guarantee proved scant security for their estates in the face of the overwhelming invasion of Anglo-Americans little inclined to respect the land rights of Mexicans. While squatting was a major problem for large landowners throughout the West, it was particularly problematic in California where Californios often didn't have the social, financial, or legal resources necessary to fight the invasion of their land.

The US created a commission to review land grants, but standards of proof were quite high and surveying too vague for the landowners to succeed often. Californio deeds, where they existed, were imprecise—land had been so cheap and the tracts so large, it hadn't mattered very much where one property left off and another began. But soon the edges mattered very much. The 1851 US Land Act, originally introduced to help Californios, required that deeds be reconfirmed, a rule that launched hundreds of lawsuits. Rancho owners were lynched, driven insane, or betrayed by Anglo lawyers—who took their clients' land in payment for defending it. For instance, the Peralta family lost their 19,000-acre estate to a swindling attorney, Horace Carpentier, who is now embarrassingly remembered as the founder of the liberal city of Oakland. In what later became

Orange County, Californios controlled 62 percent of the land in 1860. Ten years later they held just 11 percent.

> Land is not considered private property until the title to it is confirmed and patented. As the proceeding to obtain a patent may consume years, almost a lifetime, the result is that the native Californians (of Spanish descent) who were the land owners when we took California are virtually despoiled of their lands and their cattle and their horses.... They are being impoverished with frightful rapidity.... I doubt if a dozen families will escape ruin. There seems to be a settled purpose with our law-givers to drive the natives to poverty, and crowd them out of existence....
> —María Amparo Ruiz Burton,
> *The Squatter and the Don* (1885)

Sutter, like many members of the Californio elite, had trouble adjusting to the money economy of the market-oriented US. He had been more successful bartering with Miwoks, Yokuts, and Nisenans than he was paying them cash wages. Sutter's workers, European and native, had rushed to the gold fields; squatters took over his land. Even though the US confirmed the title to his estates, he did not have the cash resources to evict squatters or pay taxes. Just three years after the rush began with the discovery of gold on his land, he was bankrupt. The former baron of Sacramento died penniless in a German Moravian community in Pennsylvania in 1880.

Southern California landowners avoided many of these problems for decades and were able to prosper by selling cattle to the growing Bay Area and mining country. But they borrowed heavily to expand their operations in the face of increased competition from cattle imported from the east. An intense drought from 1862–4 devastated even the hardy longhorn cattle of Southern California. In Los Angeles County alone, as many as three-quarters died of thirst and hunger. The heavily indebted ranchos collapsed and with them most of Californio society. While some of the Californio elite joined Anglo society, for the most part, they merged into the larger community of cowboys, shepherds, and artisans who now faced a future as a segregated minority group in a land they had once ruled.

Like the Spanish and Mexicans before them, the big Anglo landowners had properties far too large to work themselves. Many of the landowning entities were partnerships and corporations, not individuals interested in living on their own land. The American elites in the 1840s and 1850s had adapted to the Mexican/Spanish system of peonage, relying on Indian labor to work their land and to prevent marauding and theft. But as the economy transformed, money began to replace barter or payment-in-kind, creating a different cultural and economic relationships between rancher and worker.

Some Indians became converts to the market economy, finding that money made trade easier and allowed them access to goods otherwise unavailable. Their adaptation brought more Indians into the workforce. The Truckee Paiutes of Nevada, for instance, crossed the Sierra Nevada to work in the mines and ranches of central California. Indians also migrated from Oregon in the 1850s and 1860s to work northern gold and silver mines, especially in Siskiyou County along the Salmon and Klamath rivers. Later many of these enterprising migrant native workers likely found jobs as farm laborers.

On the whole, the first decades of US rule in California proved devastating for the First Peoples: The disruption of the region's economy, the competition of new groups of workers, and the vast increase in population stressed native communities. Increasing economic desperation led to more conflicts, as Indians turned to raiding and stealing to survive. Worse, Anglo settlers carried deeply racist and violent attitudes about Indians that justified brutal massacres. The devastation that had begun with the Spanish invasion continued as whole tribes disappeared. Those that survived were in terrible condition. Nonetheless, some First People found ways to survive, to work, and eventually to recover under their new rulers.

By the early 1850s an oversupply of Indian and other labor in the mines and a decline in agricultural employment led to violent clashes between white miners and Indians—as well as whites and Chinese, whites and Mexicans, and whites and Latinos. The increased use of mechanical harvesters and other modern equipment, along with a new influx of Anglo and immigrant white farm workers from the east further limited Indian employment. To make matters worse, new white farmers refused to hire Indian workers.

Yet, the story is not simply one of exclusion and slaughter. Other patterns continued. Pioneer leader John Bidwell, a friend of Sutter, explained, Indians were "all among us, around us, with us—hardly a farm house—a kitchen without them." Slower growth in Southern California allowed for a continuation of Mexican economic, cultural, and labor practices. In Los Angeles, where relatively few Anglos settled in the 1840s and 50s, the new government continued the Mexican practices of labor exploitation, now legitimized through the US's own racial system. Under Chapter 133 of the 1850 state statutes, LA authorities each week auctioned off "loitering" Indians to work for whites. Somewhat better for the former mission residents were jobs as household servants that paid steady wages and provided a place to live relatively safe from the dangers of the streets and jails. In 1860, nearly

Governor Pio Pico's home deteriorated after his death.

half of LA households had live-in native servants, continuing the pre-US pattern of natives providing domestic service for whites. This pattern continued through the 20th century to this day, enabling the Southern Californian middle classes to enjoy a level of personal service in their homes, yards, and restaurants that matches the 19th century's levels of domestic service.

Despite employing natives in large numbers, settlers regularly complained about the Indian work ethic. Tejon Ranch owner Edwin Beale noticed "in my fields here for instance, if I were to allow them to work when they pleased, but little would be done, for the industrious would be... discouraged by the indolent, but as it is the indolent are punished and compelled to labor." Free native people were little interested in volunteering for this sort of life, but like many groups pulled into the vortex of

"Digger" Indians

Whites named California's coastal people "Digger" Indians to demean their food-gathering practices. Men worked alongside women, leading Anglos, who prized manly hunting skills, to see them as effeminate. Since whites also believed that Indian men were lazy, they more often employed the women. A British visitor to California in 1851 expressed these ideas: "The extreme indolence of their nature, the squalid condition in which they live, the pusillanimity of their sports, and the general imbecility of their intellects, render them rather objects of contempt than admiration."

market compulsion, they had few options. They could work for the new rulers of California, they could resist, or they could try to survive on the margins, hiding in lands they had once roamed freely.

At the same time as white settlers disdained the Indian work ethic, they were attracted and repelled by native culture and sexual practices. In the pre-gold rush days, some Anglo settlers had adopted the Spanish attitude toward interracial relationships, taking Indian lovers and wives. While most whites probably regarded these relationships as temporary, some were long-term. What the native women and their communities thought of these relationships we have very little direct evidence. After the US takeover, white men often used native women for sex, occasionally paying for sexual labor but all too often committing rape. Like the Spanish soldiers and Mexican settlers before them, the Anglo men saw native women as sexually available and powerless to resist. Desperate to survive, Indian women worked the white towns, "to provide their bread and clothing in a manner most infamous" to quote one contemporary writer. Native fighters did retaliate for rapes and other assaults, but risked extermination of their communities when they did so. Rape was rarely prosecuted since US laws would not protect indigenous women: their testimony was inadmissible in court. As a consequence of this sexual economy, native women continued to suffer from devastatingly high rates of venereal disease, especially syphilis. Indeed, VD probably caused much of the calamitous decline in native birthrate that kept the population from rebounding for decades.

Captured while moving west, pioneer girl Olive Oatman lived for years with the Mojave near Needles. She retained fond feelings for the Mojave along with traditional facial tattoos.

For some observers among the new Californians, native women's physical and sexual labor confirmed their degradation by violating the norms of femininity. According to proper middle class lady Dame Shirley, who wrote about the shockingly rough culture of the gold fields, native women were a strange mix of qualities both appalling and appealing. Indians travel in a "herd," she wrote, and were amusing in their primitive desire to "finger my gloves, whip and hat." She did happily discover one particularly beautiful sixteen-year-old girl with "her starry eyes, her chiseled limbs and her beautiful nut brown cheeks." Yet "it must be said that those who bear the name [Indian] here have little resemblance to the glorious forest heroes that live in the Leatherstocking tale." Despite "the extreme beauty of the *limbs* of the Indian women of California," she explains, "for haggard-ness of expression and ugliness of feature they might have been taken for a band of Macbethian witches."

Witches or not, native-settler intimacy continued into the US period and even led to many, perhaps more than a thousand, mixed marriages. More often, the domestic arrangements were informal and imposed on the Indians. Despite their acceptability in Mexican California, such relationships collided with Anglo fears of racial mixture and racial betrayal. Anglo men who married Indians were called "Squaw men"; their racial interconnection both feminized them and made them a bit Indian themselves. Californians passed laws against interracial marriage along with the rest of the country in the latter half of the 19th century.

US authorities sought to regulate American-Native interactions. In 1853 President Millard Fillmore appointed Edward Fitzgerald Beale, a scion of an elite East Coast family, explorer, and heroic courier in the Mexican War, to oversee Indian affairs in California. The liberal Beale was distressed by the ongoing genocide of California Indians and sought to save them by confining them to reservation lands around the state, effectively separating them from the aggressive Anglo settlers. Beale signed a series of treaties with the Indians, setting aside 8.5 million acres of land to establish five large reservations near US Army forts, including one at the southern end of the San Joaquin Valley. The San Sebastian reservation at the foot of the Grapevine Pass became the main dumping ground for Indians from the southern half of the state. In 1863, for instance, skirmishes between settlers and Paiutes in the remote Owens Valley on the eastern side of the Sierra Nevada led to the Army seizing 1,100 people and imprisoning them in Grapevine Canyon without clothes, food, or shelter. Many died that winter; the survivors were sent to the Tule River Reservation near Visalia.

The planned reservations left California's First Peoples only 8 percent of the state, but at least they guaranteed them substantial territory. The federal government further offered subsidies to Indians who agreed to settle down on the reservations and live as ranchers and farmers. The military delivered food and supplies to pacified natives. Many leaders memorized the terms of the treaties, reciting them to people who trespassed on their lands. However, whites resented the amount of land given the native people—for as much as gold, California meant fertile plentiful land to the newcomers. US citizens mobilized against the reservation funding, preferring federal money to subsidize

Edward Beale Makes Good

Beale decided to make the best of his failed reservation policy. He obtained title to a large chunk of San Sebastian, one of the proposed reservations, and turned it into the Tejon Ranch (now a publicly traded corporation largely owned by the *Los Angeles Times*'s Chandler family). He soon owned nearly 270,000 acres and gave jobs to hundreds of the same Indians whose reservation would have been on the land. Beale was a creative, modernizing landowner, even importing camels for road-building in the arid region. His wartime heroism, administrative service, and great wealth made him popular with the Republican Party. In the tradition of gilded age graft, he was appointed Surveyor General for the State. Beale used his position to enlarge his holdings and those of his friends and family until a public outcry forced him from office.

their wars against the state's first residents rather than paying for Indians to retain enormous sections of the state. Some ambitious Anglos and Californios had sought contracts to supply beef to the reservations. Yet when California's congressional delegation defeated Beale's treaties, many of these same people, including Beale, moved quickly to seize the land that had been allotted for the reservations. US Senate investigations into the land grab saw nothing wrong, a position upheld by the Supreme Court in a series of cases in the 1850s. One Senate committee put it in good 19th century legalese: "the Indian had no usufructuary [land use] or other rights therein which were to be in any manner respected."

By the end of the 19th century the first Californians were left with only four much-reduced reservations—Tule River, Round Valley, Smith River, and Hoopa Valley. The rest of the state's Indian population lived on tiny tracts throughout the state known as rancherias, native communities usually located near a Spanish or Mexican settlement. These extremely small territories averaged less than 200 acres. During the twentieth century, dozens of other reservations were founded, the largest in the southeast desert areas. Despite these official additions, today most California native lands are small, remote, and barren. Native people's territory totals less than half a million acres—a far cry from the 8.5 million promised in the 1850 treaties.

Some people went willingly to the rancherias—faced with death and enslavement in the white populated regions, the reservations held out hope of survival. But peoples in more remote regions, especially in the north of the state, resisted the new system as long as possible. Into the late 1850s and 1860s a series of wars roiled the northwest as Californian and Federal soldiers forced residents to move. Hungry and displaced from their traditional lives, the Indians responded with raids to steal cattle and horses, often simply killing the livestock as acts of revenge. The miners and most settlers, often economically desperate themselves, refused to employ Indians or even to coexist on the land with them. One of the worst examples of Anglo actions was a

The Volcan Indian School was presided over by a white teacher in the early 20th century. Located on the Santa Ysabel reservation in the mountains near San Diego, it provided a limited Anglo education for Iipay (Diegueño) children.

group of pioneers, led by lawyer Lanford Hastings, that made a point of shooting Central Valley Indians for pleasure. Eminent 19th-century historian Hubert Howe Bancroft described it as "one of the last human hunts of civilization, and the basest and most brutal of them all." Hastings was not a Free Soiler, however. He later supported the Confederacy in the Civil War, then led a colony in Brazil, where slavery was still legal. Peter Burnett, the golden state's first governor, warned in 1851 that this spiral of dislocation and violence could have "only one result: A war of extermination will continue to be waged between the races until the Indian race becomes extinct."

Burnett's warning was sadly close to accurate. Whites repeatedly slaughtered the outgunned Indians. Any Indian could be judged a vagrant and forced to labor for a white landowner. Whites in some circumstances could legally kidnap Indian children, which created a market in native kids, especially girls to be used as slave help. The native people had little recourse: Indians were barred from testifying in court against white men. Confinement to ever more limited rancherias left the natives "in a most miserable and destitute condition," according to Thomas J. Henley, the Superintendent for Indian Affairs. By the mid-1850s, they faced "disease, starvation, and death in its most appalling forms."

Brutal massacres occurred throughout the state into the 1860s as the burgeoning settler population displaced native people from their lands and forced Californio and Anglo ranch owners to get rid of Indian workers. Raiding and horse stealing had been one of the dominant forms of the native economy under the Mexicans and Spanish—an adaptation of older traditions. While the previous rulers had fought raiders, they did not seek to entirely eliminate the native presence in order to keep a supply of neophytes and peons. American settlers, however, came from a world where Indians were expected to disappear; when they didn't vanish, the settlers helped them. In 1860 San Franciscans and a national audience were horrified by the brutality of Eureka settlers who murdered between 50 and 100 Wiyot women and children on an island in Humboldt Bay. What is now called "Indian Island" was the site of Tuluwat, a Wiyot village, and location for their most holy ceremonies. Settlers in the midst of continuing conflicts with nations in the hills surrounding the new city were looking for any Indians they could kill—regardless of their involvement. The writer Bret Harte managed to expose the murders in a San Francisco newspaper, but had to write anonymously for fear of retaliation. "The pulpit is silent, and the preachers say not a word," Harte wrote. Outrage at the massacre was soon overshadowed by the appalling casualties of the Civil War, but the sense that unless something was done for native peoples they would all soon die persisted. Reservations were a stopgap measure. Indian societies and cultures, the liberals believed, could not, and should not survive intact.

Some people were able to organize violent resistance. The Modoc War of 1872–3, the last of California's Indian wars, resulted from native resistance to the reservation program. After bloody clashes between Modoc and pioneers heading to the

The Bloody Island Massacre

At Clear Lake, rancher Andy Kelsey and his business partner Charles Stone had kept local Pomo under conditions of slavery. Kelsey (for whom the town of Kelseyville was later named) and Stone effectively turned a native village on an island in Clear Lake into a prison. They whipped Indian workers for the slightest infractions, raped young girls, and limited the people to starvation rations of food. They forced native men to accompany them to the gold fields of the Sierra Nevada, but would not pay them for their labor. Finally, the two ranch owners made plans to hire out most of the Clear Lake village to Sutter's fort to replenish the work force there in 1850. Two of the Pomo, Shuk and Xasis, hatched a plan. A woman who worked in the house poured water down the rifle barrels of her rancher employers, rendering their guns useless. Five of the Pomo men then murdered Kelsey and Stone. In retaliation, a punitive expedition by local militiamen and US Army troops under the command of Captain Nathaniel Lyon slaughtered at least 135 people, most of them women and children.

The site of the village and massacre, now called "Bloody Island," has a marker explaining the incident. It is just off State Highway 20, 1.5 miles south of the town of Upper Lake. Captain Lyon later died a hero in the Civil War and grateful San Franciscans named a street after him. None of the people his troops massacred have streets named for them. The Pomo near Clear Lake today have to contend with a nearby sulfur mine superfund site, but they maintain their culture, including teaching their language, and have a traditional round house.

northwestern mines in the 1850s, the US forced the Modoc onto a reservation with their traditional enemies, the Klamath. When a band of Modoc fled the reservation in 1872 after repeated clashes with the Klamath, the US Army pursued them into the Lava Beds south of Tule Lake. For two years, 53 Modoc warriors held off hundreds of soldiers.

While the Modoc War resembled other US-Native confla-grations, US Indian policies needed to be adjusted to the contra-dictory realities of California, with its genocidal exclusiveness and its racially segmented labor system. The main policy of the federal government had been to "remove" native peoples from their lands and force them to live in territories far removed from white settlers. Yet the Mexicans and Spanish had established a system that made native people essential to the state's economy.

Rather than extend the rights of citizenship to its new non-white subjects, the new Californians sought to "reclaim the old mission Indians to the habits of industry and the wild ones too" and at the same time "to prevent them encroaching upon the peaceable inhabitants of the land" in the words of California Military Governor Richard Mason. To do this, they adopted the notorious "black codes" of the antebellum south. The govern-ment used vagrancy laws to formalize extensive controls over Indians. They could be arrested for being without employment or for quitting their jobs and then sentenced to forced labor. The government forbade Indians to gather in "crowds" or to go any distance from their mission, place of "employment," or ranche-ria without a passport. It was clear to some of the Anglos that California's natives shouldn't be treated like Indians elsewhere in the west. Pearson Reading, who received 26,000 acres in the last Mexican land grant before the US conquest, wrote a friend: "The Indians of California make as obedient and humble slaves as the negroes in the South... For a mere trifle you can secure their services for life." For the first decade of US occupation, the model of slavery competed with the model of removal and extermination.

According to the Treaty of Guadalupe Hidalgo, Christianized Indians should have been able to be citizens of the US. But the US ignored these provisions. The new state govern-ment established its own control over Indians in 1850. It denied them the right to vote or to keep their own land if whites claimed it. The new laws allowed indentured servitude for natives and severely punished raiding. Stripped of their land, they were neither *gente de razón,* useful workers, or independent nations with their own territories. The Indians, as historian Albert Hurtado puts it, had to "work, steal, or starve."

Under American rule, California's Indian population collapsed, dropping 80 percent in the 1850s alone. While in 1848 Indians had outnumbered whites by 10 to 1, the 150,000 native people who had survived the plagues, murders, and starvation

Martina Espinoza, "la Chola Martina," an Acuchama woman of San Juan Capistrano, pictured here in 1908. Espinoza was rumored to have helped her lover, the charismatic bandit Juan Flores, escape after his gang killed LA sheriff James Barton and three other men in 1856.

of the Spanish and Mexican conquest soon succumbed to a new land and labor policy and the genocidal fury of the people of the land of liberty.

By 1860 only 30,000 Indians survived in California. The population continued to drop until 1900 when there were at most 22,000 people. Many surviving native people with Spanish names and the Catholic religion merged into the urban and rural Mexican working class. Despite this erasure, pockets of indigenous society remained, preserved in isolated rancherias and reservations. Far Northern California peoples resisted cultural conquest more effectively than elsewhere in the state. No full-blooded Yurok converted to Christianity before World War I.

Ishi

Little indicates the fate of native societies more poignantly than the life of Ishi, a middle-aged Yahi from the foothills of the Sierra who appeared at an Oroville slaughterhouse, starving and alone in 1911. All of Ishi's people had been hunted to extinction by whites and he had spent his entire life hiding and running. Alfred Kroeber and Thomas Waterman, professors at the University of California, brought him to San Francisco to live in an exhibit at the UC anthropology museum. Ishi entertained and enlightened the anthropologists and museum visitors with his native handicrafts and stories. There he died a few years later after catching a cold, having lived for years without anyone who could speak his language. Theodora Kroeber, the author and wife of Alfred, wrote, "Ishi was the last wild Indian in North America, a man of Stone Age culture subjected for the first time when he was past middle age to twentieth century culture." Although Kroeber and Waterman respected Ishi's wishes to be cremated, they could not resist extracting his brain for future research. Ishi's brain eventually ended up in the Smithsonian Museum in Washington, DC. In 2000, the museum reluctantly gave up the brain after a campaign by the Yana people, distantly related to the Yahi. The Yana buried his brain in a secret location on Mt. Lassen.

Modoc Plateau

Honey Lake, Pleistocene cousin to Mono and Pyramid. The alkaline water is more opaque than fresh would be, a wide sheet of pale, glassy blue. On the far shore, low brown hills, doubled in reflection. Once past them, we spend monotonous hours driving north across the unrelentingly flat Madeline Plain. Unlike the dramatic volcanic cones of the Cascade Range to the west, the volcanic tableland of the Columbia Plateau, of which Modoc is a part, was formed by lava that extruded up slowly through fissures, spread for hundreds of square miles to form long shelves of dark red or black rock, the flat top of which is called tableland. Equally dark, long low ramparts to the west formed where the front edge of the slow flow of lava cooled enough to stop the flow.

Things still move slowly in this part of the state. At a two-building stop called Termo, gas pumps remain that were made when prices were in the two digits; modernity takes the form of "$1" scrawled next to the ancient ".39." Inside the store, old men play cards.

After the bleak tableland, Alturas offers up a surprising paintbox of pure color: carmine boxcars behind chromium yellow and green cottonwoods, black cows on viridian fields among patches of standing water that reflect blue sky. The Modoc County Museum in Alturas documents the 1905 gold strike on "Discovery Hill" and the 1912 heyday of the "High Grade" mine with tools, ore samples, and photographs. The museum is a grandma's attic of artifacts: button-up gloves, an Iron Lung, Depression-era milk glass, someone's arrowhead collection, John Bidwell's Indian Wars Decoration medal. A typed card notes that the fort named for Bidwell was established in 1865 to "protect the residents of Surprise Valley from Indians," by which is meant the Modocs. That year, under the leadership of Kintpuash, more popularly known as Captain Jack, the Modoc people had made their first attempt to return to their homelands on the Plateau from the Klamath Reservation to which they'd been herded. They tried again in 1872, but leadership was divided, and after a long standoff among the lava beds, Captain Jack was captured, convicted, and hung. His disinterred body, embalmed, was shipped off to be a carnival attraction on the eastern seaboard. The remaining Modocs were sent to Indian Terrritory in Oklahoma. By 1893, the museum placard states, "The Indian problem was alleviated." The fort, it says, was converted to an Indian school, and is part of what is yet called the Fort Bidwell Indian Reservation.

We caravan over the Warner Mountains into Surprise Valley to camp—that is, to park our campers in the Cedarville fairgrounds parking lot. We drive up to Fort Bidwell the next morning. Handsome old wood

Indian School
At Ft. Bidwell, Cal.

frame houses stand among orchards, but we see no one. Kobe's General Store is boarded up. We've already seen its contents in the museum in Alturas. The docent had told us that the store closed because "no one went there any more." But as we stroll the empty streets, we can hear someone behind a vine covered fence begin raking.

While no one we can talk to is about, semis thunder past hauling cattle trailers, and then a man appears on horseback; a cowboy, as we can see by his outfit—chaps over jeans over cowboy boots, roweled spurs. The horse's bridle is decorated with silver at the cheek straps and brow band. "Lotta cattle moving today," he observes, and explains when we ask that they are sent being north to feedlots or south for sale.

I ask him about the fort site. "Never was a stockade," he says, "just a parade ground. There was a school building, but all the remnants are gone." He gives the word three syllables: Rem-e-nants. "But there's a lotta history in the cemetery. There's cavalry names." His saddle creaks as he shifts to gesture toward the cemetery and toward where the fort was. I ask whether it would bother anyone if we looked around. "Well," he says, "They might act like your friends, but they're not. They're not." These would be the people, he said, he went to school with after having come north with his dad from Antioch in 1965.

On the way up the hill, we startle a small gopher snake getting warm on the paved shoulder of the road. Two men are working in a far corner of the cemetery as we approach. In the center sections, the usual family plots, granite plinths, rows of small inset plates sharing family names. I find only one mention of the Indian Wars, on a stone of a man born 1856, died 1932. In a southern section, graves are decorated with silk flowers, pieces of obsidian, an unraveling dream-catcher, an abalone shell. One headstone bears the photo of an old woman, white hair middle-parted and pulled up in wings behind her ears. On another, a photo of a dark-haired man in sunglasses, 1943–95. The two men have withdrawn, though I didn't see them go.

The cowboy had told us, "That's my country along Fandango Pass." Crossing back over the Warners, we stop at the pass to dance what we pretend is a fandango, as the plaque there tells us emigrants did when, seeing Goose Lake below, they thought their hard desert journey had come to an end. Beyond the lake lie the ice caves where Kintpuash made his last stand, and the Tule Lake Internment Center, to which Japanese Americans were infamously herded after Pearl Harbor.

Coming down the western slope, we see pronghorn antelope grazing. I am excited as all get out, because I thought they were extinct. I make the caravan stop. Everyone else thinks it's funny, how excited I am, but I can't help it. I thought they were gone, and yet here they are.

LAWTON, L.F.   HAVERLY'S.

CALIFORNIA LEAGUE

S.F. HESS & CO'S.
CREOLE CIGARETTES.

*1888 card for the centerfielder of the San Francisco Haverlys in the
short-lived Central California League. Some gamblers "knew who
would win three hours before the game started."* San Francisco Alta
Californian

7

The Shameless Upheaval

alifornia is very important to me," Karl Marx wrote, "because nowhere else has the upheaval shamelessly caused by capitalist concentration taken place with such speed." Marx was right: Despite its gold rush reputation as a place for a lone miner to get rich quick, the new state of California rapidly became a place dominated by large industrial and agricultural corporations, none more notorious than the railroads.

Painful busts followed astounding booms as the state's economy became more and more subject to the turmoil of the rapidly industrializing US economy. Combined with repeated and deep depressions during the last quarter of the 19th century, the integration of California into the national economy brought new opportunities, but also hurt workers, family farms, and small entrepreneurs throughout the state. The multiple economic crises of the 1870s set the pattern. The opening of the transcontinental railroad in 1869 brought new investments, but then flooded markets with cheaply produced eastern goods, destroying local manufacturers. Overproduction in the late 1870s led to a national crash. The 1880s and 1890s saw similarly intense boom-and-bust cycles. In response to a land crisis in these decades, creative developers realized as much (or even more) money might be made by subdividing land than by simply accumulating acreage. By 1900 this land development led to a population boom.

Ironically for the developers and entrepreneurs, a growing public of small landowners and burgeoning urban dwellers came to resent the power of big business, big agriculture, and especially big railroads. Responding to these problems, working-class Californians formed trade unions that affirmed both cooperative action and anti-Chinese politics. Farmers joined the cooperative, Grange, and Populist movements to counter the increasing concentration of wealth and property into a few hands.

Vast economic changes transformed all aspects of California's political economy as rapid rail transport linked the state to national markets and improved shipping connected it to foreign economies. Market-oriented farmers could succeed in national and world markets—provided they grew things that shipped easily. Wheat from the Central Valley could be packed in barrels built in San Francisco's workshops: in 1850 the state produced just 17,000 bushels a year; by 1860 it had increased nearly a thousand-fold to 16,000,000 bushels. California's wheat, like its minerals, stimulated the growth of national and international financial innovations, in particular, trading in commodity futures. The scale of the California wheat business inspired technological innovations as well. Benjamin Holt, a carriagemaker from New Hampshire who moved to Stockton in the 1880s, recognized the need for machinery to industrialize agricultural production. He and his employees invented the harvester and caterpillar tractor, expensive high-technology instruments perfectly suited to California's enormous fields and highly capitalized farming enterprises. During the 1860s, as the Civil War disrupted eastern growers, California wheat flooded world markets. The state became the second largest grower of wheat in the US. The "Grain Kings" Isaac Friedlander and William Chapman cornered the market on growing and distribution. Friedlander ran the distribution side, building almost monopoly control of shipping wheat to England, which had repealed its protective "Corn Laws" in the 1840s, opening its hungry markets to foreign wheat.

Chapman, who grabbed about a million acres in the San Joaquin Valley, sponsored irrigation projects, particularly the Kings River and San Joaquin canals, and built model villages, both to populate the valley and increase the value of his holdings. While other large farmers at the time resisted subdivision and development because it might increase taxes, Chapman's approach set the model for later developers—subdivide parts of the vast landholdings to increase population and property values while building massive water infrastructure projects. Chapman sold plots to cooperatives and to individuals. In the state's first subdivision, the Central Colony near Fresno, Chapman provided instruction and sample crops for growers unfamiliar with California's two-season climate. Another Chapman scheme, "the great aim and desire of my life" as he put it, was to change the Central Valley's climate by flooding the high desert southeast of the valley. This is a plan still ahead of its time.

But wheat production in the Plains, the Midwest, Canada, South America, and Russia grew at the same time that

California's boomed. Wheat prices plummeted from more than two dollars a bushel in 1866 to less than fifty cents in the midst of a depression in 1894. In an upheaval with aristocratic overtones, the heavily indebted wheat kings lost most of their holdings to ranching royalty, particularly the land barons Henry Miller and Charles Lux. Wheat farmers abandoned the crop in favor of more lucrative plantings. Many lost their land. California's production plummeted so far that at the turn of the century wheat production had dropped to an insignificant level. Today California grows less than 1 percent of the US's wheat, though since the 1970s it does export the crop, especially to China.

> But, no doubt, the most significant object in the office [of the wheat ranch] was the ticker. This was an innovation in the San Joaquin...The offices of the ranches were thus connected by wire with San Francisco, and through that city with Minneapolis, Duluth, Chicago, New York, and at last, and most important of all, with Liverpool.... During a flurry in the Chicago wheat pits in August of that year, which had affected even the San Francisco markets, Harran and Magnus had sat up nearly half of one night watching the strip of white tape jerking unsteadily from the reel. At such moments they no longer felt their individuality. The ranch became merely the part of an enormous whole, a unit in the vast agglomeration of wheat land the whole world round, feeling the effects of causes thousands of miles distant—a drought on the prairies of Dakota, a rain on the plains of India, a frost on the Russian steppes, a hot wind on the llanos of the Argentine.
>
> —Frank Norris, *The Octopus: A Story of California*, from his incomplete trilogy, *The Epic of Wheat* (1901)

Few developments capture the turmoil of the last half of the nineteenth century better than the construction of the transcontinental railroad and the monopoly on rail transport that ensued. Enormous distances from the main centers of national and world markets held back California's economic development in the

19th century. While shipping continuously improved in speed and safety through the decades, the powerful north to south current in the Pacific made the sea journey long and arduous. The overland route either from Mexico or the United States was even more difficult.

Railroads seemed an obvious solution, but the towering upthrust granite blocks of the Sierra Nevada were impassable for trains that could only climb gentle slopes.

Then in 1861, a bright young engineer, Theodore D. Judah, convinced four well-off Sacramento merchants and politicians—Charles Crocker, Leland Stanford, Mark Hopkins, and Collis P. Huntington—to back his audacious plan to build a railway across the towering Sierra Nevada mountains at Donner Summit. The Central Pacific railroad project broke ground in 1863 and was completed in just six years. The construction of the Central Pacific was an impressive engineering achievement—the line rises thousands of feet in a few miles, passing through tunnels drilled in granite mountains and clinging to sharply cut cliffs. Using hand tools and black powder, laborers took an entire year to carve out the Sierra Nevada's summit tunnel. The progress was slow through the mountains, impeded by sheer cliffs and heavy winter snowfall. The line is one of the most spectacular railways in the world and owes much to the original thinking of Judah, other skilled engineers, and tens of thousands of unskilled laborers.

In a sermon delivered to celebrate the project, Reverend Israel Dwinnelle told Sacramentans, "Clearly these iron bonds... hint a higher and warmer and purer brotherhood of mankind, and a snugger home feeling beneath our common father's roof." Yet the Big Four (as Crocker, Stanford, Huntington, and Hopkins came to be called) had more than brotherhood in mind. They wanted hard-working men who would do the job despite low pay and hard, dangerous work. Irish immigrant navvies, as railway and canal laborers were called, had laid most of the track in the US. But the Central Pacific wanted to pay lower wages and drive the men harder than even the Irish would accept. Chinese contract laborers—"coolies" in the nineteenth-century term that came to be an insult among whites—appeared willing to accept the dangerous and intense work. Crocker thought the Chinese were "far more reliable" than whites, "No danger of strikes among them." Chinese, who had been immigrating to California since the 1840s, were indeed on the whole efficient, fearless, and deferential workers. Their crews once laid ten miles of track in

Chinese railroad laborers not only carried enormous loads on their shoulders but also brought tea to their fellows in barrels that formerly held black gunpowder.

one day. Hanging in baskets from sheer cliffs, they hand drilled holes and set black powder charges, swinging themselves out of the way of the explosion. Ten thousand Chinese worked year-round in arid high desert and snow-covered mountains. The work took an enormous toll. Hundreds died in avalanches, explosions, landslides, and other disasters. Chinese workers were paid three-quarters of what whites made for the same work.

Disproving Crocker's assessment, 2,000 Chinese workers struck in 1867, demanding the same wages as whites. Central Pacific management refused to negotiate with them or to supply them with food in their remote mountain camps. Starving and desperate workers called off the strike after two weeks. Irish laborers also suffered a terrible toll. "There's many a man been murdered by Railroad," went an old folksong, "and laid in his lonesome grave." The names of most of the railway workers have been lost, though there are records of some of the labor contractors who acted as intermediaries between supervisors and workers. A monument to the Chinese who built the Central Pacific stands near the Sierra foothill town of Colfax on Highway 174.

Stanford swung a ceremonial sledgehammer to drive in a golden spike joining east and west when the Central Pacific and the Union Pacific met at Promontory Point, Utah in 1869. He missed. That didn't dismay one observer, who wrote: "We felt that the work there being completed meant more to this nation and to the advancement of civilization than anything else that could be imagined." Chinese workers on the scene were moved out of the frame in the famous photo of the meeting of the two lines. The first transcontinental railroad was soon joined by the Southern Pacific line, which was built for the Big Four with similar creative financing, muscle, and engineering talent over the deserts of Arizona, New Mexico, and Southern California.

Stanford, Huntington, Hopkins, and Crocker wanted riches and power—and they got what they wanted. At the end of the century their fortunes totaled approximately 200 million dollars (147 billion in 2008 dollars). The Big Four secretly owned the Southern Pacific, gaining a monopoly on rail transit across the country. They formed front corporations such as the Contract and Finance Company and Charles Crocker and Company to award themselves exorbitant loans and construction contracts. In order to get ever larger subsidies, they lied to federal commissions, asserting that the Sierra Nevada mountains started in the middle of flat Sacramento. US Government bonds paid a bonus for the construction—at a rate as high as $48,000 per mile (about $10 million in 2005 dollars, a sum that actually compares favorably to later boondoggles such as the Los Angeles subway project of the 1990s, which cost more than $300 million per mile.) The machinations of the railroad barons outraged many Americans, but their actions were typical of big business operations during the 1860s and 1870s, a period of rampant corruption known as "the Great Barbecue." The Big Four may have managed a profit of 200 percent above actual construction costs—although the exact figures will never be known because their financial records conveniently disappeared.

In addition to construction profits, the Big Four received huge land grants from the federal and state governments. Railroads received one square mile on alternating sides of the track right of way—land that immediately became valuable because a railway passed next to it. The impact of the railroad on land values was enormous. The Central Pacific chose Oakland, a small village in the 1860s, for the terminus of the transcontinental railway, a decision that set off a land boom in that town and led to its becoming the West Coast's leading port and industrial city for much of the twentieth century. With its enormous power, the Southern Pacific could create new cities or devastate towns simply by its choice of where to build stations, siding, and switching houses. The quaint city centers of the old agricultural towns of California were all made by rail lines. Using the threat that they would bypass the then small city of Los Angeles, the Big Four extorted a $600,000 subsidy and a gift of the short San Pedro rail line. By the end of the 19th century the Central Pacific's successor corporation, the Southern Pacific, owned more than 11.5 million acres of land, 12 percent of the entire state of California. To this day the SP's land company, the

Chester Crocker's enormous mansion on Nob Hill in San Francisco came to symbolize overweening wealth when Crocker built a "spite wall" (visible on lower right) to overshadow the property of a next-door neighbor who refused to sell out to the railway financier. The mansion burned in the 1906 fire.

Stanford

Leland Stanford's wealth and charisma won him the governorship in the midst of construction of the Central Pacific Railroad. In his short two-year term as governor, he appointed the Central Pacific's chief counsel, Edwin Crocker, as Chief Justice of the California Supreme Court. Edwin Crocker didn't bother to resign from his post with the railroad. When Stanford later ran for and won a US Senate seat, one journalist complained he was "better qualified to be a candidate for San Quentin than for the Senate." Stanford's legacy—a major university and huge family fortune—has had some challenges. In 1972, after Native American students at Stanford University objected to the school's mascot, the Indian, the student body voted to recognize the University's founder by changing the name to the Robber Barons. Stanford's athletic department vetoed the idea, instead calling the team "The Cardinal" for the school color.

Catellus Corporation, owns nearly a million acres in the state beyond its rail lines and rights of way.

Railroad companies were the first modern corporations. As historian William Deverell explains it "the Railroad was far more than the all-powerful, all-seeing Big Four; the Southern Pacific was a huge, extremely complex industrial enterprise strengthened by layer upon layer of bureaucratic insulation." In this new system, capitalists in faraway cities controlled the lives of people all over the country. On their decisions hung the livelihoods of thousands of employees and the millions of farms, businesses, and communities that depended on their freight lines and freight rates.

The unprecedented riches of the Big Four and other industrialists of the late 19th century shocked Americans who believed their society should not have such huge disparities in wealth and power. But while the companies and robber barons might have been hated, the trains were not. The transcontinental railroad and various regional links had been backed by California's booster press—the *San Francisco Examiner*, *San Francisco Chronicle*, *Los Angeles Times*, and *The San Diego Union*—as the motor of progress. Railroads were technological marvels that sped passengers and freight over enormous distances at low cost. Railroads changed people's very sense of time—it was in the interest of railroad schedules that Congress imposed standard time zones on people who had previously told time by the sun overhead. Not all were enthralled by the trains. San Francisco-based cynic Ambrose Bierce wrote that the railroad was "the chief of many mechanical devices enabling us to get away from where we are to where we are no better off."

While railroads, wheat growing, and ranching transformed the economies of the northern half of the state, Southern California's growth lagged behind the north. Southern California land prices collapsed amid the depression of the 1870s, making property a bargain for the railroads and other speculators who bought up the best sections for development and rights of way. Yet without a large population, transportation, and water, the investments in the south would not pay.

This Southern California citrus rancher labeled his 1930s photo to emphasize the variety of citrus he grew, but did not caption his hat.

The keys to growth—transportation and water—also created political and economic upheavals. As the economy began to recover in the 1880s from the post-Civil War drought and depression, true competition arrived with the completion of the Atcheson, Topeka, and Santa Fe line into Los Angeles in 1885. A fare war ensued—at one point, $1 bought a ticket across the country. Tourists flocked to the state just to see the Pacific Ocean. The lower fares allowed mass migration into the LA area, jumpstarting that region's spectacular population and economic growth. All through the frigid Midwest, real-estate promoters advertised cheap land for orchards and farms. Promotional leaflets capitalized on the state's image as a land of easy riches, Hispanic leisure, and eternal sunshine. Farm families from the Plains and Midwest, tired of fighting the harsh conditions and drawn to the chance to grow exotic oranges and other fruits, poured into Los Angeles, Orange, San Bernardino, and Riverside Counties. "You would have thought all of the United States and parts of Canada were on the move," recalled a railroad employee of the boom.

Central to the spectacular Southern California boom were land speculation and often fraudulent real-estate deals. Shady developers promised ample supplies of the southland's most precious commodity, water, but failed to deliver. One promoter sold lots along the San Gabriel River to unsuspecting easterners who believed the river could support paddle wheel steamers year round. The river is more accurately a giant flood channel that carries water from the San Gabriel Mountains to the sea during the rainy season. San Diego and its surrounding area experienced a similar boom in the 1880s, financed by speculative mortgages. At the peak of the region's land bubble, 1887–8, $200 million dollars changed hands in the real-estate business—equivalent to about $200 billion in 2008 dollars—in just this highly populated region.

When the farms proved hard to develop, water to be scarce, shipping prices on the railroads to be high, and markets for farm goods to be saturated, thousands went bankrupt. California land prices plummeted; sketchy developments collapsed. Worried farmers and miners pushed for an inflationary monetary policy to control their debts. In turn, jumpy British and East Coast bankers sparked a stock market crash and the economy nearly ground to a halt as the Panic of 1893 led to a severe depression nationwide. The Populists and Democrats advocated inflationary monetary policy and political reform but could not gain control of the White House. With the political defeat of the

Fruit crate labels often used bucolic California imagery.
Transcontinental Brand showed modern transportation and a mythical
golden harbor to connect their fruit to industrial and imperial triumph.

cheap money movement, "sensible" bankers like J.P. Morgan
gained more control of the economy and steered big investors
away from the most speculative land markets and the more
corrupt robber barons. E. H. Harriman, a more competent
manager for a complex transportation firm than the Big Four,
bought the California railway monopoly with financing from
Morgan in 1898 after the Depression exposed Southern Pacific's
mismanagement.

    After the Depression of the 1890s lifted, other landholders
learned from William Chapman's example and made fortunes
subdividing their property. Idyllic planned farming and ranching communities like George Chaffey's Etiwanda and Ontario,
east of Los Angeles, boomed. These projects had regular supplies
of water, due to Chaffey's engineering skills and intelligent business model. California's planned housing developments—from
Rancho Santa Fe in San Diego and Rancho Cucamonga in Los
Angeles to Rancho Peralta in the Bay Area and Rancho Cordova
near Sacramento—carried the names of the old Spanish/Mexican
land grant ranchos. Yet they were the result of more modern
ideas and ways of handling property than that represented by the

ranchos. The subdivision quickly became the dominant form of real estate transaction.

The subdivision ranch and orchard allowed small holders a chance to gain land and enter the farm market. The number of farms in the state shot up, tripling from 1880–1900 and doubling again from 1900–1925, reaching a peak of 150,000 farms in 1935. The average size of farms also dropped from almost 500 acres in 1860 to 200 acres in 1925. Nonetheless, enormous enterprises of more than 1,000 acres continued to dominate the market with their economies of scale and political power. Smaller farmers joined together—sometimes using coercion—to form agricultural cooperatives that shared in storage, process, and marketing. The most famous, Sun-Maid, packaged raisins in Fresno, and the Southern California Fruit Growers Exchange (later Sunkist), organized orange distribution. Both came to dominate their industries by the 1910s. Orange growers in particular used massive and effective marketing to sell their fruit. Sunkist, in reality a highly efficient, integrated modern industry, packaged itself to a consuming public as representative of a bucolic, healthful paradise. Under the guidance of scientific manager G. Harold Powell, Sunkist modernized packing plants to create fast-moving operations that segregated workers by sex and automated the process as much as possible. Like cattle and wheat before them, the citrus orchards had grown exponentially, from a mere two navel orange trees in 1873 to 5.5 million trees in 1900.

The stark environment of much of the state disturbed many who longed for the lushness of the east and south. One visitor described the Tejon Pass as a "most romantic and beautiful place... mother nature has almost excelled herself." Of the exact same place, a resident complained: "There is little water... No rains for many months in summer and a more dreary expanse than the parched plains you cannot imagine.... A few clouds would be such a relief, and a thunderstorm a luxury too great to be described." During the first decades of mass migration to the south, settlers built homes that recalled their Midwestern roots. Rejecting the Spanish/Mexican construction of adobe and stone, they constructed homes of two or more stories, wood framed, with peaked roofs. They planted lawns and gardens that required large amounts of water. Indeed, strolling through the older neighborhoods of Southern California's former orchard towns, it is easy to imagine one is in Ohio or Iowa rather than on the arid alluvial plains of the West Coast.

Marx's shameless upheaval may have disrupted social relations and destroyed and remade the economy multiple times, but it happened in an environment that simultaneously repelled and entranced Californians.

In the beauty of its homes and orchards and the excellence of its horticultural methods, in the organization of its fruit exchanges, and the character of its urban life and civic institutions, the Santa Clara Valley is fully equal to the most ideal localities in California, not even excepting the famous orange districts near Los Angeles.... Land is almost exclusively devoted to fruit. Farmers buy their milk, butter, eggs, poultry, bacon, and fresh meats of others. They themselves produce none of the real necessities of life, but only the luxuries.

—William E. Smythe,
The Conquest of Arid America (1900)

[San Jose] is the Champion prune town of the world. I was reported to the police this morning for ordering grapefruit.

—Will Rogers (1922)

Mechanized packing houses employed large multiethnic workforces divided by gender, as in this plant in Whittier in the 1920s.

The tallest tree in the world symbolized either leftist or national strength—depending on whether it was called the Karl Marx Tree or the General Sherman Tree.

Kaweah

Few visitors to Sequoia National Park realize that the General Sherman Tree was first named the Karl Marx Tree. Sequoia Park had been part of a utopian socialist community in the 1880s. San Francisco's International Workingmen's Association—a branch of the first International started by Karl Marx and other European radicals— created Kaweah among the giant sequoias of the Sierra Nevada. Kaweah was led in part by Burnette Haskell, "one of the most brilliant and erratic geniuses in the history of the labor movement on the Pacific Coast"and a founder of the IWA in San Francisco. Kaweah clubs around the country supported the colony with donations. Haskell described the great variety of residents: "There were dress-reform cranks and phonetic spelling fanatics and word purists and vegetarians. It was a mad, mad world..." To finance a California socialist commonwealth the founders dreamed of harvesting the enormous redwoods, then loading them on to their own ships, which would sail "the South Sea Islands, Australia, India, Good Hope, Madeira, visiting the Mediterranean and the coast of Europe... New York... Cuba, the Brazils, Peru, Mexico, home." The colony never achieved this vision, lasting less than a decade. Still, hundreds came to live at Kaweah where they organized themselves on completely cooperative principles, sharing work and expenses. They even managed to build the first road to the Giant Sequoias, 18 miles long and rising 8,000 feet. But timber companies wanted their choice land, and the federal government turned it into national park and national forest in 1890. Lawsuits ensued. The colonists were never paid back for the land, they claimed; the federal government charged the organizers with mail fraud. They were acquitted, but Kaweah dissolved in acrimony. Deeply discouraged, Haskell later wrote: "And is there no remedy, then, for the evils that oppress the poor? And is there no surety that the day is coming when justice and right shall reign on earth? I do not know; but I believe, and I hope and I trust."

San Francisco's building trade unions won the 8-hour day by 1900. Their new power allowed them to celebrate the 4th of July in style and to be a major force in city politics.

8

Before the Shaking Earth

A broad optimism brought hundreds of thousands of new residents to the state. Yet the enormous power of California's economic elites, the corruption they used to maintain their position, and the repeated crises of the economy threatened immigrants' opportunities. Powerful movements— from workingmen along the North Coast to well-off progressives in the major cities—sought to remake the state out of this disorder. The results of their efforts were not always what we might like or they might have hoped.

White California society was deeply divided about race and class issues. Wealthy elites who benefited from the ongoing racial divisions in the state often encouraged competition between different social groups—as in the case of the Big Four's use of Irish and Chinese labor on the railroad. Other Anglo immigrants to the state, who worked as laborers or small farmers, feared economic competition from the racially-mixed California workforce as much as they worried about the power of monopolistic elites.

From the natives forced to work at the missions and ranchos, to Mexican immigrants cleaning bathrooms in the 21st century, California's system of labor has always been fundamentally stratified along ethnic lines. As in the South, racial caste as much as class decided who stooped in the fields, toiled in the factories, dug the mines, and lay the track. California's legacy of Spanish mission exploitation and Mexican elite-controlled peonage, and its native-settler confrontations led to bitter labor conflicts. Indeed, the labor movement in the latter half of 1800s easily made the transition from workshop politics to the electoral realm because racially antagonistic union members united with a wider community intent on excluding Chinese workers and confining natives and Mexicans to limited occupations. Unlike the northern industrial states in the 19th century where European ethnic divisions characterized the main social fault lines in workers' lives, the racial barriers intrinsic to the organization of production confronted California's workers.

As a result, California's labor movement in the 19th and early 20th century was as much a set of organizations meant to

San Francisco.—The Chinese Must Go.

Easterners betrayed their own prejudices when they portrayed anti-Chinese rioters as a group of dark-skinned Irish thugs as in this Puck illustration.

preserve white male supremacy as it was a movement to raise up downtrodden workers.

Despite its radical sounding name, the California Workingmen's Party of the 1870s was more inspired by the artisanal republicanism of eastern trade unions than by socialist ideals. The Workingmen fought, in historian David Roediger's memorable phrase, for the "wages of whiteness." Closely connected to Irish immigrant workers, the party espoused a unity of whites against the threat of Chinese employed by white industrialists and "monopolists." The solution was not to join with their laboring Asian brothers in an economic struggle against the state's wealthy, but rather to force the Chinese from market competition. Decrying the idea that they might be reduced to the level of Chinese "coolies" the Workingmen argued "the Chinese must go."

With the charismatic leadership of sandlot orator Denis Kearney and a talented group of activists, the Workingmen's Party quickly came to dominate the streets of San Francisco. Kearney provided charismatic leadership for laborers, less skilled Irish immigrants and second-generation workers. Skilled workers in the newly formed trade unions followed Frank Roney. But

Some small Chinese communities, like this one in Monterey in 1900, survived the 19th-century ethnic cleansing. The photographer, William Letts Oliver, an explosives engineer trained in Chilean mines, was also treasurer of the elite Bohemian Club.

both groups came together in riots that tore through rail yards and Chinatown during the massive 1877 railway strike—the first nationwide labor confrontation. Although the strike began over wage cuts in a small West Virginia town, it soon spread along the country's rail network into something akin to a nationwide insurrection. The 1877 strike was part industrial dispute over wages and part national uprising against the power of industrial capitalism exemplified in the large railroad corporations. In California the strikers attacked the Central Pacific Railroad, the main employer of Chinese, and threatened to burn the Pacific Mail dock where ships brought immigrant workers from Asia. Middle-class vigilantes protected the docks. Rioters poured into Chinatown, burning dozens of laundries and other businesses, leaving 4 dead and 14 wounded.

The 1877 riot was not the worst violence against Chinese. Six years earlier, a mob of 500 people, purportedly responding to the murder of a white man, had looted and burned the Los Angeles Chinatown, killing 19 people—15 of them lynched in a

> Humboldt County has the unique distinction of being the only community in which there are no oriental colonies.... Although 52 years have passed since the Chinese were driven from the county, none have ever returned. On one or two occasions offshore vessels with Chinese crews have stopped at this port, but the Chinamen as a rule stayed aboard their vessels, choosing not to take a chance on being ordered out. Chinese everywhere have always looked upon this section of the state as "bad medicine" for the Chinaman.
>
> —*Humboldt Times* (1937)

public hanging. Similar riots occurred throughout the state for decades, making freedom of movement difficult for Chinese and forcing them to abandon many smaller communities for the relative safety of the larger Chinatowns. In 1885, whites in Eureka

Crowds in Eureka forced out Chinese workers in the early twentieth century, keeping the northwest of the state whites-only for decades.

expelled 500 people, the entire Chinese community. Humboldt County remained whites-only until the 1950s.

In 1878 when one of the sandlot workers' demonstrations turned from harassing Chinese on the streets to marching on the mansions of Nob Hill, wealthy citizens fought back. City elites organized a vigilante Committee on Public Safety that targeted the Workingmen's street fighters and leadership. The city government banned demonstrations and briefly jailed Kearney. But the Workingmen were more than simple street toughs. Within a year, their political organization mobilized workers up and down the coast, winning local and state elections. They dominated San Francisco politics, electing the mayor and taking control of the city government.

Rural ferment also grew in the post-1877 economic crisis. In the farming towns of the delta and the valleys, the Grange of Patrons of Husbandry, begun in the Midwest during the post-Civil War agricultural downturn, started organizing California farmers and ranchers. Part social club and part political movement, the Grange focused on countering the power of the railroads, banks, and insurance companies over the rural economy. The organization also enlivened the lonely country life of farmers and ranchers with its social clubs and community centers.

Grangers organized cooperative banks, insurance companies, and grain elevators to free the farmers from the domination of the "moneyed interests." They even created a small gauge railway from the rich farmlands of Salinas to the port at Monterey.

The Workingmen's Party threat in the cities and towns, along with activism among farmers mobilized by the Grange, forced the Republicans and Democrats to combine their parties and run as non-partisans in 1878—this at a time of intense partisan division nationally. The Workingmen demanded a new state constitution, which was enacted the next year. The lengthy new constitution appeased the Workingmen with many anti-Chinese restrictions, but efforts to limit the power of corporations, particularly the railroads, failed. With victory at the polls, the Workingmen lost focus. Many of its most talented organizers moved into Socialist or Democratic Party politics. Other joined the burgeoning trade unions. Kearney himself gave up his sandlot oratory and became a small businessman.

The Grange Patrons of Husbandry built halls that continued to function as social centers long into the 20th century.

> The Central Pacific Railroad men are thieves, and
> will soon feel the power of the workingmen. When I
> have thoroughly organized my party, we will march
> through the city and compel the thieves to give up
> their plunder. I will lead you to the City Hall, clean
> out the police force, hang the Prosecuting Attorney,
> burn every book that has a particle of law in it, and
> then enact new laws for the workingmen. I will give
> the Central Pacific just three months to discharge
> their Chinamen, and if that is not done, Stanford and
> his crowd will have to take the consequences.... if he
> doesn't do it, I will lead the workingmen up there...
> and give Crocker the worst beating with the sticks
> that a man ever got.
>
> —Denis Kearney (1877)

California's combination of racial and class mobilization translated into labor's greatest political victory in the 19th century: the Chinese Exclusion Act of 1882. The Act, which ended Chinese immigration to the US, passed easily over the objections of pro-immigration employers and a very small group, largely clergy, who saw Chinese as deserving of the same rights as other people. With the anti-Chinese victory secure, labor turned it sights toward what it saw as other dangers: Japanese, South Asian, and Mexican immigrants.

Labor's involvement in these powerful racist movements fulfilled a basic purpose of trade unions: to close off labor markets in order to protect their members from competition. Yet the broader, more inclusive side of labor linked the unions to the great social reform movements of the 19th century, such as the Knights of Labor, the cooperative movement, and socialism. Nonetheless, this expansiveness failed to counteract the divisive effects of racism and opposition to women in the workforce.

Despite the short life of the Workingmen's Party, its combination of class mobilization and racial hatred continued to fuel San Francisco and North Coast politics into the twentieth century. Although more conservative groups returned to power in the 1880s, the trade unions experienced spectacular growth, organizing mostly skilled craft workers. By the end of the century, the trade unions had achieved remarkable prosperity for a few workers, but at a price: their method of operation excluded the vast majority of California's working people. The patriarchal labor argument for a "family wage" that would keep wives and children out of the workforce worked—to a degree: union power won an eight-hour day for most skilled workers in San Francisco by the end of the century.

Later labor politicians followed Kearney's formula: protect craft workers, attack monopolists, and hate non-whites. A powerful synthesis of socialism and racism rallied workers and middle-class leftists first to one of the country's most successful labor parties and then to socialist and progressive movements. By 1901 labor regained power in San Francisco with their Union Labor Party (ULP). It turned out to have more in common with Boss Tweed than Karl Marx. The ULP was formed after Democratic Mayor James Phelan ordered to the police to break a Teamster's strike. Phelan was ousted and the ULP easily won elections throughout the city. Yet there was too much at stake in the bribery, kickbacks, payoffs, scams, and rackets throughout the state to end their rule.

There were exceptions to union racism. In Oxnard's beet fields during the first years of the new century, Mexican agricultural workers teamed with their Japanese fellows to organize the Japanese-Mexican Labor Association. Founded around a beet factory in the midst of thousands of acres of sugar beet fields, the town of Oxnard grew as part of a nationwide sugar boom. Overproduction in the 1900–1 recession drove prices down, and the farmers and mills cut wages. After years of frustration with the difficult conditions in the fields, the united workers fought a successful strike in March 1903. But when the new union applied to be part of the Los Angeles labor federation, they were told only the Mexicans could become members. In a rare act of solidarity, the Mexican workers refused to join without their Asian comrades. The Japanese-Mexican alliance in Oxnard may have been unusual, but Japanese farm worker militancy was not. Often led by socialist intellectuals, other Japanese farm workers'

Japanese immigrant farmworkers made possible the fruitfulness of Santa Clara orchards and other agricultural enterprises while their lowly status reinforced the racial order in the state.

organizations led successful agricultural strikes up and down the state before World War I.

The militancy of the Japanese workers and, probably more importantly, the success of some of their compatriots in obtaining their own fields and farms, led white farmers to throw their support behind the labor movement's anti-Japanese agitation. By 1905 the Asiatic Exclusion League called for a ban on all Asian immigration, not just from China. In San Francisco, Japanese school children, including teenagers, were confined to segregated elementary schools after the 1906 earthquake. This act of intolerance provoked a diplomatic crisis with the Japanese government, which protested the mistreatment of its citizens. President Teddy Roosevelt pushed a compromise. The city agreed to stop singling out Japanese children while in exchange the President negotiated the "Gentlemen's Agreement" of 1907. The Japanese government agreed to issue passports only for wives, parents, and children of immigrants or students to enter the US. Under the agreement, thousands of "picture brides," women whose marriages to men in the US were arranged by parents abroad, entered the US. The picture brides, like the "paper sons" of Chinese men who claimed unrelated youth as members of their families, allowed Asian immigrants to work around the restrictions and keep their communities alive with a trickle of new arrivals during the years of exclusion. Nevertheless the population of Asians in the US stagnated.

Racial exclusiveness typified the dominant labor movement and animated working-class politics for many decades, but radical trade unionists in the early 20th century charted a different course. The Industrial Workers of the World (IWW), an all-inclusive union formed in 1905, had an impact all over the country, but its base was in the mines and lumber country of the west. As part of its goal of uniting all members of the working class in order to "take possession of the earth and the machinery of production, and abolish the wage system" the IWW was the first organization to self-consciously challenge the racial and gender divisions of labor. The IWW achieved relatively little due to a combination of brutal repression by the government, business, and vigilantes and its own ideologically-driven refusal to sign contracts with bosses. Yet the IWW galvanized the left with its members' willingness to stand up to power, the inclusiveness of its ideology, and a style that prized working-class culture.

Radical westerners fought pitched battles with police, militias, and private officers particularly in mines in the mountain west. California's labor fights were less violent, but often dramatic. The "Wobblies"—as the members of the union were called—became a significant force in California labor, not so much for what they achieved but for the way they galvanized the left. The IWW organized and validated communities of marginalized workers from longshoremen to lumberjacks, even organizing hobo camps. It was rumored that to ride the rails in western states a hobo had to carry an IWW card or he would be thrown off the train—not by the railroad company guards, but by the other riders!

In addition to organizing marginalized workers, the IWW mobilized its members and liberal supporters for free speech fights around the state. In 1910, IWW organizers mounted an organizing campaign in Fresno, but the police kept arresting them whenever they tried to give a speech. Arrestees soon filled the city's jails. A similar effort in San Pedro in 1912 brought support from notable Socialists and progressives like Upton Sinclair, who was arrested for reading the constitution in public.

In 1913, brutal violence organized and supported by San Diego's elite, particularly *San Diego Union* owner and sugar heir John D. Spreckels, defeated a year-long free-speech campaign by the IWW in that southern city. Vigilante attacks and government repression took an enormous toll on the IWW. The free-speech fight in San Diego was won by the city elites when police arrested union activists for speaking in public. "I am going to charge some with disturbing the peace and other with offenses which I shall figure out tomorrow," explained the chief of police. The arrestees soon filled the city jails—a problem the police solved by turning over the Wobblies to a mob of respectable citizens who dragged them to the county line, beat them with pick handles, and forced them on their way.

IWW rhetoric tended to be incendiary; the group warned that "there could be no peace" as long as inequality continued. Wobblies proved unwilling to sit back and endure police attacks. At Ralph Durst's ranch in Wheatland near Yuba City in 1913, Wobblies tried to organize thousands of hops pickers but were brutalized. The strikers fought back. Two workers and a deputy sheriff were killed. The governor sent in the state militia, breaking the strike. The Wheatland Riot aside, the Wobblies tended more to suffer than perpetrate violence.

The IWW's appeal to the unskilled brought in members throughout California. By 1913 the radical unionists had about 5,000 members in the state, spread from the logging camps of the cool northwest to the massive farms of the hot inland valleys and the temperate docks of the intemperate southern cities. The IWW turned to organizing the unemployed during the rapid boom-and-bust cycles of the 1910s. In March 1914 Kelley's army of 2,000 unemployed workers marched on the state capital. In an echo of Coxey's army of the poor, which had marched on Washington, DC, in the Depression year 1894, the Wobblies were met by Sacramento police with their own army of recently-deputized middle-class vigilantes who beat the marchers, burned their blankets and tents, and drove them back across the Sacramento River from the capital.

The threat of a powerful labor movement, let alone a radical one that bridged the racial divide, terrified the wealthy who dominated California's economy and culture. Many of the small farmers and businessman who had gained a stake in the subdivision economy shared these sentiments. LA businessmen, led by *Los Angeles Times* publisher Harrison Gray Otis, who had made a fortune in land speculation, bitterly opposed unions and pledged to make LA an "open shop" town. The anti-union drive received a big boost during a strike of 1,500 ironworkers in 1910 when John and James McNamara, brothers who led an American Federation of Labor (AFL) affiliate, bombed the *Times* building, killing twenty people. Even though mainstream union leaders and labor politicians had sought to distance themselves from their intemperate brothers and sisters, the *Times* bombing justified conservatives' belief that Otis was right: all unions, not just the IWW, were a danger. Business leaders boycotted any companies that signed union contracts and blacklisted activists. LA remained anti-union for decades.

While for many in the state a strong response seemed to make sense after the upheavals of the 1910s, the state often prosecuted radicals without justice. In 1918, after hearing perjured testimony, a jury sentenced Socialist labor activists Tom Mooney and Warren Knox Billings to death for bombing a Preparedness Day parade in San Francisco and killing ten people. The trial received worldwide publicity, as it became apparent that the two men had been convicted because of their political beliefs rather than their actions. The outcry over the case convinced President Wilson to intervene. Progressive Republican Governor William Stephens then commuted Mooney's sentence and in 1939 liberal Democratic Governor Culbert Olson pardoned Mooney and commuted Billings's sentence.

For some, cooperation provided an alternative to capitalist enterprise and the basis for a new economic system. While the most successful brought together farms for marketing purposes, other producer and consumer coops thrived in the state. Cooperative mills, gins, and distribution facilities made it possible for small and middle-sized farmers to stay in business. Cooperative banks and insurance companies also thrived. Beginning in 1875, Italian farmers marketed produce in San Francisco through the Columbo Market coop, an enterprise that guaranteed set prices. Worker cooperatives were equally widespread but shorter lived. Unionized Oakland butchers, facing an open-shop drive in 1904, formed a meat cooperative that supported smaller farmers and did not purchase from big ranchers such as the Western Cattle Company. Not all cooperation grew from such positive goals. The Anti-Jap Laundry League, for instance, built whites-only laundries. The Knights of Labor, a giant nationwide organization with many California adherents, promoted a vision in the 1880s of a cooperative commonwealth. In the midst of the Depression of the 1890s, some San Franciscans tried to jumpstart the cooperative commonwealth by establishing a system of "labor checks" as an alternative currency, redeemable at local coops and sympathetic stores. It lasted only a year.

Key to the thinking of the moderate trade unionists and small business people who supported the Knights of Labor and later cooperative efforts was their belief that monopolistic land holding was the root of inequality in society. San Francisco journalist and later New York mayoral candidate Henry George promoted a "single tax" on unimproved land. George argued that "indolence and not industry should bear the burden of taxation." George's analysis appealed to unionized workers who believed his rhetoric that the tax would usher in "the Golden Age of which poets have sung and high-raised seers have told in metaphor." Too bad for the poets, seers, and George, then, that California voters rejected decisively a single-tax initiative in 1916. In general, as Ira Cross, a pioneering California labor historian, wrote in 1911, cooperation "has failed primarily because the Californians do not have the cooperative point of view." Cross explained that the state's ample resources and chances of quick wealth "made them individualists of a most pronounced type."

Most of the trade unionists of the 19th century believed in socialism and came to support the Socialist Party when it was formed in the 1890s. At its peak, the Socialist Party had 8,500 activists in 300 locals around the state. Supported by working-class voters and underwritten by the trade unions, the Socialists had a major impact on state politics, often in coalition with progressives. Socialists advocated public control over natural resources and municipalization of utilities—thus the term "sewer socialism." Socialists won quite a few municipal elections and managed to get a representative in the State Assembly. Socialists even reached out to black voters, nominated African-American candidates for office, and supported their campaigns. But the Socialists bitterly opposed Asian immigration and refused to organize in Chinese, Japanese, or South Asian communities. In Los Angeles, Socialist mayoral candidate Job Harriman won 37 percent of the vote in 1911, coming in second, and might have won the election had the Socialists not been discredited by the *Times* bombing. Harriman then helped found the Llano del Rio utopian colony in the high desert Antelope Valley. It lasted 20 years despite boycotts by LA businessmen. Berkeley elected J. Stitt Wilson, a Christian socialist, mayor that same year, a high point for the left in the state. Conservatives immediately launched a recall campaign, but Wilson survived and went on to challenge the seat of Congressman William Knowland, the conservative publisher of the *Oakland Tribune*. Wilson, a minister, explained his socialism in terms that the Marxist wing of his movement probably rejected: "Socialism is the greatest effort that has ever been made to put teachings of Christ into practice in everyday life."

Californians apparently didn't want to put Wilson's version of Christ's teaching into practice—socialism declined quickly as a political movement in the repressive atmosphere of the 1910s. But in 1906 a major outside force did intervene to shake up California's politics.

The deadly bombing of the LA Times *Building by Irish American union leaders, the McNamara brothers, in 1911 shocked the left and confirmed conservative fears of radical labor. (Security Pacific National Bank Collection/Los Angeles Public Library)*

Residents of San Francisco watch fire moving up Sacramento Street towards them just after the 1906 earthquake.

9

THE PROGRESSIVES

In the early decades of the twentieth century, Californians stood in the forefront of the nationwide movement of political and moral reform that has come to be called Progressivism. Although "progressive" today refers to a political position on the left, Progressivism then was a complex movement, at once enhancing people's lives and yet controlling them further. Progressivism existed in electoral politics as a series of reform movements and as a party dedicated to ridding the system of corruption, professionalizing administration, and making politics more democratic. Yet the Progressives' ideas and actions often contradicted themselves—by creating the initiative, referendum, and recall, they enhanced electoral democracy and then reduced it by backing the city manager form of government and other efforts at professionalized controls. They wanted to empower women by backing suffrage and limiting the hours women worked, but instituted rigid, morally-based controls on behavior through prohibition and anti-prostitution laws. Some Progressives were Democrats, a few were Socialists, but most came from the Republican Party. The Progressive Party, led by Teddy Roosevelt and California's Hiram Johnson, could not withstand the appeal of the major parties; it barely lasted into the 1920s. Despite their electoral failings, the ideas and programs of the Progressives came to dominate twentieth-century America. Yet California might not have been such a cauldron of reform had it not been for the geology of the Golden State and a few greedy San Francisco politicians.

In 1905, San Francisco Mayor Eugene Schmitz of the Union Labor Party; Abe Ruef, the city's most successful political fixer; and the whole San Francisco Board of Supervisors received hundreds of thousands of dollars in "fees" from trolley-line operator United Railroads and utility Pacific Gas and Electric, which sought to electrify the city's cable car system. This corruption, all too typical of municipal affairs throughout the country, would have gone unprosecuted but for interference from the San

On the watch for looters (valuables lie buried
t of Chinatown where frightful mortality resulted
e. San Francisco.   Copyright 1906 by C. L. W

A soldier guards the wreckage of Chinatown where, as the original caption tells us, "frightful mortality resulted from the quake." Though Mayor Schmitz tried to force the Chinese to move to Hunter's Point in the south of the city, Chinese businessmen financed the rebuilding of Chinatown as a tourist attraction. St. Mary's Church in the background still stands.

Andreas Fault on April 16, 1906. A secret committee organized by the city's wealthiest Republican families took advantage of the earthquake to expose rampant corruption in the government. Scandals revealed corporate payoffs to Schmitz and Ruef. "Boss" Ruef, a multilingual Jewish prodigy—he graduated from UC Berkeley at age 18—had once been a good government Republican, though his definition of good apparently evolved. While controlling the state Republican Party, he had handed the Party's gubernatorial nomination to a Southern Pacific-backed candidate.

Soon after the politicians made their backroom deals, the earthquake struck. The 1906 quake, estimated to have been 7.9 on the Richter scale, devastated the city and the surrounding region. The 600-mile long San Andreas fault had shifted 20 feet. The earth shook for over 200 miles from the epicenter in the ocean just off San Francisco. The fault opened the ground for miles, flipped trains off their tracks, and demolished hundreds of buildings.

It was a strange San Francisco that I gazed upon... Buildings by the dozen were half-down; great pillars, copings, cornices and ornamentations had been wrenched from the mightiest structures and dashed to the ground in fragments.... The sidewalks and roadway were covered with fallen stones, wooden signs and the wreckage of brick walls, the car tracks were twisted, the roadbed had here fallen, there lifted, and everything on every hand was either broken, twisted, bent, or hideously out of place.
—Charles Sedgwick, 1906 earthquake survivor

The destruction was enormous, but a greater disaster struck the following day as dozens of fires broke out around the city. When firefighters connected their hoses to the city's hydrants, they found no water. Without an effective water system, firefighters tried setting smaller fires to keep the blazes from spreading but inadvertently spread the disaster. The residents watched helplessly as the inferno destroyed the town. Four hundred and ninety blocks burned in three days. Hundreds died in the initial earthquake, but as many as 3,000 people died in the fire (there are no exact figures). Some estimates put the damage at $500,000,000 ($230 billion in 2008 dollars). National Guardsmen and Army troops occupied the city, providing a sense of order but also shooting suspected looters on sight. Refugees huddled in tents or fled to surrounding cities. Thousands of San Franciscans moved to the East Bay, with working-class residents moving near the West Oakland rail and dockyards and better off residents moving to Piedmont and the hill areas of Berkeley and Oakland. Asian and Latino residents had to stay in the city because of racially restrictive housing covenants elsewhere.

The natural disaster had been made much worse by the inadequacy of the city's infrastructure, which much of the public blamed on government corruption. Businessmen and good government reformers demanded change. In the widely read *Shame of the Cities,* Lincoln Steffens called for exposing the miscreants and for a system of open government. Nonetheless, in rebuilding the city after the earthquake, city officials opted for speed over safety. Rather than require new building to conform to the highest available standards, the city allowed more shoddy construction than had been permitted before the quake. The strategy worked and within a few years the city had regained much of its stature and a new skyline. Instead of focusing on problems of design and construction, reformers attacked the power of the city's trade unions and their political allies. Ironically, the Progressive movement had been stimulated in the first place by the cities' rapid unplanned growth, teeming streets, and divisive politics. Progressives believed they could only achieve electoral success in coalition with some of the same powerful people and corporations that had created the very problems they sought to overcome.

While California's economy revolved around rural agriculture and mining until the 1940s, its city dwellers outnumbered their country cousins by 1900, twenty years before the same trend caught up with the rest of the country. California's major cities may not have had the enormous size of eastern metropolises like New York, where 5 million people lived in 1910, but the growth of California's cities was spectacular. None more so than Los Angeles, which increased from 10,000 in the 1880s to 100,000 by 1900 and then ballooned to 576,000 in 1920 and 1.2 million in 1930—growing faster than an expanding use of adjectives can convey. It swelled past San Francisco, long the most populous city in the western US, by 1920. LA's growth, activist writer Carey McWilliams remarked, "should be regarded as

Los Angeles grew colorfully even before the automobile.

one continuous boom punctuated by major explosions." San Diego saw similar growth; its population grew 500 percent from 1900–20. Older cities like Sacramento and Oakland increased by a mere 300 percent during the same period, while San Francisco, restricted by the bay and ocean on three sides, followed the pack with a mere 50-percent growth rate. The populations of smaller cities—Bakersfield, Berkeley, San Jose, Santa Barbara, San Bernardino—also jumped.

Progressivism developed in response to the belief that dense urban spaces fostered political corruption, racial and ethnic mixing, radical ideas and social conflicts. Diverse cultural practices, from new kinds of foods to cultures that revolved around wine or beer-making, were believed to disturb the urban order. The anonymity of urban life, changing social mores, and growing job opportunities allowed young men and women new freedoms. Economic independence, even if only small amounts, allowed single women the opportunity to live in ways that had long been restricted to men. Dating, socializing with friends, and evenings out filled young people's social lives as never before as young people seized opportunities for fun, adventure, and sex away from the intrusive control of parents and neighbors. New technologies—streetcars, trolleys, bicycles, and for the wealthier, automobiles—allowed greater freedom of movement. Amusement parks, vaudeville entertainment, saloons, and dancehalls catered to a population increasingly prosperous after the painful 1890s. The burgeoning cities also filled with immigrants from southern and eastern Europe, Mexico, the Middle East, Asia, and India. The mix of cultures, both foreign and domestic, young and old, was heady, but appeared out of control to many.

Progressives worried about rising divorce rates, political bosses manipulating immigrant voters, unregulated corporations shutting out competition, drunken men abusing their wives and children, and public health crises from impure food and water. Labor conflicts, changing social practices, crime, and corruption—often wildly exaggerated in new mass distribution newspapers and magazines—created a powerful fear of disorder among the growing California middle class, particularly among rationalistic professionals. Along with the power over politics exerted by corporations, monopolies, and trusts, the vast ferment of society created a sense of unease. Yet the middle class and elite were imbued with a confidence that society's problems could indeed be mastered.

Hiram Johnson, Progressive candidate for governor, senator, and vice president, campaigned as a fighter for the people—as long as they weren't Asian.

Despite its wide-ranging goals, the Progressives had the greatest impact in politics after the earthquake. Republican reformers feared Boss Ruef's exposure would allow the Democrats to steal the anti-railroad issue. They used their connections with President Teddy Roosevelt to get a special prosecutor to investigate San Francisco politics. The Feds wrung confessions from Ruef and the whole Board of Supervisors, but indicted no one.

A San Francisco court convicted Mayor Schmitz of taking payoffs from "French Restaurants" (houses of prostitution), but the California Supreme Court overturned the decision. The reformers had seen enough of both the Republican and Democratic parties. They organized the "League of Lincoln–Roosevelt Clubs" and in 1908 elected to the legislature a broad slate of reformers who passed a direct primary law, taking the choice of candidates partly out of the hands of party bosses and conventions. The Republicans then nominated Hiram Johnson, a charismatic prosecutor of the San Francisco graft investigation, for governor. Johnson had broken with his assemblyman father over the elder Johnson's service to the Southern Pacific machine in the legislature. Johnson ran as the anti-Southern Pacific, pro-morality reform candidate, winning a close election over a railroad-supported Democrat in 1910.

In office, Johnson and the other Progressives quickly moved to enact a platform that attacked economic, political, and social evils. The Progressive legislature called a special election in which voters approved 22 of 23 initiatives presented. After early opposition, railroads and utility companies came to support the Progressive laws since they regulated business processes that had long been subject to the whims of bosses and vagaries of backroom deals. The Progressive voters also outlawed racetrack gambling and allowed voter initiatives and recalls. They created public utility commissions, banking reforms, and a corporate tax system.

Perhaps most significantly, the Progressives endorsed temperance and women's suffrage. Club women—the well-off ladies who had combined sociability with social reform for years—provided much of the lobbying strength of the Progressive movement as a whole. Club women worked as social workers, conservationists, and fundraisers, but they needed male allies to gain their larger goals. The suffrage campaigners had been an important part of the Progressive coalition that swept to office in 1910. After an earlier effort to enfranchise women had failed in 1896, suffragists such as Katherine Philips Edson, the LA-based head of the Federation of Women's Clubs, and Elizabeth Thacker Kent, wife of a Marin County landowner turned politician, had made women's right to vote the central dogma for reform-minded men. California became the sixth state to allow women to vote. Edson later worked for Johnson's administration, becoming head of the state's Division of Industrial Welfare, where she championed the state's first minimum wage law.

The powerful Save the Redwoods League included several prominent club women on its board. Humboldt Redwoods State Park and Big Basin Redwoods, among others, owe their existence to the initiative of women who used their connections with wealthy, powerful men to achieve their ends. The California Club in San Francisco spearheaded the preservation of a stand of redwoods in Marin County now known as Muir Woods. They succeeded by convincing Elizabeth Thacker Kent's husband William to buy the woods and donate it, along with much of Mount Tamalpais, to the state. Even the tiny Monday Club of Eureka defied the lumber industry that dominated their region to push for the creation of Humboldt Redwoods State Park. The founder of the California Federation of Women's Clubs, Clara Bradley Burdette, criticized "men whose souls are gang-saws" for turning "our world-famous Sequoias into planks and fencing worth so many dollars." As one newspaper editorial put it in 1907, "the uncouth hand of man scars and gashes the beautiful face of nature" while "the smooth and gentle hand of woman can touch the wounds and heal them."

The triumph of the suffrage movement allowed California women activists a new arena. Women Socialists, Prohibitionists, and one Democrat immediately entered races for office as soon as they became eligible in 1912. But divisions within the women's movement over their role in politics and partisanship among male supporters limited the direct impact of female politicians. Both press and public made fun of the women politicos. Mary Ella Ridle, a 1912 Democratic candidate for the Assembly from San Luis Obispo explained: "there has never been a step taken in history that has not received its share of derision. It is the usual fate of innovations of any kind. However, someone has to make a start." Ridle and the other early candidates failed; while women won local positions on city councils, school boards, and other offices, it took six more years for the first woman to be elected to state office. Three Republican women and one Democrat— Anna Saylor, Elizabeth Hughes, Esto Broughton, and Grace Dorris—won Assembly seats in 1918. Their victories, however, did not herald a string of female electoral successes. Over the next fifty years, from 1920–70, only ten more women won assembly seats. The paucity of female politicians didn't bother Edson's Federation of Women's Clubs, which advocated for non-partisan good government causes: "Suffrage has had the effect of improving the character of candidates for office, cleaner methods have been used in campaigns, political meetings more orderly, more women are present, there is less 'hot air' in the speeches and more real argument." The Women's Club assessment may have been a bit of hot air itself, but Edson, an early leader of the League of Women Voters, insisted the Club stance against electoral participation was the right one: "We believe, I am sure, that it is much more important to have solidarity among women than it is for women to be intensely partisan in their activities."

Progressives believed deeply in rationality and morality. They thought that corruption in society could be dealt with through political reform that rationalized and opened up the government process. While much of their political muscle came

Natalia Vallejo Haraszthy, great granddaughter of General Mariano Vallejo, in a portrait by fashion photographer Gabor Eder, revealed her skin and the artistic bohemian side of the new woman. Founders of California's first winery, the Haraszthy family linked the turn-of-the-century upper crust back to the Californio aristocracy and forward to the elite wine culture of Sonoma and Napa.

from business people who had been shut out of deals by better-connected competitors, progressive activists were more often highly educated professionals. Progressivism extended beyond formal politics to widespread programs of social reform of which Edson's Industrial Welfare Bureau is a good example. Social work, school programs, and efforts to control sexual activities deeply concerned the Progressives.

The greater freedom to young people afforded by modern cities led to new patterns of dating and premarital sex. The changes alarmed many reformers, who saw such sexual activity as threatening the whole of society. Progressive sexual fears led to elaborate efforts to control the sexual behavior of young people, immigrants, and people of color. A Sacramento judge explained progressive reasoning to a 23-year-old Portuguese immigrant convicted of statutory rape of a 14-year-old girl in 1910:

> Silva... all government is builded [sic] upon the cornerstone of the good homes... By your assaulting the virtue of girls... you were assaulting the very foundation of the cornerstone of the government; you are assaulting the very principles upon which the happiness of the race depends.

At the turn of the century, newspapers stories and fiction by writers such as Frank Norris, better known for his biting critique of the railroad monopoly, raised alarms at the prospect of "White Slavery," a largely mythological problem in which Chinese men would use opium to entrap innocent white women into a life of prostitution. In fact, most prostitutes working for Chinese pimps were also Asian. Nonetheless, the anti-vice movement received strong popular support because of its racial component. Eurasian writer Edith Maud Eaton (Sui Sin Far), tried to present a different portrait of Chinese life in the west. Her works, along with those of Chinese painters and photographers, portrayed a less sensationalized world in Chinatown, but could not stem the tide of anti-Asian images.

Fear also extended to same-sex sexuality. Although "crimes against nature" had been illegal in California since 1850, the vagueness of the term led the Progressive legislature to make "cunnilingus" and "fellatio" felonies in 1915 The technical Latin terms, however, violated an anti-Spanish constitutional section of the 1879 Constitution that required laws to be written in English. The Supreme Court overturned the new law. In 1921 the legislature managed to find the English words to make oral sex illegal, which it remained until 1976.

The Progressives used intolerance to maintain their tenuous hold on power. After the successes of the 1911 legislative session, Hiram Johnson had risen to national prominence and joined Theodore Roosevelt as vice-presidential candidate on the unsuccessful third party Bull Moose Progressive ticket in

1912. Returning to the governor's mansion, Johnson found the Progressive coalition beginning to fall apart. He championed the anti-Japanese Alien Land Act in 1913, finding unity for his forces in racial intolerance. The Act banned "aliens ineligible for citizenship" from owning land in California. Since federal law prevented Asians from becoming naturalized citizens, the law effectively applied only to Asian immigrants. While some international trade-minded people worried the law would further alienate the Japanese government, it turned out to be only partially effective as Japanese landowners turned over their property to native-born children or cooperatives with native-born members.

Johnson returned to the Republican fold in 1918. By 1920 the Progressive Party had no effective organization in California and was a mere shadow on the national scene. Yet the Progressive platform—government regulation of business practices, more open politics, social control by the state over the people—had triumphed. Restrictions on personal behavior, immigration, and suffrage were widely accepted or soon to be the law of the land. Johnson, elected to the Senate in 1916, became a powerful voice for immigration restriction and isolationism during his four terms. He opposed the League of Nations and led the fight against US participation in World War II.

A more positive legacy of the progressive impulse was the park system. Urban parks beautified and softened the hard edges of urban life. The national and state park system, which preserved enormous areas from development, owed much to the Progressive impulse, but also to the activism of John Muir.

Muir's writings powerfully captured what he saw as the realm of nature endangered by the massive development of the west. Responding to a "natural inherited wildness in our blood" he wandered the mountain west, especially Alaska and California. Raised in a strict Scottish Calvinist home, Muir came to see the beauty of nature as a spiritual power that could remake the human soul. "No synonym for God is as perfect as Beauty," he wrote under the inspiration of the eastern Sierra and the Owens Valley, "All is Beauty!" Descending from the mountains, Muir married Louisa Strentzel, daughter of a wealthy 49er family in the town of Martinez on the Suisun Bay, east of San Francisco. Her money allowed him to continue writing, hiking, and organizing, and gave him easy entry to the regional and national elite.

Muir made his mark with a fight over Yosemite Valley. Yosemite had been preserved in the midst of the Civil War at the

"Our Friends the Trees" as impressive tourist sites and as symbols of the human triumph over natural power.

behest of an ad hoc group of Californians led by park planner and landscape architect Frederick Law Olmstead. Along with a group of intellectuals including Stanford University president and ichthyologist David Starr Jordan, Muir founded the Sierra Club in 1892. The Sierra Club fought to make Yosemite, then under state control, into a national park. The Club's campaigns in the 1890s gained powerful allies in the Progressive movement, most importantly in President Teddy Roosevelt, who became a camping buddy of Muir's.

Despite Muir's connections, the Sierra Club's vision of wilderness clashed with the ideas of mainstream conservationists such as Roosevelt or another Muir friend, railroad magnate E. H. Harriman. The conservationist mainstream saw wild lands in terms of what they could be used for, particularly recreation and rejuvenation of people weakened by the perversities of urban life. Muir, on the other hand, sought preservation of wilderness of its own sake.

When San Francisco sought to dam the Tuolumne River in gorgeous Hetch Hetchy Valley in Yosemite Park to create a water and power supply, Muir and the Sierra Club fought but failed to stop the project. Michael O'Shaughnessy, an Irish-born engineer who had designed San Francisco's post-1906 fire hydrant

Making your way through the mazes of the Coast Range to the summit of any of the inner peaks or passes opposite San Francisco, in the clear springtime, the grandest and most telling of all California landscapes is outspread before you. At your feet lies the great Central Valley glowing golden in the sunshine, extending north and south farther than the eye can reach, one smooth, flowery, lake-like bed of fertile soil. Along its eastern margin rises the mighty Sierra, miles in height, reposing like a smooth, cumulous cloud in the sunny sky, and so gloriously colored, and so luminous, it seems to be not clothed with light, but wholly composed of it, like the wall of some celestial city....

When I first enjoyed this superb view, one glowing April day, from the summit of the Pacheco Pass, the Central Valley, but little trampled or plowed as yet, was one furred, rich sheet of golden compositae, and the luminous wall of the mountains shone in all its glory. Then it seemed to me the Sierra should be called not the Nevada, or Snowy Range, but the Range of Light. And after ten years spent in the heart of it, rejoicing and wondering, bathing in its glorious floods of light, seeing the sunbursts of morning among the icy peaks, the noonday radiance on the trees and rocks and snow, the flush of the alpenglow, and a thousand dashing waterfalls with their marvelous abundance of irised spray, it still seems to me above all others the Range of Light, the most divinely beautiful of all the mountain-chains I have ever seen.

—John Muir, *The Mountains of California* (1922)

system and the city's municipal streetcar system, supervised the construction of an elaborate dam, power station, 160-mile long aqueduct, and reservoir system. The losing battle for Hetch Hetchy split the nascent environmental movement, revealing the weakness of Muir's faction in the face of the claims of powerful economic and political interests. "So what if one valley was inun-

Lumber appeared an inexhaustible resource in California. The industry relied on a rough but highly skilled workforce like this log roller at the Red River Company in Westwood, Shasta County. The Red River Company was one of the biggest promoters of the Paul Bunyan myth.

dated," observed water expert Erwin Cooper, "there were many others equally beautiful!" Not to be outdone, Oakland teamed up with other East Bay Cities to dam the Mokelumne River, which flows from just north of Yosemite Park. The Sierra Club lacked the resources even to oppose the project. The Pardee Dam on the Mokelumne was named without irony for conservationist George Pardee, a Progressive Republican governor and Oakland mayor who had supported the creation of Yosemite Park and a vast extension of government-owned parks and forests. Pardee wanted to protect "our friends, the trees," from uncontrolled logging, not simply for his friends' sake, but because the state would need lumber and water in the future. "The relationship between streams and forests is an intimate one," he said, and the state needed the water.

Advocates of the preservation of wilderness had deeply mixed attitudes toward the native people who had lived in the parklands. The native residents of Yosemite, the Awahneechee, and other Miwok-speaking people on the western face of the Sierra Nevada had been killed or forced out by white militias in the 1850s, but had slowly moved back to their old region. In the

Cars gave easy access to camping in Yosemite Valley after the Park Service allowed them in 1916. They also brought traffic jams and air pollution to the pristine site, leading to restriction on cars beginning in the 1960s.

other early National Parks such as Yellowstone and Glacier, the federal government had forced residents to leave; in Yosemite, the Park Service continued the Californio labor system and employed the Awahneechee for menial tasks and to sell baskets to tourists. Capitalizing on native exoticism, Park Superintendent Washington Lewis had an "authentic" Indian village built in the 1920s—though only Indian employees of the park were allowed to live there. John Muir had not shared in this romantic notion of viewing exotic native people in the parks. Muir found Indians "debased fellow beings," as out of place in the wilderness as "the glaring tailored tourists we saw that frightened the birds and squirrels." After an encounter probably with Kutzadika'a Paiute near Mono Lake, Muir wrote "The worst thing about them is their uncleanliness. Nothing truly wild is unclean." On the other hand, echoing the myth of the noble savage, Muir believed that before the western conquest native people had once lived in harmony with the wild and wished that Indians could return to that harmony.

Despite the elite origins of the conservation movement, ready access to beautiful countryside drew Californians of all sorts to camping, hunting, fishing, and hiking. "California is the campers' state," one writer put it in 1910, "No wonder half the state turns nomadic in the spring." In the 1880s, Californians developed "coaching" wagons, proto-RVs with tents and sleeping gear, to make their outings simpler and more comfortable.

Until the government's economic crisis of the 1980s, the parks were free. Reformers believed outdoor experiences would cure diseases of the body and the soul. Progressives, building on the grand park ideas of the 1860s, developed extensive plans for park systems around the cities. Building on the eastern Settlement House movement, Boy Scouts, the YMCA, and Socialists, concerned about the health of city kids, created summer camps—some in faraway mountain resorts, and others within city parks, like Griffith Park in LA. In 1896, Griffith J. Griffith, who made a fortune in mining and then land speculation, donated more than 3,000 acres of the former Mexican Rancho Los Feliz to the city of Los Angeles for a park now named after him. Griffith declared "it must be made a place of recreation and rest for the masses, a resort for the rank and file, for the plain people" and endowed a trust for the park. The philanthropist apparently wasn't so generous toward his wife, whom he later shot in a drunken fit. She survived and he only served two years in jail for the attempt. Perhaps Griffith needed more time in his park.

Not content with poor kids getting the pleasure of camps, the artists, writers, businessmen, and politicians of the purportedly countercultural Bohemian Club built an outdoor retreat at the Bohemian Grove near the Russian River in 1900. As it evolved, the Club's annual hijinks brought together members of the power elite of California and the nation for drinking, skits, and informal networking. It has attracted protestors to the bucolic Bohemian Highway outside the camp.

The California that the Progressives created was better organized than the state they had inherited. Yet their efforts to control morality, to organize the cities and to rationalize society had effects that only became apparent in the decades that followed.

Resistance to moral uplift manifested itself in widespread defiance of prohibition. Resentment of urban metropolises and resistance to centralized municipal politics led to a multiplication of small towns and a spreading suburbanization. The prosperity of the 1910s turned into the bubble years of the 1920s.

Ramona

Helen Hunt Jackson championed the rights of native people to remain on their lands even in the parks. Jackson's *Century of Dishonor*, a heavily-researched condemnation of US treatment of native people, became one of the best-selling books of the 19th century and sparked a reassessment of American Indian policy. But Jackson was not satisfied with non-fiction: "If I could write a story that would do for the Indian a thousandth part that *Uncle Tom's Cabin* did for the Negro, I would be thankful for the rest of my life." Jackson turned her sights to the "mission Indians" of Southern California with her fictionalized story of their decline, *Ramona* (1884). She based the book on a tour she took in the early 1880s of Southern California *rancherias*. While romanticized, *Ramona* presented powerful women actively trying to help the debased Indians who worked on the ranchos of "old California." The character Ramona, an Anglo-Indian girl raised by the hard-edged Señora Moreno, struggles to find her place in a world that disparages her. Moreno thwarts Ramona's love with a full-blooded Indian, Alessandro. The pair run off, only to meet tragedy. Squatters murder Alessandro and steal his land. Ramona, pregnant, returns to the Moreno rancho after the Doña's death, only to see it too stolen by the Americans. She ends up marrying Felipe, Moreno's son, who had loved her for years. The two flee to Mexico where they can raise Ramona's daughter safely. They have their own children: "the daughters were all beautiful; but most beautiful of them all... the one who bore the mother's name, and was only stepdaughter to the Señor,—Ramona,—Ramona, Daughter of Alessandro the Indian." The novel did not have the effect Jackson hoped, as the book came to help boosters market Southern California's romantic image.

RAMONA PAGEANT

The Ramona Pageant is performed every April and May in Hemet, though the popularity of the story has declined from its peak in the 1920s and 30s when three films were made from the novel.

Communist artist Diego Rivera's "Allegory of California" graces the very capitalist City Club in San Francisco and includes portraits of notable Californians, such as botanist Luther Burbank. (photo: Empire Group/Stock Exchange Tower Associates)

10

THE STATE OF WATER AND POWER

A*llegory of California*, a fresco mural by the Communist Mexican artist Diego Rivera, hangs in the very capitalist San Francisco City Club (formerly the Stock Exchange Club). The mural depicts the tennis star Helen Wills Moody as "California," holding in her shapely arms the bounty of the Golden State. By portraying oil wells, freighters, miners, farmers, airplanes, engineers, piles of produce, a farm, and a tree stump—in short, many of the iconic images of 1930s' celebrations of the modern economy—the radical Rivera found common ground with his capitalist patrons at the club. Left and right agreed that mass production and modern technological sciences should transform the natural bounty of the land so that it would present its fruits to the people, as Helen Wills Moody does in Rivera's mural. (They disagreed, of course, on whom Moody should give that wealth to!) The fresco brilliantly expresses the twin beliefs in the innate potential of the land (and of women) and of the need for (male) human effort to bring it to fruition.

California, Rivera was saying, is the result of a monumental effort to transform nature into things. Rivera was right. California, from the late nineteenth century on, was the product of conscious and purposeful transformation, organized by the government and private interests and carried forward by groups of enterprising engineers to benefit, they believed, the whole of society.

Of course, the largest portion of the benefits went to the part of society with the most money. "California is the rich man's paradise and the poor man's hell," went a common saying in the 19th century. Success in California required funds far beyond the reach of most immigrants to the state and indeed even of most well-off people. From the miners' corporations of the gold rush to the venture capitalists of the dot-com boom, speculative groups of investors have creatively banded together to take on the complex engineering of large projects. But even these incorporations could not provide the basic infrastructure, the water systems, rail, roads, harbors, and eventually airports that the state needed. Only government could bring to bear the huge

California's fruitfulness, particularly in the southern San Joaquín Valley, rests on elaborate water projects, massive subsidies, and contentious politics.

investments that transformed the region. California's spectacular growth and productivity in the twentieth century was thus the result not only of individual enterprise and creative forms of teamwork but also of massive government intervention.

The great projects of the 19th century concentrated massive power and wealth in the hands of a few people such as the railroad barons. Populist anti-monopoly feelings mixed with the economic needs of groups ranging from small farmers to major landholders, merchant bankers to urban businessmen brought a new consensus in the twentieth century. The way for California to grow was to professionalize development projects and to use government to actually carry out the massive changes. With government funding and organization, a new breed of aggressive, politically savvy professional engineers transformed the face of the state.

California's water has been at the center of this history. On the face of it, using, capturing, moving, and distributing water might seem like it should just take a bit of work but beyond that be pretty straightforward. If only! To paraphrase author B. Traven, "I know what water does to men's souls."

There is plenty of water in California—but only at certain times of the year and in certain places. Tremendous amounts of winter precipitation are captured in the snow pack of the high Sierra, then released in torrents in the spring melt. In contrast, in the many mountain ranges below 3,000 feet—the Coast Range or the Santa Monicas, for example—winter rains simply and immediately flow downhill to creeks, rivers, and the sea. Little water remains above ground during the long dry spring, summer, and fall, though rich aquifers lie deep underground. Heavy winter flows alternate with long dry spells, even in the Sacramento-San Joaquin river delta, the meeting place of all the waters of the great Central Valley. Annual floods, occurring over thousands of years, deposited layer after layer of organic matter, creating some of the best agricultural land in the world, with peat topsoil over 60 feet deep in the delta. Unlike much of the rest of the state, the far northwest remains wet throughout the year.

Early water projects put local water to use. Paiutes in the Owens Valley east of the Sierra Nevada dug small canals to direct river water to their crops. The early water systems created by the First People were able to support small populations that traveled into the high mountains during the dry summers, but not the intensive agriculture of a market-oriented society based on

The difficulty of driving before the construction of the Pacific Coast Highway gave good reason to tame California's rugged environment.

private property holding and the accumulation of wealth. The Spanish and Mexicans built small reservoirs and short aqueducts. Gold rush hydraulickers harnessed nearby creeks, blasting away mountainsides to reveal buried treasures. Settlers soon exhausted the rivers, springs, and small lakes in their neighborhoods. They turned to simple engineering: digging wells and building small dams. In the Bay Area, some clever farmers and engineers figured a way to harvest the condensation in the region's pervasive fog. They constructed concrete and stone basins in the hills to catch the water from the humid clouds, funneling it into tanks and ponds. Around the fertile delta regions or where aquifers moved close enough to the surface for a well, agriculture boomed in the second half of the 19th century, while the drier, more remote parts of the valleys remained ranching land. But the demands of the market, the pressure for ever greater yields of crops, and the desire for lush plantings in housing developments, soon outstripped these early methods of water collection and distribution.

It took massive diversions of water from the region's rivers to turn the entire Central Valley into wheat farms, then into orchards and cotton fields. Water diversions, dams, and canals allowed California's arid regions to bloom with thirsty crops. By the second half of the twentieth century, developers took advantage of cheap water to subsidize sprawling developments in the deserts of Southern California. Water created huge fortunes. It made the state's astounding urban growth possible. Yet battles over water also enriched lawyers, demolished land baronies, devastated remote farming regions, created arcane bureaucracies, drained lakes, and created the modern environmental movement. "In California," Mark Twain supposedly wrote, "whiskey is for drinking and water is for fighting over."

Whatever the size of their lands, farmers all required regular supplies of water. Indeed, the proprietors of medium-

Miller and Lux

Henry Miller and Charles Lux, two San Francisco butchers, began buying up ranches to raise cattle to provide steaks to hungry miners during the gold rush. Miller and Lux proved adept at manipulating local, state, and federal laws to amass unparalleled landed wealth. For instance, the Homestead Act allowed families to claim only 160-acre plots of government land. Miller and Lux had their ranch hands claim homestead land and then turn it over to the partnership for a pittance. They loaned cattle and money to small ranchers then foreclosed on their land when the prices they had paid for the cattle left the ranchers unable to pay back the loans. Miller once boasted that he could ride from Mexico to Oregon and sleep every night on one of his ranches. But he didn't always ride over his land: in order to gain title to one ranch under the US Reclamation Act of 1850, Miller had a team of horses tow him over the dry land in a rowboat then claimed it as a swamp. Miller and Lux's holdings dwarfed even those of Richard King's enormous Texas ranch. By the late 1880s, the two partners owned 1.4 million acres outright and controlled another 14 million acres (22,000 square miles). Their properties included almost the entire eastern side of the San Joaquin Valley. These massive holdings equaled almost 14 percent of the entire area of the California, equivalent to the states of New Hampshire, Vermont, and Connecticut put together.

sized farms and ranches constituted a powerful constituency that identified with the larger companies and landowners even when in competition with them for water and markets. Another key constituency, speculators and entrepreneurs, saw the huge expanses of dry land not as worthless desert but as an opportunity for creating cities and new greatness for their state—and not coincidentally, enormous wealth for themselves.

Irrigated fields and industrialized agriculture turned California into the nation's and the world's dominant farm producer. The water systems fundamentally transformed the environment, and not only the areas drowned under reservoirs or sucked dry by water diversions. For many years only a few people understood or cared about the environmental devastation caused by water projects. The big fights were over control of the water itself. The state's many rivers, especially those flowing through the Central Valley, became the objects of intense conflict over who could use the water.

Cattle barons Henry Miller and Charles Lux's power and wealth gained from their control over the rivers and creeks that flowed through their lands. They defended this power against claims by downstream landowners Lloyd Tevis and James Ben Ali Haggin in one of the monumental legal battles of the 19th century, *Lux v. Haggin*. English common law allowed a property owner to take as much water as they liked when they owned the land on both sides of a river or creek. Lux and Miller built a canal that took all the water out of the Kern River, preventing Tevis and Haggin from irrigating their holdings downriver (or down-dried-out-ditch, in this case). Did rules developed in water-rich England apply in the arid western US? In 1886 the California Supreme Court said they did. An owner could take all of a river's flow—if they owned both banks. Lux and Miller had won.

Miller and Lux's victory over Tevis and Haggin threw into confusion the rights of farms and irrigation cooperatives all over the state. The courtroom victory inflamed the public against the "Cattle Barons." The public outrage came despite the fact that Tevis and Haggin were as much barons as Miller and Lux. Haggin, born to a wealthy Turkish family, was second in command to Tevis at the Wells Fargo Company. They were partners of Hearst and Stanford in mining operations and in the Anaconda Mining trust. Hardly modest, they built the first of the big mansions on San Francisco's pompous Nob Hill. Yet Tevis and Haggin won popular support as defenders of the little farmer against the big interests, a classic feint in US politics. In

Irrigation was and is essential to agriculture in California. Tulare's Harry Crowe watches the precious liquid pour from an artesian well his company drilled.

response to the *Lux v. Haggin* decision, the Granger-majority state legislature passed the Wright Act in 1887, which allowed for the creation of cooperative water districts. Miller and Haggin, however, had less democratic goals and soon patched together an agreement sharing the water of the Kern River, an accord that continues to this day.

"Only thirty years ago," John Muir wrote in 1901, "the great Central Valley of California, five hundred miles long and fifty miles wide, was one bed of golden and purple flowers. Now it is ploughed and pastured out of existence, gone forever—scarce a memory of it left in fence corners and along the bluffs of the streams." The new irrigation systems brought more lands under the plow. The percentage of farmland under irrigation went from 4.7 percent in 1880 to 18 percent in 1890. But high costs, complicated politics, and the Depression of the 1890s quickly doomed most of the Wright Act water districts. By 1900 the percentage of irrigated farmland had been cut by a third. Neither the invisible hand of the free market nor the clasped hands of cooperation could irrigate the west fully. Such an undertaking required a massive investment that only the federal government could provide.

The Federal Reclamation Act of 1902 responded to western farmers' needs, committing the national government to developing the dry western states. It established a massive new bureaucracy: the Bureau of Reclamation. Interestingly enough, despite western conservatives' opposition to big government, few attacked the Bureau on principle. By the end of the 20th century, the Bureau operated 58 hydroelectric plants and 348 dams, distributing 10 *trillion* gallons of water annually. The federal government subsidized the cost of water to western farmers, providing no interest loans for water projects. Farmers often paid as little as 10 percent of the actual cost of the water; taxpayers covered the rest. For the first 80 years of the twentieth century, this subsidy totaled almost a billion dollars *per year* (in 2000 dollars). There was one catch: farms that received subsidized water could be no larger than 320 acres (for a married couple) or 160 acres for an individual. With California agriculture dominated by enormous farms covering thousands, tens of thousands, or even hundreds of thousands of acres, growers found creative ways around the law—leasing land from family members, for instance. They also lobbied for an increase in the size of farms eligible for subsidized water. The giant landowners like Beale's Tejon Ranch, Standard Oil, Southern Pacific, and Tevis and Haggin's Kern County Land Company bypassed the Bureau of Reclamation. But they still liked government, preferring instead the State and the Army Corps of Engineers. The acreage limitation proved difficult to change: after nearly a hundred years of lobbying, Congress amended the Act in 1982 to allow 960-acre farms to receive subsidies.

The arid regions of the west attracted both competent and delusionary developers, none more revealingly than in the Imperial Valley. The enormous valley, formed by the southern end of the San Andreas Fault and surrounded by jagged mountains, lies in the far south of the state, its half a million acres named to honor the US conquest of the Philippines in the 1890s. Originally called the Salton Sink, the valley floor lies well below sea level. There is no topsoil in the valley; instead, silt deposited by the Colorado River when it flooded the valley eons ago lies as much as 12,000 feet deep. Ecologically part of the Colorado Desert, the area was largely uninhabited—a perilous dry place, with a few small bands of Cahuilla and Tipai who farmed flood lands.

For decades, Indian agent Oliver Wozencraft created plans to irrigate the valley, but could not find credulous private investors nor convince the federal government simply to give him the hundreds of thousands of acres he needed. Wozencraft tried to recruit George Chaffey, a brilliant engineer and developer. Chaffey refused to join the project because he thought white people would never live in such a hot, forbidding desert.

> The true opportunity of the American people... is not to impose their dominion upon distant lands and alien peoples, but to work out the highest forms of civilization for their own race and nationality... [The desert] is popularly regarded as an empire of hopeless sterility, the silence of which will never be broken by the voices of men.... Neither animal life nor human habitation breaks its level monotony. It stretches from mountain-range to mountain-range, a brown waste of dry and barren soil. And yet it only awaits the touch of water and labor to awaken it into opulent life. Much time will be required to overcome the wide and ingrained public prejudice against the Colorado Desert, but it will finally be reclaimed and sustain tens of thousands of prosperous people. It is more like Syria than any other part of the United States, and the daring imagination may readily conceive that here a new Damascus will arise more beautiful than the old.
> —William Smythe,
> *The Conquest of Arid America* (1900)

Possibly imagining himself the emir of the new Damascus, businessman Charles Rockwood convinced Chaffey that whites would indeed live in the desert—if they could bring water. With the "California Development Company" (incorporated in... New Jersey), Rockwood and Chaffey designed and began construction of a sixty-mile long ditch from the Colorado River to the valley. The unironically-named "Alamo Canal" traversed Mexican land controlled through an illegal front company. Chaffey dubbed the southern end of the Salton Sink the Imperial Valley to attract settlers and founded the city of Calexico there. Chaffey soon left the company after fighting with the careless Rockwood, who had ignored the engineer's warnings about canal reinforcement. Still, the canal began delivering water in 1903; within a year the water

The Salton Sea, hundreds of feet below sea level, was created by accident. It smells bad but supports a variety of wild birds.

irrigated 100,000 acres, stimulating a land boom. Rockwood, however, not only neglected Chaffey's recommendations, but had his crew widen the canal entrance at the Colorado River to feed thirsty farms. When heavy winter rains began in 1905, floodwaters burst through this opening and changed the course of the entire Colorado. A torrent of water rushed into the valley for two years. Without an outlet, the river filled the Sink, transforming it into the Salton Sea, a 375-square-mile lake, the largest in California. Humiliated, Rockwood resigned after turning over his company to the Southern Pacific Railroad. It took thousands of native workers from nearby villages, SP engineers, and rail crews to eventually push the river back into its old course. They built a railway bridge then drove an entire train into the river, all at a cost of more than $3 million.

The Salton Sea story didn't end in 1907—water politics and environmental disasters continued through the twentieth century. Farmers in the Imperial Valley resented Mexican control over the Alamo Canal and eventually convinced the federal government to build the more accurately named All-American Canal solely on US soil. Essentially a sump, the Salton would have evaporated years ago, except that the irrigated farms of the valley replenish it with salty, pesticide-laden runoff. Entrepreneurs, probably lacking a sense of smell, built resorts around the shores of the lake, but the romantically named towns of Desert Palm Beach, Desert

Beach, and Desert Shores failed quickly. Salton City, the last of the developments, attracted $20 million worth of investment in the 1950s and 60s with its golf course, marina, and casinos. It too went under, leaving only a small village. Despite its unpleasant smell, high salinity, and chemical content, the lake is today an important nesting ground for thousands of birds.

For decades, the All-American Canal (actually a very large unlined ditch) diverted 90 percent of the water of the Colorado, one of the greatest rivers in North America, to water the farms of the Imperial Valley. The diversion, along with the creation of enormous dams farther north, left a small trickle of the once mighty Colorado to flow to Mexico and into the Gulf of California. A 1944 treaty guaranteed Mexico about 10 percent of the river's flow, but in dry years the great Colorado no longer makes it to the Gulf—the water is indeed All-American.

Other western states resented what they considered California's control of the river. In 1922 the Colorado River Compact apportioned the river's water among the bordering states, allowing California the lion's share of the water. Even so, California continually used more water than its allotment and almost as much as all the other states combined. Decades of argument and litigation ensued, until the 1960s when the federal government began nominal oversight of the distribution. Again in the 90s, the Feds brokered a plan to reduce California's consumption. It has not yet been put into effect. Pat Mulroy of the Southern Nevada Water Authority explained, "Things have changed, but what remains the same is that California was the problem back then, and California is the problem today."

Few projects captured the power dynamics of water projects better than the Los Angeles Aqueduct. Subject of fiction and film, the aqueduct made possible the transformation of Los Angeles at the expense of the small farmers of the remote Owens Valley and eventually of the even more remote Mono Lake. Like most water projects it pitted one group of white landowners against another. The farmers, however, fought back with militant community actions and even terrorist violence to prevent their bucolic valley being turned into a desert by Los Angeles developers' insatiable thirst.

In 1905, Los Angeles was in the midst of a spectacular growth surge: the population had more than doubled in the preceding five years to over 250,000. Serious water shortages, however, put a limit on future growth and even threatened the supplies for people already in the city. Led by a brilliant chief

THE ARMY OF OCCUPATION
LOS ANGELES
ACQUEDUCT
Nov. 20, 1928

engineer, William Mulholland, the Los Angeles Department of Water and Power wanted an abundant supply of water. The cold clean streams that fed the Owens Lake seemed to Mulholland an excellent source.

The Owens Valley already had an extensive irrigation system, first dug by the Paiute people and then developed further by white settlers, who in independent pioneer fashion had forced the earlier residents out with the help of the US Army in a short 1862 war. These farmers, some of the few non-Mormons involved in irrigation in the high desert west, soon turned the valley into a valuable producer of apples, wheat, and other crops. Mulholland's organization secretly bought up property along the rivers and streams supplying the Owens Lake and constructed an enormous aqueduct—a massive 240-mile long pipeline—to bring water to the city. In a grand ceremony in the San Fernando Valley in 1913, engineer Mulholland turned on the tap, declaring, "There it is, take it!"

But the Owens Valley farmers had never agreed as a whole for LA to take it in the first place. As they watched their farms dry up and the Owens Lake vanish into a salt plain, the farmers struck back. They dynamited the aqueduct repeatedly and when that failed, in time-honored American fashion, they went to court. The city solved the political problem by buying out almost the entire Owens Valley. A San Fernando Valley land boom enriched a group of Los Angeles developers led by *Los Angeles Times* publishers Harrison Gray Otis and his son-in-law, Harry Chandler, who had earlier bought up the Valley in anticipation of the aqueduct.

The fight over the Los Angeles Aqueduct, the effort of the farmers to protect themselves against the metropolitan behemoth to the southeast, has become central to the populist history of California water. Similarly, for the developers and water engineers, the story stands for all small-minded opposition to the practical water projects of the state. In the late twentieth century, the Owens Lake, by then a barren, windswept desert, served as a warning of the environmental price of water engineering.

Top: *LA Water & Power workers open the gates for the first time to send Owens Valley water into the LA Aqueduct.*
Middle: *Owens Valley residents took over the LA Aqueduct in November 1924 and temporarily diverted water back to the dry lakebed.*
Bottom: *An Owens Valley pear orchard without Owens River water.*

While a signal engineering achievement, the Los Angeles Aqueduct is far from the only project that has had a massive impact in California. Far larger is the Central Valley Project, a gigantic undertaking of aqueducts, dams, tunnels, and canals that remade the flow of water in tens of thousands of square miles. Robert B. Marshall, who came to California in 1891 to work for the US Geological Survey, devised the basic ideas behind this massive water system. Marshall complained that the Central Valley was "the largest, richest, and most fertile body of

The Central Valley Project's Shasta Dam under construction began to fulfill Marshall's dream of no longer wasting all that water.

indifferently used or unused land in the United States, perhaps in the World." He proposed an enormous project that would shift the flows of water in California dramatically south. The Kern River's water was to be sent to Los Angeles. Enormous dams high up on the Sacramento River at Red Bluff would fill canals to flow southward replacing the water lost from the Kern.

The proposal, he argued, "would provide all the water Southern California can reasonably get and perhaps would need for 150 years." Marshall had no time for doubters of the engineering or financial feasibility of such a project: "It must be done and it will be done."

> The people of California, indifferent to the bountiful gifts that Nature has given them, sit idly by waiting for rain, indefinitely postponing irrigation, and allowing every year millions and millions of dollars in water to pour unused into the sea....
>
> Some engineers have said that the reclamation of this Valley of California and adjacent parts of the State by one great coordinated project is impracticable, but I propose to show that the possibility of reclaiming it by engineering is its greatest asset. It is a large undertaking, but this is a day of large undertakings....
>
> Consider also that our west coast, particularly that of California, needs protection, and that there can be no better propaganda for patriotism than to place owned homes in the hands of present and prospective citizens, for it is well known and recognized the world over (as has been lately and so truly exemplified in France and elsewhere) that every man will defend to the death his tract of land, his home, his castle. Place 3,000,000 more in happy country homes in the Valley of California, and she will forever defend herself from invasion.
>
> —Robert Bradford Marshall, *Irrigation of Twelve Million Acres in The Valley of California* (1920)

The state's plans for building the Central Valley Project, based on Marshall's design, were finalized in 1930—a bad time to sell bonds because of the Great Depression. The state handed the project and the problem of its funding over to the federal government; construction began in 1935. By the time it was done, the Central Valley Project alone had 390 miles of canals, 4 power plants and 20 major reservoirs. It built the largest reservoir in California: Shasta Lake, which holds 4.5 million acre-feet (an acre foot is enough water to cover an acre one foot deep with water), completed in 1944.

With the completion of many water projects in the mid-twentieth century, California came to dominate agricultural production in the country, becoming the US's most productive farm state in 1948. The farm sector remains central to the state's economy. In 2000, 10 percent of California's Gross State Product came from agriculture. In 2003, California's farm business earned more than Texas and Iowa put together. It exports agricultural products across the US, as well as significant amounts to the rest of the world, with more than half to Canada and Japan. Today the state produces nearly $28 billion in agricultural products and another $100 billion of revenue in services, trucking, chemicals, and so on. This enormous figure was a key part of making California the world's fifth largest economy by the 1980s. Without the state's water systems, this agricultural economy would never have grown.

Water policy and engineering changed other aspects of the state. The 160-acre limitation on Federal Reclamation Project water furthered the subdivision of many of the huge estates, since landowners could make more from selling off land than farming without subsidized water. The number of farms in California by mid-century reached over 140,000 individual enterprises, but, as in the rest of the country, small farmers had a hard time getting by except during war-induced booms. Family farms could not compete in the post-World War II years and a widespread consolidation took place. Federal and state subsidies and water projects contributed greatly to this consolidation—even though most included provisions to do the opposite.

Engineering allowed a few California contractors to enrich themselves while remaking the face of the land and spurring the state's overall economy. While engineers such as Marshall or Mulholland approached their work as public service, others like Steven Bechtel, George Chaffey, and Herbert Hoover pursued engineering as a path to great wealth and power. As the builders of the state, these men exercised enormous influence over the landscape and the economy. Indeed, it was their enterprise and vision that made California's sprawling cities and suburbs, its industrial agriculture, its massive roads, its spectacular bridges, and its enormous, complex, difficult water system.

Aqueduct Junction

The California Aqueduct runs the full length of the Central Valley to carry Cascade- and Sierra-drained water from the Feather River to vast housing developments in LA and Riverside counties. The Los Angeles Aqueduct brings Mono Lake and Owens River water from the Eastern Sierra to the City of Los Angeles. Both projects bring the water up 2,000-ft Tehachapis. The aqueducts cross somewhere in the Mojave Desert. We set out to find that spot.

We choose the back route out of the LA basin, Highway 138, which follows Cajon Canyon northwest when it departs from Interstate 15. We pass the massive piles of boulders that have been the backdrop for Hollywood westerns for decades. Descending into the Mojave, we have our first encounter with the California Aqueduct. The road runs west across the back of the San Gabriel Mountains, the San Andreas crumpling their base.

Long before we are anywhere, we begin to pass numbered roads, ridiculously high numbers—233rd Street East, 227th Street East— that are no more than gravel tracks. At times, the state highway is also Fort Tejon Road. Though we are hours away from the visitor's center at the top of the Grapevine, we are within the vast holdings of the Tejon Ranch, 270,000 acres that was the San Sebastian reservation until the US Senate refused to ratify its treaties with the Indians it had rounded up and sent there.

For some time, the aqueduct runs alongside the highway. We stop at the ruins of Llano del Rio, the utopian socialist community whose plans to survive in a market economy by selling orchard fruit and streambed clay pottery were thwarted when the LA business community boycotted their goods. Half walls of riverstone set in concrete, jagged with half windows. The remnants of tent cabin platforms, the solitary fireplace and chimney of the Llano del Rio Hotel.

We cross the aqueduct again, run parallel to it for a time, the deep, straight blue channel a strange contrast to the stark brown hills and sparse sagebrush.

State Highway 138 becomes Pearblossom Highway, and we pass through all two blocks of town, registering too late the rows of bagged peaches arranged for sale on shelves outside the general store.

Highway 138 meets 14, the six-lane, elevated freeway that commutes 90 miles to LA. We skip the sprawling towns of Lancaster and Palmdale whose green subdivision trees render the desert's greens gray. We exit at the old Lancaster Road, now Avenue I. We see signs for recreation facilities, detention facilities. We find ourselves in another number grid, counting out: 110th Street West, 170th Street West. To the south we can see the geometrically precise levee walls of the aqueduct between us and the stark hills going gold in the changing light. At 235th Street West, the open aqueduct, angling north, crosses under the highway. Shortly after, we cross a pipeline in a filled ditch running in a straight north-south line: the Los Angeles Aqueduct. We can see its descent down the back slope of the Tehachapis on the far side of the valley. We know the junction must be nearby. We take the first turn north. Where this road goes over the open aqueduct, we park.

We cross the road bridge on foot, walk next to the open channel, where a series of V's drags out from a string of bobbing floats. Then, directly ahead of us, creating a scene simultaneously surreal and pastoral, the LA pipeline crosses at a right angle over the open canal. The shiny ribbed steel casts a striped reflection on the creased blue sheet of what the warning signs call "cold, swift, deep water." On either side, the white-sloped concrete of the canal is lined with cyclone fencing, the fencing surrounding the pipeline and its valves is topped with razor wire. The long plain of the valley stretches out behind, darkening with evening shadows. A constant light wind sometimes smells of arid dirt, sometimes of water. Signs welcome us and instruct us not to loiter.

Wooden posts decorated with familiar emblems for hikers and horses indicate that not only are we at the junction of the two aqueducts, we are on the Pacific Crest Trail. We could walk to Mt. Whitney, to Canada, or, in the opposite direction, to Mexico. Instead, we walk on the wide bowed back of the pipe. It is made of thick curved black steel plates, bound together by rivets the size of large chocolate kisses and much the same color, two inches apart, a double row to hold together the overlap that makes the circle, a single row where circular sections are joined. We count the ones we can see, multiply by the guessed circumference of the pipe. We estimate, 140 rivets all the way around, 50 for every side joint. We figure 400 miles of three-foot sections with 190 rivets each means 133,760,000 rivets.

After the sun is gone, from the houses in the small, isolated subdivision a realty pamphlet calls "Holiday Valley" we hear the cry of peacocks and sheep bleating. A woman on an ambling horse passes slowly in the distance. The dirt bike rider whose incessant whine has been the backdrop of our explorations explodes past, standing on the pegs in nothing more than baggy basketball shorts. The sky stays light for a long time. Against the dark mass of the mountains in the distance, the lights of the next pumping station begin to come on.

REAR-ADMIRAL EVANS' FLAGSHIP "THE CONNECTICUT"
HEADING THE FLEET THROUGH THE GOLDEN GATE.

THE MOST POWERFUL FLEET EVER GATHERED UNDER THE AMERICAN FLAG

| CONNECTICUT | MINNESOTA | KANSAS | GEORGIA | RHODE ISLAND | MISSOURI | ALABAMA | KEARSARGE |
| LOUISIANA | VERMONT | VIRGINIA | NEW JERSEY | MAINE | OHIO | ILLINOIS | KENTUCKY |

The White Fleet sails through the Golden Gate in 1908 on its round-the-world voyage to show American power.

State of War

California has been profoundly shaped by its close relationship to the US military economy in the twentieth century. One simple statistic illustrates this: nearly 1,300 military bases, camps, installations, forts, depots, and other sites are located within the state. While some of these were tiny, such as shore batteries to defend the coast, others were and are massive—hundreds of thousands of square miles devoted to bombing ranges and training bases in the wilderness and just offshore, more millions of square miles are now reserved for Naval training. Edwards Air Force Base in the Mojave Desert covers almost 500 square miles. More to the point, the state's six military graveyards, particularly for the casualties and veterans of the Philippine War, Second World War, Korean War, and Vietnam War, cover more than 2,000 acres and inter the remains of more than half a million people.

Beyond its occupation of the land, the US military created entire industries in the state, driving the economy for decades. War brought millions of people to California to train on the bases, to depart for, or to recover from the challenges of war. Millions more came to work on the bases and in the state's ever growing defense industries. The economic impact and the movements of so many people changed California profoundly, bringing about a transformation as profound as the gold rush—but one far less memorialized.

By the end of the 19th century, California had begun to fulfill its promise as a gateway to an American empire on the Pacific. California-based fleets provided the muscle for the US as it expanded its presence in Asia. Naval squadrons from San Francisco and later San Diego and Los Angeles seized strategically important islands in the Pacific like Guam and Samoa. They participated in the coup that brought Hawai'i under US control. San Francisco was the main staging ground for forces heading to fight in the Spanish American War in the Philippines (1898) and the more prolonged Philippine-American War (1899–1912) in which 5,000 Americans and 200,000 Filipinos were killed.

Launching ceremony of the battleship USS California *in 1919, which was built at Mare Island in the San Francisco Bay. The* California *became the flagship of the Pacific Fleet and survived sinking during the Japanese attack on Pearl Harbor in 1941.*

A monument to Commodore Dewey, who led the US Navy to victory over the Spanish fleet in Manila Bay during the Spanish American War, stands in San Francisco's Union Square. *Los Angeles Times* publisher, Major General Harrison Gray Otis, not to be outdone by the commodore, was honored for his role as an officer in the Civil War by a statue in MacArthur Park in LA, which included the figure of a US soldier (until it was a hit by a car), in the Philippine-American War.

The US entry into World War I brought a substantial mobilization of Californians as thousands trained at bases throughout the state then served overseas. California-based Navy ships seized German islands in the Pacific, though the bulk of the impact of the war occurred further east. Nonetheless, technological advances necessary to fighting the brutal conflict overseas led to greater American investment on the West Coast. The Navy developed its first submarine base in Los Angeles as a cost-saving measure; the brass thought it would be cheaper to patrol the Pacific Coast with submarines than surface ships. The success of undersea warfare in the Atlantic, however, led to a big expansion of the submarine program, particularly in San Diego. By the beginning of World War II, San Diego had become the major US Naval port on the West Coast, with dozens of bases and installations. Sailors, military employees, and contractors rolled into the small city, fueling a dramatic population and construction boom even into the Great Depression.

No industry was more profoundly connected to the military than aviation. Initially, California's aviation industry was an expression of the character of the adventurous young men who took to the skies in the early years of powered flight. California's climate and wide-open spaces fostered a creative culture for young pilots. Glenn L. Martin, with the help of mechanic Roy Beal, built his first plane in an abandoned church in Santa Ana in 1910. Within a couple years, Martin gained local fame thrilling audiences at air shows at county fairs. But perhaps the most famous of California's macho, risk-taking, young pilot-engineers was Howard Hughes, a Cal Tech graduate. Hughes won a variety of land and air speed records as a pilot and driver.

> We know the psychological moment when we see it, we Aces. There are things of the past; let them lay. There are things of the future; we will come to them. There is this one thing of the palpitating, pulsating present, this aviation, an aggressive, vital thing...
>
> We couldn't possibly be persuaded that anything more wonderful than the conquest of the air has happened in the last thousand years. It isn't a thing to be conservative about. It's young—breathlessly expectant of all the things it will do.
> —"We Talk of Ourselves," *The Ace* (1919)

Yet the flyers were more than dashing young men, they were pioneers of a major new manufacturing and transportation industry. Hughes, for instance, parlayed a small fortune into a giant one with his business acumen, showmanship, and government contracts. His empire eventually included pioneering passenger carrier TransWorld Airlines, aircraft manufacturing, tool making, casinos, and films. T. Claude Ryan started the country's first regular air passenger service, flying between LA and San Diego in 1922. Ryan went on to build the plane Charles Lindbergh flew across the Atlantic in 1927, the Spirit of St. Louis. Glenn Martin, the Loughead [Lockheed] brothers, John Northrop, and Donald Douglas all began with small aviation businesses in Southern California. Donald Douglas, the first person to graduate from MIT with a degree in aeronautic engineering, began building four planes for the navy in an abandoned movie studio in 1923 with capital from land developer and *LA Times* publisher Harry Chandler. The Navy paid Douglas almost $200,000 (worth $23 million in 2006 dollars) for the planes. Wealthy venture capitalists in the east also took chances with the new companies. Daniel Guggenheim provided the money for the first commercial airline, Western Air Express. Guggenheim money, made mostly from mining, also underwrote early research programs at Cal Tech.

Many of the aviation companies failed in the Depression, but by 1938 military orders started to revive the industry. Military contracts in World War II provided the money for the Lockheed, Douglas, and Hughes companies and North American Aviation to grow into enormous corporations. Aviation employment in California took off, rising from little more than 1,000 in 1933 to 280,000 in 1943. California made nearly half of all the airplanes in the US in 1940. The Douglas Company alone built more than 29,000 planes for the Navy and Army Air Corps. While the industry shrank in the later 40s, the Korean War and the larger Cold War pushed up military budgets and contracts for bombers, fighters, transports, and experimental planes. Using designs and equipment developed for the military, commercial aviation also rose in the postwar era. By the late 60s, Douglas's successor company, McDonnell Douglas, was the world's largest military contractor. It merged with Boeing in 1997.

The culture and society of aeronautics and defense contracting extended far beyond charismatic individuals. Whole cities depended on the enormous plants; hundreds of thousands of people spent their days designing and building advanced weapons and transportation—a single Douglas plant in Long Beach employed 160,000 people by the end of World War II. Even after postwar cutbacks, the factory employed around 100,000 in the 1950s.

While the aerospace industry in California grew in importance, naval forces remained the main strategic focus as the US military expanded out of the old presidios of the Spanish era and remote forts of the Indian fighting years. At Monterey, the Spanish presidio was succeeded by US Army Base Fort Ord. The former Spanish *castello* at the entrance to San Francisco Bay

Planes under construction at a Curtis-Wright training center in Glendale during World War II.

San Francisco National Cemetery in the Presidio holds the remains of soldiers from the Mexican-American War, Civil War, Indian Wars, Boxer Rebellion, Philippine War, World War I, Korean War, and Vietnam War. Photo courtesy of US Dept. of Veterans Affairs.

RAND

With the maturing of the aerospace industry, the culture of the aviator and entrepreneur gave way to the culture of the engineer, the machinist, and the scientist. As part of Douglas's wartime research program it created the Research and Development (R and D) group, which after the war spun off as the RAND Corporation. RAND provided mathematics-informed analysis and research for critical Cold War innovations, including the ideas behind apocalyptic technologies such as multiple warhead missiles. It also outlined basic Cold War strategies such as the training of modern third world military forces and the development of nuclear deterrence. After RAND analyst Daniel Ellsberg leaked the Pentagon Papers in 1971, which exposed the government's pattern of lies about the Vietnam War, the organization went through a major overhaul, though it remains a key part of the military-industrial economy. RAND has branched out to provide a broad range of policy analyses in areas such as healthcare and education, but its main work remains in the mathematical social sciences funded by the Defense Department. Like the elite RAND analysts, highly trained, college-educated aerospace workers supported a new sort of conservative politics in California—libertarian, anti-communist, futurist. Heirs to the visionary engineers who built the state, these men believed in a rational future, one based on science, power, and—despite being the beneficiaries of massive government spending—individual enterprise.

became Fort Point and the Presidio became the Headquarters of the US 6th Army. In contrast, San Diego's presidio didn't become an army base; San Diego became a Navy town and the Marines developed Camp Pendleton further up the coast on the site of the former Rancho Santa Margarita y Los Flores, with San Clemente Island conveniently situated for bombing practice. The first US submarine base was in San Pedro. World War II, with the deadly fighting in the Pacific, led to the creation and expansion of many bases for all the armed forces, more than fifty for the Army alone, totaling hundreds of thousands of acres.

After substantial base closings, California is still the home to 27 major military installations. Fort Point is now a museum under the Golden Gate Bridge (best remembered as the spot where Kim Novak jumped into San Francisco Bay in the Hitchcock film *Vertigo)*, the Presidio is part of the Golden Gate

National Recreation area, and the Letterman military hospital
as been renovated into the Letterman Digital Arts Center, home
of filmmaker George Lucas's Industrial Light and Magic, which
brought us *Star Wars*. In the 1990s, Fort Ord became the site of
Cal State University, Monterey Bay. Camp Pendleton is alive and
well, still bombing San Clemente Island, a piece of California
whited-out on Google Earth's maps.

California's military growth and industrialization depended
on an infrastructure built up during an oil extraction and refining boom. Prospectors had found oil in the 1860s, mostly in the
Central Valley, creating a small industry. Then, in 1892, previously unsuccessful miners Edward L. Doheny and Charles
Canfield made a spectacular find in the Echo Park area of LA.
Soon, derricks sprouted around the city. At its peak, Signal Hill
in Long Beach produced more than 250,000 barrels per day. The
Lakeview gusher, a single well in the Central Valley, produced
45,000 barrels a day for its first two years. News of this incred-
ibly productive well drove down oil prices nationwide. Union Oil
nearly went bankrupt because it had too much petroleum. Since
the first strike, California has produced more than 25 billion of
barrels of oil. Indeed, the black gold extracted in California has
been worth far more than all the actual gold ever mined in the
state. The large oil companies were started by the usual suspects of
California enterprise, such as Lloyd Tevis. Still, the rapid growth
of the industry made fortunes for an enterprising few like Doheny
and Canfield or former piano teacher turned "Petroleum Queen"
Emma Summers, who controlled a majority of Los Angeles's
fields in the first decade of the twentieth century. Soon the companies consolidated either as independents, such as Union Oil, or as
subsidiaries of John D. Rockefeller's Standard Oil.

Oil towns from Bakersfield to Brea attracted thousands of
workers and entrepreneurs. Dominated by Standard Oil, the
industry created relatively isolated communities—residents
of Long Beach sometimes lived their entire lives only visiting
downtown LA once or twice. Oil fields surrounded houses in
formerly rural enclaves. Derricks, wrote one breathless observer,
were "springing up in every direction, as well paid happy workers are piercing the bowels of mother earth [for] that wonderful
liquid gold." Others were not so sanguine. To them, oil towns
were places full of "squalor, where garbage and decaying vegeta-
ble matter, tin cans, old rags and scrap papers lie in heaps about
temporary structures or are strewn over vacant lots. Flies swarm
and the atmosphere reeks with offensive odors."

ORANGE
COUNTY
California

Nature's Prolific
Wonderland—

The land of the orange blossom,
With its mountains, vales and hills,
Its wealth of olive, fruit and oil,
And sunny, singing rills;
The home of the palm and
poppy, the blue Pacific too,
Orange County, Nature's
wonderland, is calling,
calling you.

Spring Eternal

This 1920s brochure promised "Spring Eternal" in Orange County's mix of bucolic farmland, pleasant beachfront resorts and industrial petroleum extraction.

More urbanized areas, such as central Los Angeles, also suffered from the ecological and social impact of the drilling, pumping, and refining. Natural gas in wells blew derricks into the air, creating toxic flammable geysers. In remote areas, the gushers were a problem, but in the densely populated cities they were disasters for everyone living nearby. Hundreds of oil fires lit up the night sky and filled the air with dense pollution years before the region's famous smog made its appearance. Pipelines split open, sending

The reality of the oil industry was somewhat different. The Lakeview gusher spilled 378 million gallons of crude oil in the Central Valley, at least 150 million gallons more than the 2010 Deep Water Horizon spill in the Gulf of Mexico — but was also a major tourist attraction in 1910-1911.

oil pouring down residential streets. Regular leaks covered the LA/Long Beach harbor in a slick of oil four inches deep. Perhaps the worst disaster occurred in 1926, in Brea in Orange County, when a Union Oil tank farm burst into flames, burning more than 2.25 million barrels of oil, 8 times more than the Exxon *Valdez* was to spill in Alaska years later. Oil pollution decimated the south coast's already stressed fisheries. Cancer and lung diseases plagued the area's residents. Like gold, oil production had far-reaching effects. "Pollution, overproduction, and profligate waste were the consequences of unchecked oil development in the Los Angeles basin," writes historian Nancy Quam-Wickam "consequences that reached crisis proportions in the 1920s."

The oil boom provided great wealth for some and steady jobs for many more, yet its hazards and boom/bust cycle caused some working-class towns like Redondo Beach to restrict oil development. Redondo Beach's actions in the 1920s fore-shadowed coastal resistance to the oil industry that eventually culminated in California's opposition to coastal drilling in the 70s. In response to the pollution and fires, the industry bought up property near refineries and reduced the presence of derricks and pumps in built up areas. In LA fashion, however, they often disguised pumps and other facilities—sort of the opposite of the stucco fantasy building built in the shape of the commodity they sold, like the hot dog stands shaped like hot dogs. Venoco, which currently operates platforms offshore also built flower-bedecked towers in the middle of Long Beach and on the campus of Beverly Hills High School. In 2003, environmentalist Erin Brockovich sued Venoco on behalf of cancer victims who had attended the school, but the company settled with regulators. The oil compa-nies no doubt would have preferred to operate in less populated regions. As one oil company attorney complained, "They ruined a perfectly good oilfield by building a city on top of it."

The result of the boom in the southland, wrote muckrak-ing attorney and journalist Carey McWilliams, was "one long drunken orgy, one protracted debauch." With its frenetic, disorganized growth, LA's population doubled between 1920 and 1930 to 1.24 million. McWilliams saw the city as built on a "vicious economic underworld" full of "two bit predators out to con the ignorant and fleece the innocent." Other observers agreed, warning that LA had an "insistent element of specula-tion that permeates all walks of life." The city was "particularly ripe for heedless financial adventure."

The most notorious case of corruption came in 1923 when oilman Edward Doheny bribed US Secretary of the Interior Albert B. Fall with $100,000 to gain access to the Central Valley's rich Elk Hills fields. Along with Harry F. Sinclair's larger bribe to obtain the Teapot Dome fields in Wyoming, Doheny's effort to provide green lubrication for the wheels of government created the largest political scandal of the 1920s, implicating not only Fall but also the Secretary of the Navy and President Harding. Fall resigned his post and ended up in prison. Doheny avoided conviction, while Sinclair went to prison for contempt of Congress.

With its booming industries, swelling populations, federal funding, and substantial capital from investors willing to gamble on advanced technologies, California, particularly the southland, seemed to be creating a far more advanced society than much of the rest of the country. The state only needed places for the new people to live and ways to get the story out. It soon had them.

Technocrats

Building on California's military-industrial culture, the Technocrats, a group made up largely of engineers, sought to rationalize society. Started by a group of New York engineers under the influence of economist Thorsten Veblen and efficiency expert Frederick Winslow Taylor, Technocracy Inc. thrived in California in the late twenties. At their peak, the Technocrats claimed a half million members (they only excluded politicians and non-citizens) who supported their approach to the political economy. Founder Howard Scott argued that scientific rationalism, the most effective approach to society's problems, would eliminate politics: "Marxian economics were never sufficiently radical or revolutionary to handle the problems brought on by the impact of technology in a large size national society of today." Rather, via technical analysis, all social problems could be seen in terms of an expenditure of energy. With this method, unemployment could be solved and people would only have to work 4 hours a day. But even this sort of rationalization wasn't enough for California's Technocrats, who began to refuse to recognize the irrational around them. Technocrats started referring to the states by their longitude and latitude. The most extreme stopped using given names and instead, like one man who addressed a California rally, started taking ID numbers such as *1x1809x56*.

Sabato Rodia started the Watts Towers in 1921, when it was still possible to create your own kind of building in Los Angeles. He named them "Nuestro Pueblo" and worked on them for another 33 years.

Suburbia and Hollywood

Revolutionary upheavals swept the world in the 1910s and 20s. In California, refugees from the turmoil of the Mexican revolution swelled the population. While these new immigrants were generally apolitical, some anarchists, influenced by the Magon brothers and other Mexican revolutionaries, tried unsuccessfully to create radical organizations in the US. Later, after the unsuccessful right-wing Cristero uprising in Mexico, conservative Catholic refugees straggled across the border. Misunderstanding the Christian symbolism of the Ku Klux Klan's crosses, a number of former Cristeros attempted to join the San Diego Klan branch in 1934, failing to understand that their conservative ideology did not compensate for their new ethnic identity as Mexican immigrants. The Cristeros were not alone.

The victories of the Progressives in the 1910s and the growth of the labor movement during the war appeared to promise a shift leftward in California's politics. But opposition to radicalism had actually grown stronger during the war and the political tide turned quickly. The year 1919 saw the largest wave of strikes in US history nationwide, but the strikes ended up reducing union power. In California, the most bitterly fought battles were the 1920–1 maritime and longshore strikes that sank union power on the docks and at sea. In the postwar period, political and cultural repression also reached a peak with a red scare and the deportation of alien radicals. At the same time the triumph of Progressive social reforms launched society on an ambitious program of cultural remaking: the passage of national women's suffrage and Prohibition. But more than these changes in government, little captures the 1920s in California better than the invention of the Hollywood system and the construction of streetcar suburbs filled with California bungalows. As in the movies, however, California's growth was not always what it seemed.

The film industry began as a slightly unsavory business of bawdy and slapstick shorts shown at vaudeville theaters, carnivals, and amusement parks. During the 1910s and 20s, it trans-

Glamour, fecundity, and racial hierarchy in the orchards as silent film star Dale Fuller poses with oranges, her picking boss, an overseer, and pickers.

formed itself. The number of movie theaters in the US jumped from a few hundred nickelodeons in the first years of the century to more than 14,000 on the eve of World War I. A group of patent-holding trust companies controlled filmmaking back east, but California was far from their control. The state's cheap land, weak unions, and good weather began attracting large numbers of filmmaking companies in the early 1910s. Before World War I, Hollywood was just another small Southern California town. But the war created a shortage of films from European producers, particularly the French, a gap that American producers quickly filled. Then Carl Laemmele, Adolph Zukor, and William Fox applied modern business principles to what had been a fairly independent, haphazard business. Production skyrocketed. Combining efficiency and centralization with astutely marketed stories designed for the largest possible audience, Hollywood became mythmaker for the nation and the world.

By 1920, Hollywood produced more than three quarters of all American films and two thirds of all films in the world, a domination that continued throughout the twentieth century. Before Hollywood, filmmaking was much more democratically widespread. For a few hundred dollars, anyone could make a film. But the Hollywood system quickly found the powerful

The iconic shape of the Brown Derby restaurant on Wilshire Avenue in LA signaled sophistication and excitement. You might bump into Hollywood bigwigs while you ate manager Bob Cobb's most lasting contribution to American cuisine, the Cobb Salad.

market appeal of well-produced, mass-marketed, politically safe entertainment. With the construction of elaborate movie palaces in towns throughout the country and the production of ever more elaborate and higher quality films, the movies became a part of everyday life for all classes of Americans—and an extremely profitable business. Wall Street investors and large banks funded studio expansion and by the end of the 20s a few large companies dominated the industry. The moguls of Hollywood built fully integrated businesses controlling the writing, production, marketing, and distribution of the movies—from the original concept to the popcorn audience members munched in their seats.

In addition to films, Hollywood produced myths about itself. The studios sold glamour and star appeal as much as they did reels of film. The creation of a star system with massive publicity for a few actors drew audiences to theaters to see their favorites as much as the movie themselves. An elaborate system of premieres—roped-off red carpets, extensive press coverage of the films and the actor's personal lives—fed audience fascination with wealthy, often scandalous lives seemingly far from their own. In Hollywood productions, actors played themselves rather than other characters since this helped audiences be sure of what would appear on the screen. Nonetheless, the best Hollywood films—whether action, melodrama, romance, or comedy—rose above their studio-imposed formulas. The draw of seeing a favored star perform wonderfully in a beautifully produced story brought millions into the theaters and millions into the Hollywood studio coffers.

> Hollywood—the motion picture capital: a community of dissolute actors and actresses and others of the movie industry; the worst of them unspeakably vile, the best suspicionable; a colony of unregenerates and narcotic addicts; given to wild night parties commonly known as "orgies"; heroes of the screen by day and vicious roisterers by night; a section of civilization gone rottenly to smash.
>
> —Thoreau Cronyn, "The Truth About Hollywood," *New York Herald* (1922)

Yet the focus on celebrity had a flip side, a fascination with the lurid and scandalous. No scandal had a bigger moralizing impact than the murder and rape trial of Roscoe "Fatty" Arbuckle, the biggest comedy star of the 1910s. After a wild party at the St. Francis Hotel in San Francisco, one of Arbuckle's companions, the actress and clothing designer Frances Rappe, died from a burst bladder. A friend of Rappe's said Arbuckle raped her violently but after three trials, he was never convicted. Nonetheless, the scandal, which filled newspapers for months, ended Arbuckle's career. Will Hays, Postmaster General and a devout Presbyterian, convinced Paramount's owners Adolph Zukor and Jesse Lasky to ban Arbuckle's films from distribution (they are now available on DVD).

Other scandals kept Hollywood on the front pages in ways that embarrassed the studios. Less than a year after Rappe's death, someone killed the popular director William Desmond Taylor. When police arrived at Taylor's bungalow in what is now the MacArthur Park neighborhood of LA, they discovered a studio employee sneaking embarrassing papers out of the house. At first, the murder of the debonair Taylor was attributed to a love triangle, then rumors surfaced that he regularly attended gay opium parties and even belonged to Aleister Crowley's Ordo Templi Orientis, which practiced an arcane religion associated

The death of actress Virginia Rappe, supposedly after being raped by comedy star Fatty Arbuckle at a wild San Francisco party, scandalized and fascinated the public.

with black magic. More scandals followed when an actor and a producer died of drug overdoses.

Though the scandals, along with daily gossip about affairs and divorces kept their industry in the headlines, studio bosses worried about a government crackdown, since films were not protected by the First Amendment. Then Paramount, along with the other studios, hired the redoubtable Will Hays to oversee the morality of the films. By the early 1930s, Hay convinced the studios to create a code to govern what appeared on the screen. The Hays Code gave a seal of approval to films that limited scandalous behavior and exhibited patriotism, respectful treatment of religion, and an overall prudery. The rules forbade scandalously bad words (like "nuts" or "hell") or the portrayal of married couples sleeping in the same bed, along with representations of graphic violence, homosexuality, or nude bodies. The Code began to falter in the 50s when the Supreme Court ruled that films were indeed protected by the First Amendment. The Code sanitized Hollywood's products until 1966, when the studios agreed to replace it with the current rating system.

Hollywood's studio system gave great power to a few studio heads and notoriety to a few stars, but it had much less to offer many of the industry's other workers. Bitterly anti-union studio owners resisted cantankerous artists and skilled craftspeople alike. Unions grew in the 1920s, but many fell under the control of mobsters, though the craft workers' union, International Association of Theatrical Stage Employees (IATSE), did win major studio contracts in the 20s. With the labor upsurge of the 30s, militant leftist studio employees founded the Conference of Studio Unions and revitalized the more conservative IATSE. Screen actors, writers, artists, and directors, along with workers in more traditional unionized crafts like electricians and painters, created a vibrant and powerful union movement. Despite the conservative tendencies of the studio companies, Hollywood in the 30s and 40s was open to many radical creative people. Communists played important roles in the industry and in the unions. Bitterly fought strikes in the those decades secured union control, but the Red Scare of the 50s led to defeat for some of the unions and the expulsion of radicals.

While Hollywood's portrayals brought images of the good life, passionate love affairs, silly antics, and mythic adventures to a wide audience in the US and around the world, they also helped create a rich fantasy life for Americans, one in which people lived in modern city apartments and country mansions. In real life, most people's homes were far less impressive, but in California a combination of easy credit, simple house design, cheap land, and suburban rail construction created a boom for comfortable, if modest, housing. The kit house and bungalow developed at the turn of the 20th century allowed working-class people the security of a well-built home. Industrially finished lumber, trim, and hardware had made houses much cheaper and faster to build in the latter half of the 19th century, while bringing elaborate decorations within the reach of the middle class. Such tracts had little appeal to the elite and to architects—or for that matter architecture critics and historians—which makes it hard to find the modest bungalow in architectural guide books.

What passes for bungalows in such works are gargantuan luxury homes such as the Parsons "Bungalow" in Altadena, listed as "one of the finest most characteristic California bungalows to be found anywhere." It is not. Most characteristic are the stucco-fronted or shingled houses with deep porches supported by thick geometric columns that line the streets of every older town in the state. Often built by the owners or small contractors from kits or plans supplied by Sears Roebuck and other companies, the bungalow dominated residential construction in the first third of the twentieth century.

Aimee Semple McPherson healing a woman in 1921.

Radio Priestess Love Scandal

Charismatic preachers led a religious revival in the 1920s, using the new medium of radio to broadcast the word of God. Few achieved the notoriety of a divorced woman, Aimee Semple McPherson of the Foursquare Gospel Church, who combined sentimental preaching with jazz age showwomanship that used radio, film, and even aviation stunts. McPherson had remade herself after serving as a missionary in China and was one of the first ministers in California to realize the evangelical power of mass-produced, high-tech radios. Her sermons attracted thousands over the airwaves.

McPherson claimed she could heal by faith. A room at her church was full of wheelchairs and crutches no longer needed by people who had been cured by her preaching. In 1926, however, she mysteriously vanished. Accusations surfaced that she had been kidnapped by Mexicans, but a few months later she was discovered shacked up with the radio operator from her Angelus Temple. Despite this fall from grace, McPherson found forgiveness and recovered enough to consider a run for vice president in the thirties. At her death in 1944, her church had 400 congregations in North America and hundreds of overseas missions.

Because land was so cheap, working-class Californians could often afford small plots where they could then camp out while building their homes themselves. Developers in LA basin towns like Compton, South Gate, or Vernon helped struggling families get easy credit for purchase of unimproved land. In contrast to the sameness of later developments, these homemade homes varied dramatically, depending on the skill and taste of the owner-builders. As "jack knife" builders worked, their homes grew room by room as they saved the money to buy more materials. Often the houses were tiny, at times only 18 feet across. Historian Becky Nicolaides quotes one observer: "Here is a perfectly

The recently-built Stewart family bungalow, around 1905 in San Juan Capistrano.

cubical building about half the size of a one-car garage covered with tar paper. It is not a chicken coop or a rabbit pen but the home of a family." Despite the poverty and overcrowding, the combination of young families, common experiences, and outdoor living created lively neighborhoods in the new subdivisions.

It helped that the bungalows were cheap. Before World War I, a relatively ample five-room bungalow cost as little as $2,000. Even cheaper, in Ramona a developer offered tiny shacks without a bathroom for only $625. Kit houses that buyers assembled themselves or bought prefabricated could save families hundreds of dollars. In 1924, when the average home in LA cost more than

$3,200, an assembled kit home cost less than $2,500. While the houses were often small and of poor quality, many Angelenos could buy their own homes. The high rate of home ownership fit into the industrial open shop vision of the Chamber and Commerce and the Merchants and Manufacturers Association. LA, wrote the Chamber, "is a land of smokeless sunlit factories surrounded by residences of contented, efficient workers."

Others doubted that utopia had arrived. In 1916, for instance, Women's Trade Union League activist Frances Noel complained "the mode of owning homes in Los Angeles while in itself ideal has produced more and more outright slaves in the labor world than perhaps any other condition we have had in Los Angeles."

> I never saw California looking more beautiful. The tremendous rains have washed away all the real estate signs.
> —Will Rogers, *Los Angeles Times* (1927)

LA, famous for its sprawling geography, originally expanded outward because of rail transit. Henry Huntington, who inherited the fortune of his uncle, Southern Pacific robber baron Collis Huntington, invested in Southern California trolley and rail systems. He and his Pacific Electric Railway came to dominate the LA region in the first years of the twentieth century as the towns of the basin were laid out along rail lines. Expanding from rail into land speculation and urban development, much like the *LA Times*'s Chandler and Otis, Huntington created developments all over the region, and his power and wealth spread. The founders of Huntington Park named their city after the rail heir when he agreed to extend a trolley line through their town. He sold his company to Southern Pacific in 1911 and devoted himself to buying European art and libraries as he had once bought land and railways. Huntington, who married his uncle's widow to consolidate the family fortune—and perhaps to emulate his adored relative—later donated his grandiose estate and enormous collections to create the Huntington Library, now one of the premier archival libraries in the world. His rail system dominated the geography of LA, enabling far-flung industrial growth largely separate from street-car-served suburban development. At its peak, the system included 1,000 miles of passenger

Whittier residents were happy to have the Pacific Electric Trolleys in 1903; they made LA's original sprawl possible.

and freight lines that carried over 100,000,000 people a year. In 1945, the Huntington estate sold the LA Railway to a consortium of General Motors and oil and rubber companies. The new owners, hardly enthusiastic about public transit, underfunded the lines and substituted less expensive buses for the trolleys. At the same time, new freeways, low gas prices, and post-World War II prosperity made automobile commuting practical. The last of LA's trolley system was "motorized" in 1963. Today, throughout the basin, wide boulevards divided by grassy strips mark the old Pacific Electric routes. Many of the new Metro light rail lines are built on old PE right-of-ways.

Although the city of Los Angeles grew rapidly along the rail lines, not everyone liked the city's expansion. In order to avoid the higher tax rates of LA as well as those of San Francisco and Oakland, developers, manufacturers, and farmers resisted incorporation into the metropolises. By incorporating separately from the big cities, suburban towns gained more control over their taxes and the direction of development. Yet without the tax base provided by industry and commerce, the municipalities relied extensively on volatile sales tax revenues. When the economy declined, as it did in the Great Depression, cities had to raise taxes on homeowners, generating resentment from people facing hard times themselves. Early anti-tax movements led by trade unions had roiled the working-class suburbs of LA and Oakland in the 1930s. By the 50s the promise of lower taxes, along with modern, spacious houses, made life in the suburbs that much more appealing. Burgeoning home sales taxes and generous government programs amply funded schools, parks, and other city services. It was a system that worked fine—as long as the communities continued to grow.

Developers and realtors ran many California cities, creating development almost without restriction. The developers and contractors overwhelmed the small town councils or took advantage of unincorporated areas. They offered struggling farmers and ranchers windfalls for their land. The suburbs, with their limited public services and few municipal attractions, nonetheless satisfied the needs of young families seeking a piece of the suburban American dream: land, security, and, not least, uniformity.

The uniformity of neighborhoods was enforced through a number of means. The culture of segregation during the 1920s was also reinforced by groups like the Ku Klux Klan, which was both a social club and terrorist organization. Although its largest influence was in the South and Midwest, the Klan created powerful branches in California's cities and small towns with its blend of clubiness, anti-Semitism, xenophobia, Protestant moralism, and racism. Klan members, campaigning for racial purity and moral probity, ran openly for office, elected sheriffs, controlled grand juries, and won complete control of the city of Anaheim. Despite its popularity, the Klan collapsed as an organization after scandals caused by almost predictable financial and sexual improprieties among the group's charismatic national leadership.

Segregationists in California also used Klan-style terrorism as a last resort. While Klansmen did target the state's small black population, they directed much of their ire at Mexican immigrants. Mobs lynched as many as 350 people between 1849 and 1934. Probably two thirds of the victims were Mexican or Mexican Americans. Lynching had declined in California (and the US) in the first decades of the 20th century, but during the border turmoil of the Mexican Revolution, these murders increased substantially. Lynch mobs generally attacked their victims for the crime of murder or rape, not for moving to the wrong neighborhood. Still, minority residents of the state lived in fear of such violence.

Far more common than terrorism in maintaining the segregation of the burgeoning cities of the 1920s, however, was the rise of the use of restrictive racial covenants and other less formal mechanisms. While California had largely avoided the comprehensive Jim Crow laws that ordained formal segregation for the South, it had nonetheless maintained racial separation and hierarchy. Racial covenants, legal agreements in real-estate contracts that restricted sales or rentals to Christian whites, were a key element in maintaining community purity. Banks and other mortgage lenders embraced redlining and other discriminatory practices, making it almost impossible for non-whites to buy homes in the suburbs and even to get loans for homes in the neighborhoods they could live in. The separate incorporation of suburbs also fostered segregated enclaves, as characteristic boosters proclaimed proudly until the 1960s. Huntington Park, proud of its rails, also boasted its residents were "100 percent American of the white race."

By the end of the 1920s, the effect of the separation of city and suburb divided the working-class vote in the central urban areas and made regional planning decisions increasingly unwieldy. Yet these proliferating small towns with their rows of modest homes on wide, tree-lined streets, and their easy access via street car to industrial and white-collar work in the older urban centers had enormous appeal to working- and middle-class people desiring security, comfort, and sameness. These communities became the building blocks of modern California's enormous sprawling metropolises. As the 20s drew to a close, the prospects for the suburbs' growth seemed unlimited. Home prices continued a steady rise. The search for security for some meant easy riches for others. Fortunes large and small from real-estate construction, financing, and sale inspired a new housing bubble in the state. It was, in the words of promoters, a "new era," in which the economy would only continue to grow. But as economist John Kenneth Galbraith later observed, "The United States is afflicted with new eras."

Filipinos working in pole peas.

from Texas

Pea picker from Texas.

Future voter & his Mexican fa[...]

All races serve the crops in California

Photographer Dorothea Lange and her husband, Berkeley economist
Paul Taylor, publicized the plight of California's farmworkers for the
federal government in this 1935 report. It became the basis for their
popular book on the Okie migration, An American Exodus.

13

THE GREAT DEPRESSION

The massive economic collapse and the human disaster of the Great Depression scarred a generation and remade American politics for decades. The stock market crash in October 1929 plunged the US into a Depression that had already sucked in much of the world. Hundreds of thousands of desperate migrants took to the roads looking for something better in California. Others joined demonstrations, marches, and strikes, demanding relief, employment, solutions. Many embraced radical ideologies or sought solace in a new religious revival.

At the worst moment, 1.25 million people were out of work in the state, almost a third of all workers. Hunger, homelessness, and a host of attendant problems haunted families and individuals. The economic collapse shattered middle- and working-class confidence in the country's business and political leaders and challenged people's sense of self-reliance. Remembered today in powerful images from documentary photography, the literature of the era, and family memories, the poverty and insecurity of the Depression was a wrenching experience for many millions.

Particularly hard hit was real estate. The 1920s population growth and speculation had propelled housing construction to new heights, but the Depression brought a new low. Housing construction effectively disappeared, down almost 90 percent by 1933. The evidence of the crash is all over the state—every town has neighborhoods full of modest bungalows constructed during the boom years, but almost no 1930s homes. The economic crisis also devastated the state's enormous agricultural industry. While national agricultural output dropped by more than a third from 1929–35, California's farm income, reliant on sales of "luxury" fruits and nuts, plunged 50 percent. Farm subsidies and stop-gap efforts to bolster agricultural prices led to the dumping of California citrus and dairy. Like others across the nation, California farmers had taken on increasing debt to pay for expansion in the 1920s. Prices for other commodities—minerals, lumber, cotton—also plummeted. Drought and collapsing prices

Families from the Dustbowl faced a difficult passage west on Route 66. Photographer Dorothea Lange documented their plight.

in the first years of the Depression made it impossible for the farmers to pay their loans, leading to thousands of bankruptcies, displacement of families, and auctions of land. It was a mark of how bad things were in the rest of the country that California remained a magnet for migrants.

The victory of the Democrats and their leader Franklin Roosevelt at the national level in 1932 ushered in a new era of reform. Government now tilted more toward the needs of the poor and unemployed—though such reforms were made politically possible with subsidies and bailouts for industry and agriculture. New Dealers pushed through elaborate business regulations and even expensive social programs like Social Security. California benefited substantially from the new Democratic administration's answer to the Depression: a whole panoply of

Despite the depression, California's farm business continued to provide work for migrants, which the Federal government recorded in photographs by notable artists like Lange.

programs, some of which offered immediate relief to desperate workers and farmers in the form of temporary jobs and work programs. The Civilian Conservation Corps provided rural and wilderness jobs and the Works Progress Administration built public works large and small. Other New Deal innovations that directly affected Californians were crop price supports to farmers, rural electrification, and new labor laws. California conservatives were not pleased with the reforms or the reformers. Still only a few diehards on the far right clung to the seemingly outdated ideas of unregulated markets and small government. While the *LA Times* sourly accused Roosevelt of trying to obtain "dictatorial authority in administering government affairs," liberals dominated both major political parties in the state by the end of the decade.

Governor "Sunny" Jim Rolph took such a hard line on crime he was dubbed "Governor Lynch." Elected five times as mayor of San Francisco, he made sure city hall was larger than the state capitol building.

Despite the Democrats' national ascendancy, Republicans continued to control California state politics. The charismatic former mayor of San Francisco, "Sunny" Jim Rolph, won the governor's race in 1930. His stance against taxes and relief programs followed conservative Republican orthodoxy. Rolph's pandering to anti-crime feeling led him to approve the lynching of two men accused of the kidnapping and murdering of the 20-year-old son of a prominent San Jose family in 1933. The lynchers beat a Santa Clara County sheriff guarding the men and hung the pair from a tree. Rolph's open endorsement of the San Jose action shocked the *New York Times*, which nicknamed him "Governor Lynch." That two white men had been murdered in a way usually reserved for the darker races gave legitimacy to the anti-lynching movement that had been carried largely by black civil rights campaigners since the late 19th century. The San Jose events were the last lynchings in California, although such crimes continued in the South for decades. When Rolph died on the campaign trail in 1934, he was succeeded by Lt. Governor Frank Merriam, another conservative Republican. Merriam soon faced a political earthquake.

Former Socialist and muckraking author Upton Sinclair charged into the 1934 governor's race championing a plan he called EPIC—End Poverty In California. Sinclair, a prolific writer with more than 100 books of fiction and non-fiction to his credit, was most famous for his investigation of the Chicago stockyards, *The Jungle*. As a Christian Socialist he had been drawn to the plight of the poor and founded a short-lived utopian community in rather un-utopian New Jersey. Determined to change the politics of the state, Sinclair initiated his campaign with—surprise—a book. In *I, Governor of California*, Sinclair proposed "a new cooperative system for the unemployed" in which a barter system would replace dollars, allowing unemployed people to "work and support themselves and thus take themselves off the backs of the taxpayers." In an echo of 19th-century San Francisco reformer Henry George's plans to counter monopolies and speculation with a "single tax" on land, Sinclair proposed funding his system with a tax on large property owners. The idealistic EPIC campaign thrilled left-leaning voters; hundreds of thousands swept Sinclair to victory in the Democratic primary over George Creel, who had been President Wilson's propaganda chief in World War I.

But California's wealthy and conservative businessmen were not entranced. Governor Merriam warned that EPIC was "flimsy and unreal... utterly misguided... completely impossible of realization... dangerously unsafe and destructive." The Republican Party and its allies in Hollywood, particularly studio head Louis B. Mayer, mounted the first modern multimedia counter-campaign for conservative incumbent Merriam. Merriam supporters declared that EPIC was communistic: "Your personal security is at issue—the welfare of your home and family; your American citizenship, your rights of self-rule and freedom of worship—your job and your independence." The vituperative media effort paid off when voters gave the dull Merriam a narrow victory. The hyperbolic election, observed the sidelined Creel, had offered voters "a choice between epilepsy and catalepsy."

Nonetheless, in 1939, Culbert Olson, a left-leaning Democrat who had been Sinclair's running mate, won the governorship. Olson's election signaled a seismic shift in California's electoral politics. Only ten Democrats had ever been governor and most of those had been before the Civil War. Since 1887, Republicans had occupied the governor's mansion with only one exception. In the 70 years after the Merriam-Sinclair race, California's politics shifted back and forth, right to left, practically with each administration. After Olson's election, the moderate right recruited Alameda County District Attorney Earl Warren for Governor in 1943. Warren was succeeded by liberal Democrat Pat Brown, who in turn lost to right-winger Ronald Reagan. Elections remained tight and landslides rare.

The shakeup in state politics reflected a wider ferment in California during the Depression years. In addition to electoral politics, creative activists offered provocative solutions to the social and economic disaster of the decade. Under the slogan "Youth for Work, Old Age for Leisure," Dr. Francis Townsend, a Long Beach physician who retired in poverty at age 66, devised one of the most popular of the relief proposals. The Old Age Revolving Pension, the Townsend Plan, would have paid all seniors whose "past life is free from habitual criminality" a pension of $200 per month. Townsend Clubs spread throughout the state and then the country, reaching a membership of one and a half million by the middle of the decade. Despite the passage of the Social Security Act, the plan kept its popularity into the 1940s because of its more generous payments. Townsend's movement was probably the first mobilization of senior citizens as a political pressure group.

Victor Arnautoff, an assistant to Diego Rivera, directed the WPA frescos at Coit Tower in San Francisco. Despite his open Communism, he became a professor at Stanford University.

The cleverly named Ham 'n Eggs relief proposal also gained ground in the late 1930s. Served up by Robert Noble, a far less savory operator than the venerable Townsend, Ham 'n Eggs demanded the government hand out thirty dollars every week to everyone in the state. How the plan would be financed, Noble wouldn't say. Like the Townsend Plan, the passage of the Social Security Act failed to satisfy the plan's wide range of supporters. A Ham 'n Eggs initiative endorsed by Olson and Senator Sheridan Downey in 1938 gained 45 percent of the vote—and that despite campaign literature like:

Let's stay away from politics
Regardless of who hollers
Let's not be fooled by childish tricks
LET'S GET OUR THIRTY DOLLARS

Violent confrontations along the San Francisco waterfront in 1934 led to a general strike that pressured the government to help settle the bitter maritime conflict.

Government-sponsored relief plans, both harebrained and reasonable, responded to the inability of the society's existing services through churches and private charities to address the scale of suffering in the Great Depression. Still, religious organizations made substantial efforts with traditional charity, providing free meals and shelter. More activist approaches also gained ground in the churches. Aimee Semple McPherson, the radio preacher, departed from the typical Pentecostal rejection of politics to endorse President Roosevelt and the New Deal. The Catholic Worker, which had been founded in New York by former Oaklander Dorothy Day, established centers and retreats, particularly in LA, providing organizing help to the unemployed and support for union drives.

Further out of mainstream religion, Guy and Edna Ballard, a mine promoter and a medium, published a bestseller, *Mighty I Am,* in 1934. The book launched a nationwide religious group. St. Germain, one of the "Ascended Masters," apparently met with Guy Ballard at Mt. Shasta and told him how he would shine violet light rays as an "atomic accelerator" on those who

Harry Bridges at his 1934 trial. Repeated attempts to deport the radical Longshoremen's Union leader failed.

needed it. The atomic light of St. Germain would wash away "all that is not constructive" and allow the Ballards' followers to gain love, happiness, power, and wealth. Apparently, the light weakened a bit after Guy's death in 1940 when Edna and their son were convicted of mail fraud. Believers have kept a small organization alive since then and still publish the Ballards' books.

The state's political and religious turmoil, however, was dwarfed by the dramatic rebirth of the labor movement. The federal government's National Recovery Act (NRA) of 1933 stimulated an explosion in union organizing. Dramatic strikes were fought in the fields, docks, and workshops of the state.

Dockworkers and sailors fought one of the most dramatic and successful strikes in US history in 1934. Radicalism had reappeared during the Great Depression among sailors and longshoremen who found that syndicalism made sense in the rough, macho maritime industry, which depended on close cooperation on deck and in longshore gangs. The maritime workers lacked effective unions after the disastrous 1921 strikes.

An Australian, Harry Bridges, and a group of militants mobilized longshoremen angered by the hated daily labor "shape up" on the docks—a humiliating experience for men desperate for a day's work. In the spring of 1934, a longshore strike quickly spread to the ships as sailors and stewards walked off the jobs. Attempts by the ship owners and stevedoring companies to bring in strikebreakers (the UC Berkeley football team volunteered) were met with mass pickets on the San Francisco Embarcadero. Repeated confrontations with police led to the killing of two strikers at the corner of Mission and Steuart streets (a sidewalk memorial marks the spot today). The deaths enraged more moderate trade unionists in a city that, unlike LA, remained a strong labor town. A silent, mile-long funeral procession accompanied the men to their graves. The next day 130,000 people walked off their jobs in a general strike that lasted four days. Eventually the maritime workers won a hiring hall, shorter hours, and strict safety regulations.

The *San Francisco Chronicle* and many conservatives labeled the strike a "red conspiracy." Bridges was indeed a secret member of the Communist Party and the union welcomed many radicals, but the strikers actually sought traditional trade union goals—job security, higher wages, and safer working conditions. Bridges's skill as a union leader and his popularity among the independent-minded dockworkers kept him as president of the radical West Coast International Longshoremen's and Warehousemen's Union until his retirement in the 1970s. Despite his political beliefs, Bridges later pushed the union to moderate its Depression-era militancy and reach accommodation with management in the 1950s and 60s. The union embraced mechanization on the docks, a strategy that dramatically reduced the number of longshoring jobs, but gave the remaining dockers some of the highest blue-collar wages in the world.

Further inland, an explosion in organizing brought thousands into newly formed or revitalized unions. Often led by immigrants and radicals like Bridges, the newly formed unions made inroads even in bastions of anti-unionism such as the Los Angeles film industry and the fields and packing-houses of the Central Valley. At the same time, migrants from impoverished Southern states flooded into California, displacing Mexican workers in the fields. The widespread labor upheavals of the 1930s depended on a great social transformation among immigrants, particularly Mexicans, who worked with new Anglo migrants.

The Depression also reinforced anti-immigrant sentiment in California. Opposition to immigration had peaked nationally in the 1920s with the passage of federal laws that restricted immigration from Southern and Eastern Europe while banning it from Asia. Mexican immigration, however, had not been restricted. From a mere 50,000 people in 1910 (though this is an undoubtedly low number, given problems with the census), by 1930 the Mexican and Mexican-American population of California had soared to approximately 400,000.

Most Mexican immigrants and Chicanos worked in California's fields, orchards, and ranches. Farmers turned to labor contractors, generally immigrants or Chicanos themselves, with good connections in the community to recruit the armies of hands needed for the seasonal harvests. Migrants moved from south to north through the growing season. In a single year, a typical picker might find work harvesting winter fruits in the Imperial Valley, oranges in Riverside, cotton in the San Joaquin, peas on the coast, grapes in Fresno, and hops along the Sacramento River. Given the low pay, itinerant life, and backbreaking labor of field work, people with other options took them whenever possible. But during the Great Depression, such options were limited. While Anglos had enjoyed the fruits (and vegetables) of low-wage Mexican labor that had replaced the excluded Asians, they now blamed them for high levels of unemployment and burdensome relief payments.

The post-revolutionary wave of Mexican immigrants largely overwhelmed the existing Californio/Mexican-American communities. They brought new cultural traditions, mostly from the northern and western states of Mexico, and merged these with existing institutions. Many revitalized congregations around the old mission churches or established vibrant new parishes. Others built community institutions such as the Mutualistas, which provided insurance, death benefits, and other forms of social security as well as opportunities outside of the church for social connection. Some immigrants were able to attend integrated schools and to move into small businesses or professional jobs. The most prominent Mexican-American intellectual of his generation, Ernesto Galarza, an immigrant from Nayarit State, Mexico, went to a multiracial school in Sacramento full of Korean, Portuguese, Japanese, Slav, Italian, and Polish kids. He later attended Occidental College and received a PhD from Columbia University. His teachers took their acculturation work seriously: "The school was not so much a melting pot as a griddle," he writes, where his teachers "warmed knowledge into us and roasted racial hatred out of us."

Mexican immigrant experiences were often more alienating than Galarza's, particularly in the larger barrios of Los Angeles or in small valley towns. In the southland, discrimination on the part of Anglos and community building on the part of immigrants kept the groups separate. Social discrimination was also prominent, with Mexicans excluded from pools, restaurants, and other public areas. Orange County school authorities developed

a "Jaime Crow" policy that kept Mexican kids out of Anglo schools.

Then in 1931, Hoover's Secretary of Labor William Doak blamed illegal immigrants for the country's unemployment woes and staged raids to deport immigrants throughout the southwest. While the Department of Labor had few resources at the time, Los Angeles politicians and police soon joined in the deportation effort. Charles P. Visel, who headed an anti-immigrant pressure group euphemistically called "The Los Angeles Citizens Committee on Coordination of Unemployment Relief," agreed with the Labor secretary: "it would be a great relief to the unemployment situation if some method could be devised to scare these people out of our city." Over the opposition of the LA Chamber of Commerce, the LA County Board of Supervisors endorsed a program to repatriate Mexican immigrants, who they blamed for the high cost of relief payments in the city.

Mexican immigrants and Mexican-American citizens did not actually get a disproportionate amount of relief. Anglo politicians, however, thought all Mexicans were illegitimate recipients and not truly part of the city. Citizenship was actually cultural, not a legal status, LA officials apparently decided, and demanded the "repatriation" of many citizens and legal residents. The LAPD responded in February 1931 by seizing more than 400

Mexicans being repatriated from LA in 1949. Roundups and deportations resumed after World War II, rising dramatically in the post-war recession of 1949 and peaking with "Operation Wetback" in the mid-fifties.

people in a spectacular raid designed to scare the Mexicans into fleeing the country. It worked.

No one knows exactly how many people were forced or scared into leaving the country, but nationwide about 350,000 people were pushed out—an enormous number, given that the Mexican-born population of the US was probably 650,000 in 1930. Loaded onto trains all through the southwest, Mexicans and Mexican Americans found themselves in desperate circumstances. The atmosphere on the trains back to Mexico was one of defeat, as one person reported: "The majority of the men were very quiet and pensive... most of the women and children were crying." The repatriated Mexicans often tried to return later in the 1930s, but had to go through a difficult application process even if they or their children were citizens.

The repatriation movement failed to change the low-wage nature of much of the Californian economy. Rather, new waves of desperate workers soon filled the jobs left by repatriated Mexicans. Sustained drought and poor farming practices turned huge regions of Oklahoma, Texas, and Arkansas into the "dust

Grower-vigilantes shot and killed three Mexican cotton strikers and badly wounded many others in the Central Valley towns of Pixley and Arvin in 1933. The shootings led to widespread protests organized by the Communist-led Cannery and Agricultural Workers' Industrial Union, but no arrests were ever made in the cases.

bowl," forcing a mass migration of "southwesterners," as these immigrants called themselves, to the West Coast. Even more migrated from the more densely populated eastern regions of the same states because of the collapsing economy. Almost half a million white southerners made the trek along "the Mother Road," Route 66, the main east-west highway in the United States. The name Okie, at first a derogatory term, came to be accepted by the migrants as time passed. While the migrants predominantly came from cities and towns, many of the most desperate were farmers with skills, temperament, and hunger that fit California's agriculture business. As desperately poor people, often with little more than the clothes on their backs, they soon took fieldwork formerly held by repatriated Mexicans.

Some white Californians were shocked by the desperate plight of southwestern farm workers—after all, it was rare to see white, Protestant, native-born Americans living and working in such appalling conditions. The liberal *San Francisco News* wrote the migrants "are Americans of old stock. They cannot be handled as the Japanese, Mexicans, and Filipinos." Despite the liberals' assertion of the migrants' whiteness, they received a prejudiced and patronizing response from most of California's press and politicians. Some school districts claimed Okie students' accents were actually speech defects. "Negroes and Okies" had to sit in the balcony in one Central Valley town's movie theater.

Muckraking journalists, photographers, writers, and filmmakers like Dorothea Lange, Paul Taylor, John Steinbeck, and John Ford compellingly portrayed the migrants' lives to wide audiences. Responding to this powerful reporting from the fields, the Federal Resettlement Administration (which became the Farm Security Administration) was set up in the early years of the New Deal to deal with the crisis migrations by establishing migrant labor camps throughout California. These camps, numbering eighteen in the state by 1941, provided a modicum of decent life for the migrants. They had their own governments, newspapers, and social committees. Mexican and Anglo families lived side by side in the camps. Both migrants and government administrators viewed the camps as temporary, but low wages and intermittent work kept people in the camps longer than they had hoped. The desperate migration of the 1930s shook the migrant's sense of self:

> The way I've been treated sometimes I wish I was dead
> The way I've been treated sometimes I wish I was dead
> Cause I've got no place
> To lay my weary head.

Agricultural workers joined in the wave of labor unrest that began in 1934. Despite their history of small landholding or of anti-union urban life, some of the migrants proved willing to join in labor struggles in the fields. Anglo Communists and Mexican radicals supported *Confederación de Uniones Obreros Mexicanos* when it struck Japanese-owned berry farms in El Monte, just outside LA in 1933. Soon the militancy spread through the farm worker camps throughout the state. The grower's organization,

*Despite the fame of the Golden Gate Bridge, the San Francisco–
Oakland Bay Bridge was an even greater technical challenge. Both
bridge projects provided much-needed economic stimulus to the region
in the midst of the crisis of the 1930s.*

the Farmer's Alliance, claimed that the union was merely a
Communist tool and thus not a legitimate union. Farm owners
and local vigilantes met a strike by Anglo and Mexican workers
in the cotton fields of the San Joaquin Valley with brutal attacks.
At peaceful rallies in the valley towns of Pixley and Arvin,
dozens were beaten and three strikers killed. The union and its
urban supporters called it "Farm Fascism."

Labor organizing in the fields in the later 1930s, when Okies
predominated, was even less successful than in 1933–4. The
southwesterners believed that as Americans they had rights to
jobs and fair treatment, that they should be able to gain a decent
life through hard work. When this opportunity seemed impossible, as it did in much of the Depression, they proved willing
to fight. Nonetheless, southwestern migrants for the most part
neither deeply espoused instead the left-wing ideas of the 1930s
nor trusted California's elites. They embraced a "plain folks
Americanism," to use the phrase of historian James Gregory,
which later turned into a more conservative populism. As the
Depression eased, many moved to jobs as permanent ranch
hands, supervisors, and managers, and began buying their own

land. Others moved to working-class areas of LA, Sacramento, and the Bay Area.

The FSA's work with farm workers was only one of the many ways that government agencies attempted to help those in dire straits. The Works Progress Administration and the Civilian Conservation Corps (CCC) provided jobs for migrants and longer-term California residents. The CCC, known for its martial organization—the Army ran the Corps—and its hard outdoor work, proved a difficult experience for many. Yet its jobs provided an alternative to the hobo life for young men displaced by the economic crisis. The CCC had hundreds of camps in the state, where thousands of corpsmen labored planting trees in the wilderness, restoring creeks, building trails, roads, and parks. Efforts to provide more elaborate education and job training for the CCC floundered, but the CCC legacy can be still be seen today in parks and wilderness areas throughout the state. A museum to the CCC and to the newer California Conservation Corps (a much smaller but similar program started under Jerry Brown's administration in the 1970s) is in San Luis Obispo on the grounds of the California National Guard's Camp San Luis Obispo on Highway 1.

The Lieutenant sure is hard-boiled
His hands and clothes are never soiled
When I come in all day I've toiled
Oh, why did I join the CCC?

These O. D. clothes sure is hot
They'll make you scratch a whole lot
They'll make you wish you'd never got
Into this old CCC.

—CCC song

While conservatives opposed New Deal programs aimed at reducing poverty or empowering labor, few opposed the largest government undertakings. The massive construction projects of the New Deal era—the Hoover Dam, the Golden Gate Bridge and San Francisco–Oakland Bay Bridge—had their origins in 1920s heroic engineering, but early Depression efforts at economic stimulation brought them to completion. The Colorado River states had bitter conflicts over the river's water. But contractors

The Bakersfield Sound

Before World War II, southwestern migrants settled mostly in the Central Valley. Bakersfield and other cities soon had a thriving music scene replete with radio programs and nightly performances in honky-tonk bars. The music played in the fields was more traditional: based on Anglo-Celtic traditions, gospel, and blues. Tommy Collins, who later helped to develop the postwar Bakersfield sound, explained: "The music was simple but powerful, played by simple-living people. They weren't apt to go for fancy music."

Southern white and black music in the thirties and forties had little appeal to outsiders. But during the forties and fifties, a younger generation of white musicians, such as Billy Jack Wills, brother of the famous Bob Wills, and Spade Cooley absorbed multiple cultural influences to create a driving version of western swing. Cooley broke out of the southwestern ghetto, appearing as a singing cowboy in numerous films and then on a pioneering LA television show. His

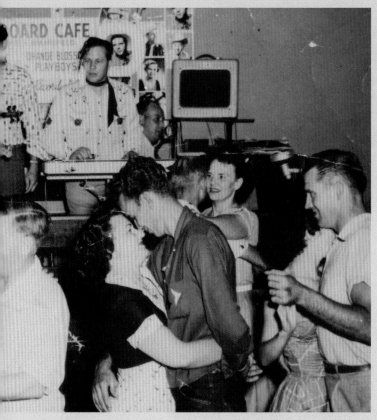

Buck Owens and the Playboys playing at the Blackboard Café where they were inventing rocking country music, the Bakersfield sound.

career ended in tragedy in 1961 when he killed his wife in their Mojave home in front of their 14-year-old daughter.

In the early 1950s, Okie musicians created a distinctly Californian synthesis, the "Bakersfield sound," an electric and steel guitar-driven style of country music. The music came of age in the tough oil and ranching city in roadside honky tonks such as the Pumpkin Center Barn Dance, the Blackboard Café, and the Rhythm Ranch. The bars were dark, smoky, loud, and full of drinking, dancing, and fighting. Guitarist Tommy Hays recalled, "They kept it dark on purpose: a lot of people didn't want to be recognized." Buck Owens and Merle Haggard made the Bakersfield sound famous, but it was a music that grew out of a place and a people. Ferlin Husky, a guitarist with Owens, explained: "All those Okies and Arkies and Texans had a lot of hard times and good material for beer-drinkin', tear-jerkin' music."

from California and Utah, cheered along by such odd allies as the Mormon Church and Otis Chandler of the *LA Times*, built the Hoover Dam in record time. Perhaps the largest public works project in history, the dam supplied water, power, and flood control around the southwest. The project made contractor Bechtel Corporation into one of largest construction firms in the world and turned Bank of America, which had started in San Francisco's North Beach neighborhood as the Bank of Italy, into the world's largest bank.

Combined with the large relief programs, the massive construction projects drew equally massive amounts of federal funding. The Golden Gate Bridge and its less glamorous sibling, the San Francisco-Oakland Bay Bridge, also signaled that the Depression would not prevent tremendous engineering achievements. San Francisco promoters had been pushing for bridges across the Bay since the 1870s. Joshua Norton, the self-proclaimed "Emperor of United States and Protector of Mexico," had ordered bridges built in 1869. Unlike his self-printed promissory notes, which bought him drinks and meals in most San Francisco bars, Emperor Norton's proclamation was not honored. The equally grandiose but reportedly more sane Chester Crocker first proposed a bridge across the Golden Gate in 1872, but it took engineer and contractor Joseph B. Strauss, with the support of the city's Hetch Hetchy engineer Michael O'Shaughnessy, to convince San Francisco's business elites that a Golden Gate Bridge could be built. As part of an ambitious development program for the Bay Area, voters supported a bond measure in the prosperous 1920s, but the economic collapse made the bonds unmarketable. A. P. Giannini's Bank of America came to the rescue and bought up all the bonds, allowing construction. Overcoming difficult and dangerous conditions, Strauss, the contractors, and the bridge workers completed the bridge on time and under budget. The day it opened in 1937, more than 200,000 people walked across it. It still draws thousands of visitors every year, though among them are depressed people who use the bridge to commit suicide. As many as 1,200 people have jumped to their deaths from the span.

Unlike the Golden Gate Bridge, the San Francisco–Oakland Bay Bridge rarely draws suicides—there is no walkway on the bridge and a jump into the muddy bay from its girders doesn't have the same melodramatic appeal. Its chief engineer, Charles Purcell, a career state employee, lacked the charisma of Strauss. Yet despite its more mundane setting, the Bay

Bridge is an even more impressive technical achievement than its glamorous neighbor. It is far longer and more technically complex than the Golden Gate Bridge. It also cost more than twice as much—almost $80,000,000 Depression era dollars ($13 billion in 2008 dollars). Given this massive amount, bond sales failed to provide adequate funding. The federal government, at President Hoover's behest, stepped in to fund the bridge using the Reconstruction Finance Corporation. Hoover, himself an engineer from the Bay Area, recognized the achievement represented by the Bay Bridge construction. The American Society of Civil Engineers declared it one the seven engineering wonders of the world, "the outstanding wonder among the bridges of the United States."

The labor strife and growing labor union power of the 1930s and 40s looked to many observers liked harbingers of revolutionary change. In reality the workers, their unions, and the wider left crafted something quite different than the overthrow of capitalism. General strikes, riots, working-class community mobilization, and sympathy among the middle class for workers' predicaments actually gave rise to the welfare state. Most people wanted a decent living, respect on the job, housing, and a better future for their kids; they saw militancy and government intervention as a way to these goals. California voters, long in the Republican column, shifted decisively to the Democrats. Numbers of registered Democrats soared from a mere 20 percent of the electorate in 1930 to 60 percent by 1936. Even the Central Valley, known for its conservatism, began sending Democrats to Congress and the State legislature in the 30s, beginning with the election of Texas immigrant Rev. Henry Elbert Stubbs. Democrats swept the state in 1938, gaining control of the Senate, Assembly, and governorship. But despite the massive Democratic majority, voters displayed a non-partisan streak and continued to elect Republicans until the late 1950s. Communists, independents, Democrats, and moderate Republicans, most famously Governor Earl Warren, elected to an unprecedented three terms starting in 1943, shared common goals of more effective planning and management of society. Warren himself championed such un-Republican programs as universal healthcare, road and other public works construction, water conservation and development, and the mediation of worker-management conflict. The political synthesis at mid-century reflected a fusion of the interests of California's diverse population and responded both to the push of reform-minded elites and the pull of working-class constituencies in the cities.

Grevillea Trees

In Raymond Chandler's 1943 *Lady in the Lake,* detective Philip Marlowe drives a suspected killer back to the scene of his crime, from the fictional Bay City, a stand-in for Santa Monica, to the equally fictional Little Fawn Lake, somewhere in the San Bernardino Mountains, perhaps Big Bear or Arrowhead Lake. Marlowe describes stopping for breakfast at Alhambra and driving out "Highway 70" past "fat straight rows of orange trees" that "spin by like the spokes of a wheel." Highway 70 lies along a combination of the current Valley Boulevard and Interstate 10, which passes over the ridgeline that divides the San Gabriel and Pomona Valleys at what is called Kellogg Pass. On the other side, the old route lies along Holt Avenue.

Nearing Ontario, Marlowe tells his passenger, "We'll switch over to Foothill Boulevard and you'll see five miles of the finest grevillea trees in the world." We set out to see Marlow's beauties ourselves.

We take Holt east out of Pomona in search of fat citrus and fine grevilleas. We don't find much. The "Sunset Trailer Park" still sports its tin sign, neon tubing broken off over the scrolled and squared-off Moderne-style letters. While the trailers remain, the last form of non-subsidized, low-cost housing around, what Marlowe called "rolling ranch country" is filled with strip malls, auto parts stores, appliance repair shops. The main entrance to a brand new housing development is a street named "Appaloosa."

Between the crammed rooflines of the walled subdivisions, one lone orchard house, deep-porched, four-gabled, faces the road, backed by a mere two rows of citrus; mature, dense trees, leaves so green as to be almost black beneath a thick coating of dust. Two avocado trees shoulder the bungalow. Behind it still also stands a gray corrugated-metal oblong fruit-packing shed, a grilled fan turning slowly. A wire cyclone fence separates the rusting bucolic from the cinder block commercial: Quality Thrift, Clinica Medica, Top Nails, Roxy's Bridal, 1-Hr Photo. The next cross street is Ramona Avenue, no doubt named for the "olive-skinned" heroine of the eponymous novel Helen Hunt Jackson hoped would be the *Uncle Tom's Cabin* for the plight of 1880s native Californians.

After Ramona, we pass only one other orchard house, this one with riverstone pillars supporting the porch roof, surrounded on all sides by used car lots and no trees at all.

It wouldn't have suited Marlowe for Chandler to mention the First Christian Church's four fat two-story-tall pillars and rows of high blue-green milk glass windows. The Iglesia del Cuerpo de Cristo, its

A trailer park in the 1940s.

side wall painted with "La Vox Que Clama in el Desierto" wouldn't likely have been across the street, either, given the racial segregation of the 1940s.

Chandler calls Euclid Boulevard a "splendid highway." The grevillea trees make it still so. They are unmistakable, beginning north of G Street (except where one section was cut down to provide a more open view of the Rite Aid parking lot). The grevilleas are high as churches, closely planted, for such large trees, eight to a block in grassy parking strips wide enough for their roots to expand. The center divider, where once the Red Car trolley ran, forms a long green uphill aisle. We drive and drive, stop counting. The trees go on for miles, "five miles of the finest," according to Marlowe, according to us.

Although less glamorous than the nearby Golden Gate Bridge, the Bay Bridge integrated the economies of San Francisco and Oakland, furthering the region's wartime boom. It's not bad looking either. (Copyright © Doug Frost)

14

The Story of Modern California

Modern California began in earnest with World War II, when hundreds of thousands of war workers, soldiers, and sailors flooded the region as part of the largest migration in US history. More than 16 million people left home to join the military, fought and worked overseas and around the nation. Probably an equal number left their homes in small towns to migrate to war jobs in urban centers around the country. Farmworkers fled the fields for industrial jobs, creating a farm labor shortage that was soon filled by hundreds of thousands of Mexican contract laborers, the Braceros.

Few places were affected as much as the West Coast cities. Already dense, San Francisco's population shot up 40 percent in five years from 630,000 to almost 900,000 (far larger than its 2006 population of 744,000). Even more spectacularly, Richmond, an industrial town of shipyards and refineries, added 70,000 people to its overcrowded neighborhoods, an increase of nearly 300 percent. Similar population explosions occurred in Southern California: San Diego more than doubled during the war to more than 400,000 people.

The war confirmed the working-class nature of the coastal cities. San Francisco, for instance, was the quintessential port town. Fifty thousand longshoremen worked the docks and hundreds of thousands more labored as sailors and shipyard workers, in manufacturing and service. Millions of soldiers and sailors passed through the region on their way to the war in the Pacific. San Francisco's relatively restricted geography forced much of the Bay Area development east to Oakland and the surrounding towns. Los Angeles, sprawling already, absorbed the growth more easily.

Wartime jobs provided working-class people of all races, particularly women, with incomes far greater than they had ever hoped for. War-worker money stimulated the economy of booming coastal cities and the racially circumscribed black neighborhoods within them. Women—white, black, and Mexican—stepped into jobs vacated by white men going off to war. These

This young officer and his wife wait at the dock in San Diego for him to ship out for the Korean War in 1950. Their faces express the fear and uncertainty brought by California's connection to overseas warfare.

"Rosie the Riveters" enjoyed the money, though the jobs were hard and the hours long. California working-class real wages (adjusted for inflation) rose an astounding 25 percent between 1940 and 1945.

Most enjoyed the prosperity. War workers, soldiers, sailors, and their sweethearts flooded into movie theaters, restaurants, and bars. Nightlife thrived, not only in the central cities but in outlying areas as well. Chicana war worker Mary Cordova recalled: "we used to go to the Hungry I, to Bimbo's 365 [today strip joints] in San Francisco—that was our entertainment—all dancing.... We used to have a good time—used to go out dancing every weekend, Fridays and Saturdays." All-night movie houses, coffee shops, and bars catered to folks working late shifts at the docks or having a last fling before shipping out to face death in the Pacific war.

Lively downtowns, major factories, colossal shipyards, booming commerce, cramped housing, and widespread prosperity characterized wartime society. Yet it was still wartime; the surface bravado covered powerful anxiety and fear. More than 23,000 Californian soldiers and sailors did not return from the war. Those who were lucky enough to make it make back suffered from debilitating physical and emotional wounds.

Japanese Americans paid the highest price domestically for wartime fears. The Japanese internment, one of the worst crimes ever committed officially by the US against its own citizens, came about in the tumultuous aftermath of US entry into World War II. The internment was the culmination of decades of anti-Asian practices in the West. Overt discrimination against Asian immigrants was perfectly legal and socially acceptable. Asians could not live in white neighborhoods and faced many other forms of legal discrimination such as school segregation. Laws prevented Asian immigrants from becoming citizens or owning land in California. While two thirds of the internees were citizens, the first-generation immigrants, the Issei, were non-citizens.

The attack on Pearl Harbor stimulated an unprecedented outbreak of fear of an imagined Japanese menace at home. Although there was no evidence of spying or sabotage by Japanese Americans, wild charges gained credibility in the fearful aftermath of the attacks. Few doubted the story, for instance, that a Japanese farmer in Visalia had plowed his field into an arrow pointing toward a nearby airfield for Japanese bombers. Front-page stories in the press fanned the flames of these fears with alarmist reporting, while more careful editorials inside the papers weighed the nation's security against the civil rights of Japanese Americans. Even the relatively tolerant *San Francisco Chronicle* explained: "we have to be tough, even if civil rights do take a beating for a time." State Attorney General Earl Warren, later known for his liberal positions about race as a US Supreme

Japanese-American internees arrive at the Santa Anita Race Track, where they had to live in horse stalls until being moved to more permanent camps inland.

*A family moves their belongings into Manzanar, the first intern-
ment camp. The camp, located in the desiccated Owens Valley, was
surrounded by barbed wire and towers armed with machine guns. Dead
trees and dust storms at the camp were the result of the Los Angeles
Aqueduct carrying the valley's water to the south.*

Court Justice, warned that it was impossible to tell loyal from disloyal Japanese "when we are dealing with the Caucasian race we have methods that will test the loyalty of them... but when we deal with the Japanese we are in an entirely different field and we cannot form any opinion that we believe to be sound."

President Roosevelt authorized the relocation and internment with executive order 9066 in February 1942, which allowed the military to exclude "any or all persons" from sensitive military areas, in this case, the entire West Coast. The federal government also created a War Relocation Authority to run the camps. In May, Lieutenant General John L. DeWitt, head of the Western Defense Command and a veteran of the Philippine-American War ordered "all persons of Japanese ancestry" to report to temporary facilities around California, Oregon, and Washington. "The Japanese race is an enemy race," DeWitt warned; anyone of Japanese descent was a "potential enemy." His strongest argument for interning citizens was a deeply logical one: "the very fact that no sabotage has taken place to date is a disturbing and confirming indication that such action will be taken."

Indeed, 120,000 Japanese Americans and Japanese aliens—92,000 from California alone—were forced from their homes, farms, and businesses. Few organizations and individuals outside the Japanese community stood up for them. Bused first to temporary holding areas around the state, sometimes quartered in horse stalls that still reeked of urine and manure, the Japanese were then sent under guard to remote internment camps in California and other western states. There the non-citizens spent the rest of the war. Many of the Nisei, second-generation American citizens, eventually left the camps to join the military or to complete college in the east. The internment was the largest single officially sanctioned act of racial discrimination by the federal government. "It was so degrading for people to live in those conditions," recalled civil rights activist Ernest Uno, "it's almost as if you're not talking about the way Americans treated Americans."

While interned, the Japanese lost control over their property, often because of the legal maneuvers they had gone through to avoid the Alien Land Law and because competing farmers pressed for aggressive enforcement of the same law in order to seize Japanese farms whose owners were interned. The California Supreme Court supported local governments' efforts to seize internee's land under the medieval common law of escheat, which gave control of ambiguously deeded property to the local lord. The US Supreme Court later declared this procedure unconstitutional—but only after the panic of the war years had faded.

The internment exacerbated cultural divisions within the Japanese-American community. The dominant community organization, the Japanese American Citizens League (JACL), promoted cultural Americanization and fought for civil rights. Yet it refused to oppose the internment. It instead advocated that Japanese prove their loyalty by quietly obeying the government. As one Fresno merchant told his fellows, "If the Army and Navy say we are a menace, let's get out." During the war, the JACL pushed Nisei to enlist in the military, an effort that led to the creation of the Nisei 442nd Regimental Combat Team, a segregated but highly decorated force made of volunteers from the camps. Other Japanese Americans, however, took a more resistant stance—refusing to enter the camps and filing lawsuits against the internment. Some embraced aspects of nationalist Japanese culture that had been weakening in the communities before the war. The Kibei, Nisei who had studied or lived in Japan, tended to assert anti-US feeling more than their more conciliatory fellows who were more likely to join in the pro-US JACL.

> We had abandoned our homes and most of our belongings, taking only what we could carry, and were transported to the camps. It was a dark time, filled with hostile images, a time of desperation and a clouded future.
>
> —William Hohri

Little is left of many of the camps. Japanese Americans make an annual pilgrimage to some of the sites, particularly to Tule Lake and Manzanar. The pilgrimages started in the mid-1970s as part of an effort to gain public recognition and redress for the internment. Tule Lake was particularly appropriate. It was the largest of the internment camps, housing more than 18,000 at its peak. The government sent the most recalcitrant and distrusted internees to Tule Lake, particularly the "no-no" boys, so called because they had refused to renounce loyalty to Japan and swear "unqualified allegiance" to the US. At Tule Lake 5,500 Japanese Americans renounced their citizenship, engaged in strikes and other defiance of the authorities. In an irony noticed by many of the internees, Tule Lake is also Modoc country, the location where Captain Jack fought off US troops in the Modoc War. Resistance occurred at other camps as well. The most open and violent incident occurred at Manzanar, on the eastern slope of the Sierra Nevada, in December 1942, after months of disgruntlement at the camp administration and a growing dispute between JACL and pro-Japanese youth in the camp. Guards fired at demonstrators in the camp, killing two and seriously wounding ten.

After the war, more moderate Japanese Americans marginalized the "renunciants" and draft resisters. Japanese Americans acculturated further and faster than most other immigrant groups. Having lost their cohesive communities and much of their property, the Nisei and their children took advantage of the growing postwar economy and educational opportunities. Japanese Americans have the highest out-marriage rate of any ethnic group in American society and as a whole are among the most economically and educationally successful. Still, many ex-internees refused to move back to California, instead creating new communities in the Midwest and East, particularly in Chicago. In 1970, activists inspired by the civil rights movement pushed the JACL to seek redress for the wrongs of the internment. The campaign succeeded to a certain degree with the Civil Liberties Act of 1988, which provided nominal payments to internees and an official apology from President George HW Bush. William Hohri, who filed one of the first lawsuits seeking compensation for the internment, wrote: "though the payment was nominal and the apology tepid, the act of redress was well received."

Racial politics intensified in the cities the Japanese had left. The 1940s brought powerful racial and cultural change to the state as hundreds of thousands of southern and southwestern black and white immigrants moved west. Industrial towns in the LA region and the Bay Area, such as Long Beach, Compton, Fontana, Richmond, and Oakland had been largely white before World War II. The Bay Area's black population tripled in the war years, reaching 60,000 in 1945, while LA's black population doubled to more than 110,000. California's total African-American population tripled during the 1940s and doubled again in the 50s, almost catching up to the number of the "Spanish surnamed," to use the Census Department's term. Latino immigration also added 300,000 people to the state in the

40s. This "Hispanic" population also doubled in the 50s, hitting 1.4 million in 1960, far outpacing the growth of any other group. Mexicans, Central Americans, and southern blacks came for the jobs that began opening up in previously segregated shipbuilding and airplane plants. Black migrants hoped to find a state free of the Jim Crow racial restrictions they suffered under in the South. They did find jobs, though California's less formal but still prevalent discrimination limited their opportunities.

Wartime prosperity did not extend to housing, particularly for newly arrived blacks. Migrants poured into the state's historically black neighborhoods like West Oakland, Hayes Valley in San Francisco, and Central Ave, West Jefferson, and Watts in LA. Many blacks also began moving into formerly Japanese-American neighborhoods in smaller coastal towns. The conditions for most war workers were difficult, but in black neighborhoods they appalled observers. LA deputy mayor (and minor Hollywood actor) Orville Caldwell explained that visitors to "Bronzeville," the newly renamed Little Tokyo, "will see life as no human is expected to endure it."

The small prewar African-American communities in California had a few middle class leaders before the boom. Limited capital and opportunities within black America at the time made their survival through the economic crisis of the 1930s even more challenging than for whites of a similar status. Vada and John Somerville, University of Southern California-trained dentists who developed hotels in the 1920s, went bankrupt during the Depression. They became administrators of New Deal programs in the next decade. Dr. Carlton Goodlett, an MD and Berkeley grad, published San Francisco's *Sun-Reporter* for decades, but depended on subsidies from the likes of Charles "Raincoat" Jones and other "businessmen" who ran gambling joints in West Oakland. By the 1940s, the new migrants reinvigorated the depression-battered African-American middle class. Charlotta Bass, for instance, the pioneering publisher of LA's leading African-American newspaper, the *California Eagle*, renewed her campaign to end the racially restrictive covenants that confined blacks to ghetto housing.

Black civil rights activism across class lines grew in assertion, most apparent in the Port Chicago Mutiny. At Port Chicago, the Navy, a segregated institution during World War II, used poorly trained black sailors to do the dangerous, hard work of loading munitions on ships bound for the Pacific war. In July 1944, two munitions ships blew up, killing 320 men and injuring hundreds more. It was the worst homefront disaster of the war. The next month, hundreds of sailors refused to load ships under the same dangerous conditions that had led to the explosion. Faced with mutiny charges, most soon returned to work, but 50 black sailors still refused. They were arrested, convicted, and sentenced to years in prison. The black press widely publicized the case and the NAACP sent their top lawyer, Thurgood Marshall, to argue their appeal. Despite the help, they lost, though the men received amnesties after the war.

Black neighborhoods bursting at the seams overwhelmed community institutions and networks. The older elites found their leadership challenged as the newcomers joined radical labor unions such as the Longshoremen and embraced more militant ideas during the war. Following a national trend, black trade unionists took the lead in pushing for equality in the state. Segregationist unions like the Machinists and Shipyard Workers were forced by the government to admit blacks and women. Meanwhile, more militant unions organized pickets at restaurants and other businesses that refused to serve people of color. Some black leaders were drawn to the left as well. Bass, who had started her newspaper as a Republican, moved steadily to the left during the war years. She ran unsuccessfully for Congress as a Democrat, but then joined the Communist Party, becoming the vice presidential candidate for the leftist Progressive Party in 1952.

The black migration also brought a revitalized African-American culture to California. Jazz clubs and blues joints proliferated along with small record labels producing "race" music. Central Avenue in LA, Fillmore Street in San Francisco, 7th Street and Telegraph Avenue in Oakland jumped with country blues, swing, jump, jive, bebop, and R & B. The names of the clubs expressed the spirit of the scene: Bop City, Club Alabama, Shepp's Playhouse, Esther's Orbit Room. Small record labels and late-night radio shows brought the music to wider and wider audiences. Along with the musicians, dancers, writers, and visual artists created a dynamic working-class culture. While the origins of the music and dance could be traced back to the South and East, Californians added their own flavors, particularly in rhythm and blues and cool jazz after the war.

The growth of vibrant black communities took place in the midst of wider social conflict over racial change that broke to the surface in 1943, the second year of US involvement in World War II. Riots and smaller violent incidents swept the country. Most of the conflicts came about as the wartime mobilization

LA police resorted to violence to control the streets during the zoot suit riots in 1943.

thrust previously segregated groups together. Governor Olson promoted intolerance with a crackdown on Mexican youth after a fight among teenagers resulted in the death of a young man at the Sleepy Lagoon reservoir in LA in 1942. Trying to find the killer, LAPD officers rounded up hundreds of Chicanos. Dozens of young men were convicted in an unfair mass trial that was later overturned. The trial became a cause célèbre for the LA left, bringing together a multiracial defense committee and leading to a new political awakening in Mexican LA.

Conflicts among young men mobilized for war soon got out of control. In Los Angeles confrontations between white sailors and soldiers and zoot suiters, young Mexican-American and black men, led to widespread violence in June 1943. Gangs of military men roamed the city for weeks beating up zoot suiters, whose distinguishing dress and self-possessed attitudes made them obvious targets of the troops who themselves were grappling with the disruption of the war and the possibility of impending death in the Pacific. Eventually the military made large portions of LA off limits, bringing a slow end to the violence.

The zoot suit riots were the most dramatic racial violence of the era, but similar if smaller conflicts abounded. Hate strikes— where workers walked off the job to protest the hiring of women and minorities in previously whites-only jobs—disrupted production throughout 1942 and 1943. For the authorities, these disturbances threatened the social order needed in the mobiliza-

The acquittal of the young men charged in the Sleepy Lagoon murder was celebrated widely in LA in 1944.

tion for total war. The conflicts also offended adherents of the country's multinational ideology of anti-fascism that valued the different races and peoples united in the fight against the Germans and Japanese.

Outright violence was not the only danger worrying the authorities in wartime California. As floods of men were drawn into the military to be transformed into soldiers and sailors, the specter of homosexual contagion alarmed the military and led to extensive screenings and purges of suspected gays and lesbians. Military police joined forces with local police and sheriff's departments up and down the coast to patrol urban night spots in the hope of keeping order amid the floods of young men prone to wild partying, drinking, and fighting. Military psychiatrists devised new methods of screening gays and lesbians and dishonorably discharging them from the service, not for specific acts of "sodomy" as had been done in earlier wars, but for homosexual identity. Screened out of the military, gay men and lesbians often decided to stay in San Francisco or Los Angeles, swelling the queer communities there.

At the same time, gays and lesbians found new communities near the docks and red light districts of the big cities and military towns. No cities openly welcomed queers but San Francisco's South of Market, Embarcadero, and inner-city Tenderloin had bars, clubs, restaurants, and hotels that were less hostile than elsewhere. Smaller though similar neighborhoods could be found in LA and Long Beach. These institutions had their roots in the radical working-class bohemianism of the interwar years, a subculture that had survived despite the cities' periodic attempts to clean up "vice."

The 1940s' countercultures had roots in earlier moments of upheaval from the Gold Rush through World War I. Repression had played an important role in forming these communities. San Francisco's Vigilance Committee of the 1850s and the anti-Chinese drugs and prostitution campaigns of the later 19th century were precursors of the homophobia of the 1940s. Similar movements had led to the suppression of the legendary Barbary Coast red light district in San Francisco, which began with a series of raids in 1909 and culminated in a complete shutdown of the area during World War I. These police and civic actions had certainly restricted criminal activity in the cities, but they also constricted the spaces available for non-conforming people, particularly sexual and gender minorities.

Yet alternative neighborhoods and communities managed to survive, buoyed by moments of cultural opening. The 1920s and 30s popularity of jazz and African-American dance forms, as well as their West Coast Latino and Asian variants, pushed a countercultural stance to the center of American consciousness. Prohibition increased the acceptability of widespread defiance of the law. Ironically, while Prohibition had been meant to purify society of the ills caused by alcohol, its legal sanctions ended up reinforcing them through a celebration of underground activity and a strengthening of criminal industry. Speakeasies prolifer-ated in West Coast cities, in San Francisco and LA particularly, but no town, especially no port town, was without them. Tens of thousands of illegal drinking establishments existed in California during Prohibition. It was an enormous underground world—sometimes literally underground, as enterprising liquor businesses located themselves in basements and even at times beneath major streets in San Francisco, Los Angeles, and West Hollywood. Small towns had fewer speakeasies but more boot-legging (a term, by the way, arising from the practice of carrying bottles of whiskey in boots covered by baggy pants).

Because of market demand and police corruption, urban red light districts survived after Prohibition ended in 1933. A California Supreme Court decision in favor of the bohemian San Francisco club, the Black Cat, found that the city could not simply shut down a bar because of its clientele—unless they were actually caught in an "illegal or immoral act," such as gay sex or female impersonation. Relatively powerless homosexuals and other minorities periodically became targets for politicians hoping to make their mark as civic reformers, but the police often seemed to understand that vice could only be regulated, not eliminated. Their roundups, especially at whorehouses, pick-up joints, speakeasies, and gay bars, did not eliminate these institutions but only restricted them to particular neighborhoods. Cops willing to go lightly on the trade could receive a "gratuity," whether in the form of free drinks, food, money, or sex. Police corruption continued after Prohibition, particularly in San Francisco. An effort to professionalize the police after World War II and come to grips with the boom in wartime countercultures shifted the dynamics of the police department and resulted in more raids on gay bars. Corruption continued however, as was revealed most famously in the Gayola scandals of 1961 when San Francisco police were caught taking payola from the owners of gay-frequented taverns. To prove themselves above bribery, the police then made several major raids on gay bars, including one at the Tay Bush Inn that netted 95 people.

Despite the wartime turmoil, repression kept the urban countercultures confined to transient neighborhoods, especially dock areas and red light districts. In these bars, nightclubs, all-night coffee shops, and SRO hotels, queers found each other and began to embrace new identities and to achieve a new sense of community. This community identity drew on multiple sources. One of these sources was a new science of sex and gender that saw homosexuality and gender differences as parts of a range of human possibilities rather than perversions or personal failings. One of the pioneers of this new medical view was Dr. Harry Benjamin, an endocrinologist who kept offices in San Francisco and New York to treat his clientele of wealthy elderly patients and transsexuals seeking medical assistance in changing their physical sex.

Radical social movements, especially of labor, were another source of countercultural ideas. Many in the nascent counterculture had experience in the radicalism of earlier years. Out of these transient radical connections arose a class-consciousness based not on demands for social respectability as in the mainstream labor movement, but rather on a rejection of conformity. This sensibility arose out of the rough-hewn world of the docks, ships, and lumber camps, a violent macho world to be sure, but one that often tolerated idiosyncrasy and prized independence. These workers' sense of dignity, their organizing ability, and critical vision contributed a powerful heritage to later movements. While the growing prosperity of maritime workers reduced their marginalization in the 1940s and 50s, their political radicalism and commitment to multiracial unionism provided a cultural milieu that protected marginal cultures. The Communist-led Marine Cooks and Stewards Union, for instance, became widely known not only for its multiracial corps of officers but also for its large number of queens.

Although the Cooks and Stewards did not explicitly embrace gay issues, the movement for homosexual rights grew directly out of this milieu. Harry Hay, a pioneering gay activist who started his political career as a member of the Communist Party but left because of its homophobia, used a Communist-style cell structure and organizing techniques to found the International Bachelors Fraternal Order for Peace and Social Dignity in 1947 in Southern California. The International Bachelors renamed themselves the Mattachine Society a few years later. In the midst of the pressures of the early 1950s under the leadership of Hal Call and Ken Burns (not the filmmaker), the organization forced the radical Hay out and reorganized with more somewhat more moderate goals. Along with the Daughters of Bilitis (an organization for lesbian rights and community-building founded in the mid-50s by two college-educated professional women, Del Martin and Phyllis Lyon), Mattachine became the core of a "homophile" movement for civil rights for homosexuals. In the turmoil of the 1960s, the Mattachine Society fell apart while the Daughters of Bilitis embraced radical lesbian feminism; changes that reflected a wider queer and countercultural rejection of moderate strategies in favor of the cultural radicalism championed by Hay. Hay himself thrived in the 1960s and 70s, embracing the druggy counterculture and gender-bending parts of the gay liberation movement. Martin and Lyon stayed together and were the first couple to be married in San Francisco City Hall in February 2004 when the mayor declared same-sex unions legal in the city, and once again in June 2008, after the State Supreme Court ruled such marriages constitutional.

By the late 1940s and early 50s, California, especially the Bay Area, became the place to be for bohemians of any race or ethnicity trying to make their way as writers, artists, musicians, or other sorts of hipsters. They lived within the tenuous world of a counterculture, impoverished, often desperate, hustling, drinking, and using drugs to excess, but nonetheless finding others who shared their critical, creative perspectives.

I've never seen so many bars, drunks, homosexuals, prostitutes, and all other kinds of Devil-worshipping evils.... I can't understand why God-fearing Republicans chose this Sodom for the place to carry on their Divine-inspired work. I praise my Heavenly Father that I am not forced to live in such a sinful place so full of Satan's evil followers.

—Salt Lake City visitor to Republican Convention, San Francisco (1964)

The Beat scene grew from the intersection of the queer and multiracial working-class culture of the docks and the ghettos with the more elite literary world of the academy. Many of the prominent figures of that movement (if it can really be called a movement) came from radical and working-class backgrounds. In the early 50s, San Francisco poet Lawrence Ferlinghetti and publisher Peter Martin, son of the famous anarchist Carlo Tresca, founded City Lights, a bookstore and publishing company, to promote the works of cool new writers. Coffee shops and clubs nearby in San Francisco's North Beach provided meeting places. World War II conscientious objector Lew Hill founded KPFA radio, the nation's first listener-supported, non-profit

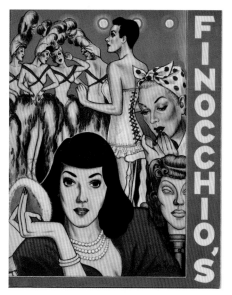

High-end venues in post-Prohibition red light districts drew broad audiences to see "female impersonators" in the 1940s and 50s. Finocchio's in San Francisco was among the most famous.

radio station, in Berkeley in 1949. The station broadcast poetry readings by the Beats and the seemingly endless lectures of Alan Watts who promoted Zen Buddhism to American audiences. Older writers such as Kenneth Rexroth and Kenneth Patchen, along with open-minded academics from Berkeley and Stanford, provided a wider legitimacy for the authors.

In 1957 Ferlinghetti published Allen Ginsberg's poem "Howl," but the SF police stopped the bookstore from selling the book and arrested Ferlinghetti and a clerk at the store for peddling obscenity. The local ACLU decided to take up the cause, and the ensuing publicity made the poet, the publisher, and the book famous. *Howl and Other Poems* became the top-selling single book of poetry in US history, selling nearly a million copies. The same year, Kerouac's best-selling novel *On the Road* appeared in print. The more creative Beats found audiences for their work, indeed, made careers if not wealth out of selling their poetic and artistic vision of America on the margins. Some, such as Ginsberg, Kerouac, Robert Creeley, and Gary Snyder, became national symbols of countercultural vision in the 1960s.

Witty *San Francisco Chronicle* columnist Herb Caen derided the writers and their hangers-on as "Beatniks"—pointing out, "They're only beat, y'know, when it comes to work." The name stuck. The cultural radicalism of the actual Beats had little effect on national culture at the time other than to reinforce their marginality. With the Beatniks, bohemianism became a 50s' pop culture phenomenon, as beret-wearing, goateed men and women with straight long hair and black turtlenecks came to symbolize a pretentious intellectual pose. Beatniks were easy targets for ridicule in films and television. For most bohemians, the journey to the other side was simply a tour. But many others, limited by their sexuality or politics, took a one-way trip. While the Beat phenomenon eventually included people around the country, the originators and key figures tended to be men, gay or bisexual, working-class, and from immigrant backgrounds. For them, the bohemian world was their own—and perhaps their only—place.

Drawn to California for its place on the Pacific, many Beats looked to Asian cultures, particularly religions, as counterweights to what they believed was the soulless brutality of American society, what Ginsberg named "Moloch," a "sphinx of cement and aluminum" that "bashed open their skulls and ate up their brains and imagination." Despite their radicalism, the Beats often ignored or demeaned women. Even their admiration of

Poet, publisher, and bookstore owner Lawrence Ferlinghetti helped get other Beat writers into print. City Lights Bookstore remains a San Francisco icon.

African-American and Asian cultures was tinged with a fascination with the exotic and forbidden that mainstream culture buried and ignored. Still, a few people of color were involved in the Beat counterculture, most famously the poet Bob Kaufman. Kaufman, a powerful improvisatory poet and former merchant marine sailor, developed a debilitating drug habit (as did many of the Beats). His drug use and his street corner recitations were too much for the SF police, who supposedly arrested him for disorderly conduct 39 times in 1959 alone. Dismayed by the assassination of President Kennedy, he took a vow of silence in 1963, which he kept for ten years.

The countercultural and minority communities survived on the margins of the basic structures of California's economy

and culture—its war-related heavy industries, its vast agribusiness, its modern cities, its segregated suburbs, its official cultural
uniformity, its prosperity, and its political orthodoxies. These
communities sheltered and empowered people who experienced
and interpreted the world differently than did the dominant
storytellers in the state. Yet the California countercultures and
the larger minority communities at mid-century always felt the
pressure of their second- and third-class status.

Smog

In July of 1943, as race riots spread through the country and the
world suffered another summer of the most deadly war in history,
a deadly cloud descended over LA. Angelenos thought it was a gas
attack. Actually, it was the area's first recognized smog. In the postwar
period, LA became famous for its dirty air, caused when the beautiful
mountains surrounding the city created summertime inversion layers
that trapped polluted air and cut visibility to a few hundred feet. LA's
huge industrial boom and increasing dependence on automobiles,
buses, and trucks for transportation contributed to the deadly
pollution problems. Chronic asthma, bronchitis, and increased death
rates led to multiple protests starting in 1953 by city residents angry at
the destruction of their Edenic environment and wanting government
intervention.

Immediate success against smog was difficult to achieve, though
helpful people in Oregon sent packages of "pure air" to the city's
Optimist Club in 1954. The state established air quality boards to try
to regulate pollution, but they had only limited power and constantly
attempted to balance the needs of industry and commuters with the
need of people to breathe. Some proposed impractical schemes:
shipping clean mountain air in trucks to the city or building enormous
fans on the tops of the mountains. But the Air Quality Board took
slow, eventually effective steps to reduce the amount of pollution,
banning the burning of garbage in 1952, and occasionally closing
down the worst polluting factories. The state managed to impose
reductions in auto tailpipe emissions starting in 1966—the first state
in the US to do so. Still in 1967, LA had 121 smog alerts. The air has
slowly improved with better pollution-control technologies and the
decline of the region's heavy industry. Yet despite deindustrialization
and extensive regulation, the LA basin continues to have the worst
air quality in the US.

Ann Rosener's photo of Richmond shipyard workers heading home captured the daunting work experiences of many Rosie the Riveters.

A rocket heads to space carrying a reconnaissance satellite from Vandenberg Air Force Base in 2006. In the Cold War, the enormous base provided the site for developing ICBMs and the Space Shuttle.

THE BIGGEST STATE

Intense wartime growth continued for decades—California surpassed New York as the most populous state in 1962. This growth came about largely because California had—and continues to have—a fundamental economic dependency on federal money, especially preparations for war and military spin-offs such as the high-tech industry. The military-industrial complex touched many aspects of California life, none more so than the modern suburb.

California's coastal cities had long depended on military contracting and defense industries to power their economies. Aerospace provided the economic and intellectual stimulus for the expansion of the state's university system and the creation of its computer industry. By 1948, the state had cornered more than half the country's airplane contracts. In the early 1950s, defense spending was more than half of the state's economic activity. California drew the lion's share of defense contracting—a fifth of all dollars awarded. Between 1950 and 2004, California military contractors received $750,000,000,000 from the government (not corrected for inflation).

Los Angeles benefited even more than the rest of the state. It had 4,000 separate "war plants" in 1944 and won nearly half of all the defense contracts awarded in the state. While before the war it had been considered a "branch manufacturing" area (where production was in plants owned by eastern firms), by 1945 it was the second largest manufacturing center in the country. The transition to a postwar economy proved rocky. California and the nation slipped into a serious recession in 1948–9. But the Korean War and Cold War revived military spending, providing a much needed economic stimulus. Then 50s prosperity increased civilian demand, which California's factories also met by churning out non-military goods: automobiles, chemicals, petroleum products, steel, aluminum, and countless other items.

Most of the rockets that lifted satellites and astronauts into space were designed and built in Southern California. In the 50s, contracting for the advanced electronics and control systems for aeronautics stimulated the development of high-tech industries and labs near major universities, particularly around Stanford, in what was to become Silicon Valley. Cal Tech's Jet Propulsion Lab (JPL), founded in the 1930s by Hungarian Jewish émigré Theodore von Kármán, provided the engineering, chemistry, and physics expertise for the country's new space program and for its military and scientific missiles. Von Kármán, paving the way for later scientists-turned-entrepreneurs, founded Aerojet Corporation, which developed some of the country's first jet engines and rockets. Later NASA's California contracts provided billions (half the agency's budget) in revenue to the labs and factories in the state.

The physicist Edward Teller, another Hungarian émigré, pushed the country to develop a second nuclear weapons lab to

SRI and the Gold Rush

Modern computing, robotics, and the internet all had their origins in war work, but Silicon Valley also had deep connections to the gold rush, the post-conquest land grab, and a very big amusement park. SRI, which started out as the Stanford Research Institute, was a key to Silicon Valley's scientific growth and received the lion's share of its funding from the Defense Department in the early days. Stanford University first created the Institute after a faculty confab organized by oilman Atholl McBean at the Bohemian Grove, a country retreat for San Francisco's elite. McBean, no self-made man, was an heir to the fortune of Henry Mayo Newhall, a gold rush merchant and partner in the Southern Pacific Railroad. Newhall had gained control of the Santa Clarita Valley after the dissolution of the Rancho San Francisco in the drought of the 1860s. McBean's family company later created the city of Valencia, site of the Six Flags Magic Mountain theme park, but McBean's heart remained in the Bay Area, where he was a key patron of the sciences at Stanford.

complement the facility at Los Alamos, New Mexico that had developed the first atomic bombs. The Livermore Labs, founded in 1952 in a sparsely populated valley east of San Francisco, became the center for advanced weapons development in the US. Livermore scientists designed and developed the hydrogen bomb, a weapon thousands of times more powerful than the bombs that devastated the Japanese cities of Hiroshima and Nagasaki. The Jet Propulsion and Livermore labs, although drawing much of their budgets from weapons research, also engaged in basic research, space exploration, and alternative energy projects. The various labs and testing facilities changed the character of the surrounding communities—even if they were located in remote areas such as Livermore, or even farther afield, such as Ridgecrest, on the east side of the Sierra near the China Lake Naval Air Weapons Station (which was run by the Navy and Cal Tech). By the 1960s, Livermore, previously a dusty cow town known regionally for its annual rodeo and old vineyards, boasted the largest proportion of PhDs of any city in the US. Not only doctorates: California's strategic role gave the state the dubious honor of housing more nuclear weapons than any other.

Many scientists openly rejected government weapons policy, lobbying against weapons programs or simply avoiding such research. Some, disheartened by science's increasing militarization, left the field entirely. One JPL founder, Frank Malina, became an artist and UNESCO official. Another JPL founder, Chinese scientist Tsien Hsue-shen was kept under house arrest for years after losing his security clearance. He eventually returned to the People's Republic of China and led his homeland's rocket development program. Some scientists opened wineries in the Livermore Valley.

The freeway, which more than any other structure epitomized California in the postwar era, had connections to the military. Early highways had opened in the 1910s and 20s: the 3,300-mile Highway 50 (the nation's first transcontinental highway, built along the old "Lake Tahoe Wagon Road"), the spectacular Pacific Coast Highway, and Route 66, memorialized in song and story. These highways, however, proved inadequate for heavy traffic. Caltrans, the state agency responsible for road construction, promoted some new ideas. The first limited access road in California, the Arroyo Seco Parkway, also known as the Pasadena Freeway, now I-110, opened in 1940, confirming the region's modern identity. By the early 50s, Californians excelled at the construction of freeways. Los Angeles had the Harbor, Hollywood, and Long Beach freeways. Within 25 years, California had 2,500 miles of interstate.

Conservatives first saw the freeways, originally called "interregional highways," as part of a system of creeping socialism. As one congressional opponent wisecracked in 1944, it was a system "under which the future life of all of our citizens was mapped

Physicist Edward Teller in 1958 with photos of a cyclotron and a nuclear explosion. A brilliant scientist and sharp political infighter, Teller directed the US nuclear weapons research program from the Lawrence Livermore National Labs.

Teller & Oppenheimer

Edward Teller, brilliant and outspoken, clashed over the future of weapons development with his mentor, UC Berkeley's Robert Oppenheimer, a renowned physicist who had directed the Manhattan Project. Oppenheimer, like many scientists who worked on nuclear programs during World War II, came to doubt the wisdom of American weapons policy in the Cold War. After the bombings of Hiroshima and Nagasaki, Oppenheimer was overcome with guilt, explaining to Harry Truman, "Mr. President, I feel I have blood on my hands."

Teller, who advocated for the "peaceful atom," argued that the opposition to weapons research by scientists was inappropriate: "Science gives them no special insight into public affairs. There is a time for scientists... to restrain their opinions lest they be taken more seriously than they should be." Despite his contribution to the nation's military power, Oppenheimer eventually lost his security clearance in 1954 because of his connections to the Communist Party during his years as a professor at Berkeley and, most importantly, because of his doubts about the morality of nuclear weapons. Testimony from Teller further doomed Oppenheimer's career.

out and planned and controlled and regimented, not only from the cradle to the grave, but for a considerable period beyond." But a large serving of old-fashioned political pork had changed the right's thinking. The interstate freeway system, begun by the wartime Federal Aid Highway Act, was more than just a clever way of getting funding for local highway construction. The freeways ostensibly created a system of limited access roads that would allow the rapid movement of the military in the event of an invasion of the US. Rather than being the highways to socialism, in fact, the freeways functioned as enormous subsidies to auto and truck manufacturers, to real-estate developers, and to state politicians unable to raise taxes from the public. The federal spigot started flowing in the 1950s, creating a system that fundamentally reorganized California's social geography.

Highway promoters—auto companies, urban planners, and real-estate speculators—envisioned a network of roads speeding people without interruption from suburban subdivision to sleek workplace to well-packaged recreation. Highway promoters proposed that tiny San Francisco be encased in elevated roadways. Freeway planners promised residents of Los Angeles an entrance every mile onto the glistening, high-speed network. Visitors and residents alike were entranced by the vision of efficiency and freedom, the modernist vision of a city without the crowds and disorder of eastern metropolises. The freeways earned their name from the absence of tolls, but the title also intellectually connected them to the imagined freedom of the expansionist "West."

Angelenos, in particular, took to the roads with a passion. Already an auto center rivaling Detroit, LA spawned distinctive cultures of automobile use and customization. The car allowed a profound change in social geography and spawned such important cultural institutions as the drive-in restaurant and the drive-in church. Young backyard mechanics in the 1930s and 40s "souped up" old cars from the junkyards that littered the LA outskirts. Hot-rod races proliferated on country roads and, for the truly dedicated, on the dry lakebeds of the region. Hot rodders felt passionately about their carefully modified vehicles—California servicemen during World War II supposedly carried as many pictures of their cars as of their girlfriends. Hot-rodders and "lakesters" usually jacked their cars up in the back for traction upon acceleration and removed any unnecessary parts of the car, such as hoods and bumpers. Southern California's carmakers and clubs used creativity, easy access to wartime salvage, and proximity to desert proving grounds to achieve a series of speed records. Chicano

Opening the Arroyo Seco Parkway in 1940, California's first freeway.
(Photo © California Department of Transportation)

hot rodders in the late 50s, in contrast, began reducing the height of their vehicles to make a visual statement while cruising slowly down East LA's Whittier Boulevard or other barrio avenues. The lowrider and the cruise became key expressions of urban Chicano culture in the 1960s and 70s. Cruising, now banned in most localities, spread to Anglo youth in small towns around the state, though the lowrider itself remained a largely Chicano style.

> The freeway experience... is the only secular communion Los Angeles has. Mere driving on the freeway is in no way the same as participating in it.... Actual participation requires a total surrender, a concentration so intense as to seem a kind of narcosis, a rapture-of-the-freeway. The mind goes clean. The rhythm takes over. A distortion of time occurs, the same distortion that characterizes the instant before an accident.
>
> —Joan Didion, *The White Album* (1979)

The car, customized or stock, along with the super-highways and the subdivisions that they made possible, came to symbolize the

Alex Xydias in his belly tank streamliner during a run at El Mirage Dry Lake in 1948 at 132.93 mph for a first in class. Hot rodder Bill Burke invented the tankster after seeing airplane fuel tanks during the Pacific war. (American Hot Rod Foundation/Louis Senter Collection)

state's opportunity for individual choice and self-fulfillment—while hiding a reality of government-funded environmental and social destruction. The sprawling growth cemented a system of public subsidy for private development. Unlike people reliant on crowded plebian trains and buses or living in apartment blocks owned by the government or distant landlords, Californians in their cars could come and go when they chose to their own comfortable homes, effectively flying over decrepit slums on the elevated freeways. Drivers reveled in the speed and choice of where they went, fulfilling a modern ideal of American independence.

The dream of the freeways was part of the modernizing 1940s and 50s. The California suburban vision combined the utopian myths of the convivial small town and the small holding farm with the avarice of land speculation. The suburbs, however, were hardly the compact communities of an imagined agrarian past. Rather they were the product of a pro-real-estate federal housing and tax policy that provided loans and enormous tax breaks for the construction and purchase of single-family homes, but not apartments or cooperatives. Suburban developments promised prepackaged utopias, safe from the social conflict, racial intermingling, and urban density of California's older cities. Returning veterans and their families could buy into a real world as carefully constructed as the fantasy world of Disneyland, the theme park that opened in suburban Anaheim in 1955. Whites—working class and middle class—fled urban centers for the suburbs' segregated towns and schools.

After the war, the city centers of California experienced a steady population decline despite the state's continued rapid growth. San Francisco's population declined precipitously after the war while the suburbs grew continuously until the 1980s. By 1980, SF's population was almost as small as it had been in 1940. Los Angeles, because it included massive suburban districts, continued its wartime growth, adding 1 million people in the 50s. LA passed Chicago in the 1960s to become the nation's second most populous city. This was no anomaly: the growth occurred almost entirely in the suburban San Fernando Valley (watered by the Owens River), while the central portions of LA stagnated and the downtown emptied out. Single-family homes predominated in California's cities, making them far less dense than comparable cities in the east. Los Angeles, as one writer put it in 1940, is "the most sparsely settled large city in America. There is no shortage of elbowroom." New towns sprawled over their neighbors. Farms, ranches, forests, grasslands, wetlands, even deserts disappeared underneath housing tracts, malls, and industrial "parks." The world's most extensive network of finely engineered roads and highways encouraged this sprawl and sustained the car culture that made sprawl inevitable.

While Los Angeles, Oakland, and San Diego had grown extensive streetcar suburbs in the first half of the twentieth century, the freeway suburbs of the later years extended the region's metropolitan areas. Californians lived farther and farther from their jobs and from urban centers. Outlying areas soon were drawn into the matrix of freeways, subdivisions, and strip malls. At the peak of development, more than 100,000 acres of farmland were turned into housing every year. This rate has slowed considerably today, but still, during the 1980s and 90s, approximately 50,000 acres of farmland per year were converted to urban and suburban uses. Realtors and developers dominated the politics and economics of the 1950s and 60s in the suburbs, both inland—in places like the San Fernando Valley, the San Gabriel Valley, the East Bay, or Riverside County— and on the wealthier and warmer southern coast from Santa Barbara to San Diego.

Race and segregation played a key role in the proliferation of suburban towns. Whites, disliking the multiracial schools

*Anti-black demonstrations at Fremont High School in South Central
LA in 1947 were part of the larger battle against racial integration.
Ironically, Fremont High had early been a segregated Mexican school.
By the 1960s, it was overwhelmingly black. Its ethnic makeup shifted
dramatically once more in the 1980s. It again became more than 90
percent Latino by the end of the millennium.*

and communities of the city centers and seeking larger, more
comfortable housing, took advantage of cheap loans to buy
mass-produced single-family homes in segregated suburbs. To
protect these enclaves, developers and suburbanites incorporated
hundreds of small towns and later developed the idea of the
"gated community" to limit the impact of the dangerous world
outside and to enforce community standards inside. LA County
alone encompasses 63 cities and over 1,000 government entities,
making regional planning almost completely impractical. A
quarter of these cities were incorporated in the 1950s and 60s.
This trend was key to the expansion. Between 1945 and 1980,
Californians incorporated 143 new cities, more than half of them
between 1955 and 1965, practically matching the massive land
boom of the late 19th and early 20th centuries that accompanied
the break up of the ranchos.

The racial and economic makeup of inner-ring suburbs and
urban neighborhoods of the Bay Area and LA shifted as whites

moved farther away. African Americans and, later, Mexicans succeeded whites in places like East Oakland and Compton. The white population of inner-city areas plummeted—Oakland's white population, for instance, dropped from 85 percent in 1950 to below 40 percent in 1980. Whites fled cities all over the state: Inglewood, next to LAX, LA's airport, was a whites-only town as late as 1960, with 99.2 percent of the city's residents white; by 1980, non-Latino whites made up less than 15 percent. Often the integration of neighborhoods was only part of the impetus to flight. School desegregation also encouraged white flight. Demonstrations roiled Pasadena, once known as America's "white spot," when liberals on the school board tried desegregating the schools in the 50s. Anti-integrationists held sway until a court order in 1963 desegregated the schools. Half of the city's whites pulled their children out of the public schools in the wake of the decision, and 25,000 moved out of the city.

In contrast, outer-ring cities like Huntington Beach, Simi Valley, Riverside, and Santa Clarita, outside of LA, or Santa Rosa, north of San Francisco, maintained their mono-color character, with populations over 75 percent white into the 1980s. This whiteness was maintained despite astonishingly rapid growth for these suburbs—Santa Rosa grew from a mere 17,000 in the 1950s to 83,000 thirty years later. Unincorporated Simi Valley had barely 2,000 people in 1960, but 77,000 in 1980 as the new city filled with people who commuted into multiracial LA. Appropriately, Simi Valley is now home to the Ronald Reagan Presidential Library.

Public policy and private sector practice before the mid-60s supported the flight of whites out of the cities and the growth of segregated suburbs. Federal Housing Administration and Veterans Administration loans provided the capital for suburban expansion, but their rules limited investment in poorer segregated neighborhoods. Private banks redlined poor and minority neighborhoods. On the other hand, credit was relatively cheap in the new suburbs. A few developers, like Joseph Eichler, whose company built thousands of iconic modern ranch homes around the state in the 1950s and 60s, resisted the openly discriminatory policies common in the business, selling houses to African Americans and Asians in Palo Alto in the early 50s. Most developers, however, tacitly supported racial restrictions, at times openly refusing to sell to non-whites or steering them away from white neighborhoods.

WALT DISNEY'S *"Magic Kingdom"*

Disneyland

60 acres of Fun, Thrills, Excitement! *Fantasyland*, dream world of Peter Pan and Snow White, Mickey Mouse and Dumbo, the Elephant . . . *Tomorrowland*, blueprinting the world of the future, of space stations, moon rockets and push-button living . . . *Adventureland*, the "wonderland of Nature's own design" . . . *Frontierland*, authentic re-creation of America's thrilling pioneer past, from Revolutionary Days to the Southwest settlement . . . *Main Street, U.S.A.*, small-town America at the turn of the century brought back to life . . . all these are DISNEYLAND, "The Happiest Place on Earth."

"60 acres of Fun, Thrills, Excitement! . . . The Happiest Place on Earth." What more can we say?

Few places reveal the cultural and political side of suburban sprawl better than Orange County, home to Disneyland. For decades, Orange County represented the conservative, rational, suburban utopia. The county had a long history of conservatism, making it as much the center of the right as the Bay Area was the center of the left. Its ranchers and farmers had long enforced an intolerant racial and labor system by occasional terrorist acts against workers and people of color. By the 1950s, the county had established itself as the center for nationalist right-wing groups such as the John Birch Society. For some on the right, the dominant liberal internationalism of American politics in the 1950s and 60s raised fears that the US was being taken over by a conspiracy organized by the United Nations, international bankers, and their Communist allies, who were carrying out nefarious plans through subversion of the US's most important institutions, from the State Department to the Army to local schools. Anyone, even President Eisenhower, might be a Communist

tool. The danger even extended to municipal water systems, which arrogant Communist-inspired bureaucrats were poisoning with fluoride (pretending it was only to prevent cavities in children's teeth). The local paper, the *Orange County Register,* had an editorial policy to the right of even the *Los Angeles Times* and inveighed against socialist plots like public schools. The county fostered the careers of national right-wing figures, most importantly Richard Nixon and Ronald Reagan, who never lost sight of their connection to the local extremists. Numerous right-wing groups of the 50s were either born in Orange Country or had significant supporters there.

For many suburbanites, de facto racial segregation was only one part of a larger concern with uniformity. Perhaps nothing expresses this drive better than Orange County's city of Irvine— named for a landholding family, whose founder, gold rush merchant James Irvine, turned several Spanish/Mexican land

Children riding the bus in 1977 from South Central LA to their school in largely white Van Nuys, more than 25 miles away in the San Fernando Valley. The massive LA school district's desegregation plan sparked a powerful reaction among whites.

grant ranchos, including one from a branch of the Sepúlveda family, into a major fortune. Irvine landholdings totaled over 185 square miles. The Irvine Company sold off land to create the cities of Santa Ana and Tustin. Like the Big Four and the cattle barons who had donated land for schools and municipal buildings to spark development that would enrich themselves, the family donated land for the University of California's Irvine campus and then profited enormously from the town built to surround it. The City of Irvine, incorporated in 1971, is an entirely planned community where covenant restrictions in residents' property deeds limit paint colors and even how many minutes in a row residents can leave their garage doors open. Irvine is not alone in this; in many small suburbs, cars may not be parked on the street overnight. The Irvine Company continues to develop, in its own words, "safe, balanced, sustainable master-planned communities where people choose to live, work, shop, play and learn." For most whites in California in the 1950s and 60s, "safe, balanced, sustainable" meant culturally, economically, and racially uniform.

Efforts to counter white flight in urban areas of LA and San Francisco, spearheaded by the Jewish left in East LA for instance, generally failed to stop the outward movement. Related efforts by civil rights activists to integrate the suburbs began in the 50s, but successes for black integrationists were few and far between. Firebombing attacks and cross burnings met blacks who bought houses in white neighborhoods in LA and San Francisco. Once black families moved in, whites moved out quickly. The white populations of integrated neighborhoods dropped quickly, and once school busing for integration was established in the 60s, white flight became a mass migration.

The experience of Asian Californians in the postwar era began similarly to that of blacks, but with their growing economic success in the state and the importance of US-Asian alliances, social mobility became more common. For instance, in 1952 Sing and Grace Sheng put a deposit down on a house in an all-white development in San Francisco. Since the development excluded Asians, Sing Sheng proposed a referendum for residents to decide if they would want a Chinese-American family to move in. The residents voted the Shengs down by a margin of 6 to 1. "I congratulate those who voted against me, and I hope you will enjoy living here," Sing Sheng commented bitterly. "May your property values go up every three days." Anti-Communist politician Jack Tenney joined the controversy. Tenney had backed an initiative in 1946 to make the Alien Land Act a part of the state constitution. Tenney hailed the vote on the Shengs: "If people don't have the right to vote on their neighbors, they don't have the right to vote on their president."

But despite the Shengs' exclusion, the tide was shifting in the state. Tenney's 1946 anti-alien proposition failed by an almost 20-point margin—the first time an anti-Asian ballot initiative had been defeated. Within a few years California's Supreme Court overturned the Alien Land Act and a California Superior Court ruled that discrimination in public housing was unconstitutional. In 1955 a realtor prevented Army Major Sammy Lee, a Chinese American, from buying a house in a Garden Grove, Orange County tract. But unlike in 1952, political support for housing integration came from conservatives. Republicans, including Vice President Richard Nixon and Governor Goodwin Knight, denounced the discrimination. While a substantial Asian suburban migration was still years away, the public outcry over the Lee case signaled a change in the social status of Asian Americans. In Monterey Park, white residents protested black homebuyers but failed to raise an outcry against Asians (who began to move to the city in large numbers in the 1960s and now constitute the vast majority of residents).

The shift in California's racial attitudes toward Asians had begun, ironically, in the midst of World War II, when anti-Japanese sentiment reached its nadir with internment. In 1943 the US Congress repealed the Chinese Exclusion and Anti-naturalization Acts to signal its support of its ally against the Japanese. After the success of the Chinese Communist revolution in 1949 and the Korean War in 1950, conservatives rallied to the side of anti-Communist Asians, a support that translated into tolerance of Asian-American mobility at home. Congress repealed laws barring the naturalization of Filipinos in 1946 and other Asians in 1952, though it maintained highly restrictive quotas on the numbers of Asian immigrants until 1965. After the 1965 reforms, immigration to the US rose quickly and by the last decades of the century, Asians constituted 40 percent of legal immigrants to California.

From the late 1940s onward, much of California barely resembled the bucolic place that so many imagined it to be. Rather, California, though still dependent on mining, timber, and agriculture, had become an industrial and military power-house, with the fastest-growing, most modern cities in the US, all tied together with an intricate network of rail and highway. The war had confirmed California's major cities as industrial centers, tied to the military economy. Cars, airplanes, steel, and a myriad of other industrial goods were produced by well-paid unionized workers in the most efficient of plants.

> We have been changing at a speed with which nothing in our past can logically be compared, neither the colorful gold rush nor any other dramatic period in our history brought quite so many new people or caused the same sweeping changes to our economy and social life. We find that the war has caused us to actually jump into our future.
>
> —Governor Earl Warren (1944)

LA, as a sprawling multi-city metropolis that resulted from the process of incorporation, annexation, tax avoidance, segregation, and redevelopment, defied American expectations of what a city should be. LA cities, in the words of activist journalist Carey McWilliams were "a collection of suburbs in search of a city." Many have attempted to come to grips with what this city was (and is), none more creatively than architect Reyner Banham. Writing in 1971, Banham celebrated LA's "four ecologies": "Surfurbia," the beach cities where "Sun, sand, and surf are held to be ultimate and transcendental values"; the foothills, "upper crust enclaves, where wealth and power correspond to altitude"; and "the plains of id," "an endless plain endlessly gridded with endless streets, peppered endlessly with ticky-tacky houses." Banham's final ecology, "Autopia," the freeway system, was a realm that united the other ecologies and deserved celebration in itself as a "single comprehensible place, a coherent state of mind, a complete way of life."

Science Fiction Capitalism

In the realm of technological fantasy, Los Angeles led the way. The film industry celebrated flying and pilots in numerous movies and in the forties and fifties embraced the future with a series of shlocky but popular science fiction films. The films owed much to the skills of futurist writers. The LA Science Fiction club, the oldest Sci Fi fan club, celebrated the field beginning in 1934. The club claimed in 2000 that it was ready for the next millennium, exclaiming: "Why, it's been ready since 1934!" Perhaps the most successful fantasy writer was Ayn Rand, an anti-Communist Russian-Jewish émigré and Hollywood screenwriter turned novelist. She parlayed her novels' celebration of capitalist self-interest, sex, and rationalist atheism into a full-blown ideological movement she called "Objectivism." Rand's books remain immensely popular: one survey by the Library of Congress in 1991 found that after the Bible, Rand's *Atlas Shrugged* was the country's most influential book. Among Rand's adherents are many business leaders and economists, including former Federal Reserve Board Chair Alan Greenspan. Greenspan, during his term on the Fed, followed strict monetarist policies that fit well with Objectivist goals: limiting inflation and promoting speculation in stocks and real estate. The Ayn Rand Institute, a think tank started by her self-making followers, is appropriately located in defense industry-dependent Orange County.

Carnegie Clay

Less than a mile past the Livermore Labs, the Tesla Road heads east. Mud-covered trucks and SUVs haul trailers loaded with dirt bikes and off-road vehicles to the Carnegie State Recreational Vehicle Park. You can't drive to the town of Tesla, for which the road is named, because it is no longer there. Tesla was built in 1890 to house the workers of the Tesla Coal Mine, named after electrical inventor Nikola Tesla by its optimistic founder, John Treadwell, who hoped to sell coal-generated electricity to the Bay Area. He never managed that, but did ship 80,000 tons of coal a year to Stockton for several years. Tesla was made up of "residential neighborhoods" with names like Treadwell Row, Jimtown, Darktown, and Chinatown—guess who lived where!—and, following solid coal mining tradition, for compensation, the company issued coupons and tokens that the workers used to purchase merchandise and food in the town.

While Tesla still appears on some maps, Treadwell's second company town, Carnegie, after which the ORV (off-road vehicle) park is named, does not. The Eocene formation that laid down the coal 50 million years ago also deposited clay. When coal began to lose ground to fuel oil, Treadwell turned to clay mining and brickmaking, in 1902 naming his brickworks after another of his heroes, the industrialist-turned-philanthropist Andrew Carnegie. Using the existing rail line to Stockton, the brickworks sent hard-edged, glazed, characteristically yellow bricks, freckled with specks of black coal, all over California, where the Eocene clay became part of the landscape in a different way: in the walls of the Sheraton Palace Hotel in San Francisco, the Natural History Museum in Los Angeles, and even coming home again to Livermore in the form of the Carnegie Library at 2155 Third Street.

These hills—the Diablo Range, named for the double-peaked mountain that rises over all of Contra Costa County, the peak by which Frémont was finally able to orient himself when lost in the Sierra—are also good for wine. The Livermore wineries boast lineages as old as Napa's. Like those, wineries such as Retslaff offer summer entertainment on their grounds, outdoor Shakespeare or jazz, or special wine and food pairings. We attend a performance of *All's Well That Ends Well* on a Sunday evening in August. We learn later that the temperature that day—113 degrees—surpassed the previous century's record, though by the time we arrive, it surely had dropped to the mere 100s. It's good for the vines, presumably, and was pleasant to picnic in. During the intermission we bought bottles of limited-edition wine, each one hand numbered. The stepping-stones in the grass are made up of yellow bricks, stamped with the name "Carnegie."

A multi-ethnic group of miners at the Tesla Mines pose for their portrait at the end of the 19th century—note the child workers. The mine was then the largest coal producer in California, but a series of deadly accidents and financial mismanagement shut the pit by 1916.

The Atlantic Richfield Corporation (now ARCO - BP) tore down its elaborate Moderne Style headquarters in downtown Los Angeles in 1969 and replaced it with two dull but tall glass and granite towers.

16

REDEVELOPMENT, REPRESSION, RESISTANCE

In 1960, the West Coast's powerful Longshoremen's Union agreed to support the modernization of the region's ports. It was a momentous decision that ushered in a new era for labor and management on the docks. Containerization allowed far greater efficiency in loading and unloading ships—a freighter that might have taken a week to unload and load, pallet by pallet, could now be turned around in a matter of hours. More importantly, the Mechanization and Modernization Agreement was key to vast social, geographic, and economic transformations of the Bay Area and the LA region, changes that soon contributed to the social eruptions of the 1960s. Yet the union might not have agreed to such vast changes if it hadn't been for the Red Scare of the late 1940s and 50s.

California's Red Scare began quietly in 1940 with the appointment of Jack Tenney as head of the state legislature's Committee on Un-American Activity in 1941. At first the left could ignore Tenney and his committee, but after the war his influence grew. The committee sought to identify subversive elements around the state in multiple industries—a goal mainstream politicians could support—but like Wisconsin Senator Joe McCarthy's Senate Internal Security Subcommittee, it indiscriminately attacked liberals as communist stooges. Tenney at one point accused Eleanor Roosevelt, the president's widow, of working for communist "front" organizations. He hounded real and imagined communists in the labor movement throughout the state, but his hectoring style and broad brush stood out in the midst of the growing moderate consensus in state politics. The *San Francisco Chronicle* even explained in verse:

> A Communist is any
> who disagrees with Tenney.

Despite the ridicule, Tenney was far from a lone crank during this period. Anti-communism expressed a political drive to

State Senator Jack Tenney (second from the right) and other members of the Legislature's Fact Finding Committee on Un-American Activities listen to Frank Spector, a Communist labor activist, in 1948. Tenney had been a songwriter, composing the Gene Autry hit "Mexicali Rose," and won election originally with support from the Communist Party. He later ran for US vice president on the extreme right-wing Christian National Party ticket.

conformity as much as the suburbanization revealed a cultural interest in safety; it made sense that Tenney later became involved in pro-segregation politics. In the Popular Front period of the Depression and war years, communists and other radicals had prospered when they had forged alliances with more mainstream groups. After Republicans gained control of Congress in 1946 and the Truman administration began to conduct purges of suspected subversives, the political right discovered that the liberal's Popular Front alliance with the left was an easy target.

Tenney's investigation of subversion coincided with the pursuit of the House Un-American Activities Committee (HUAC) of suspected communists in Hollywood. Hollywood had embraced the Popular Front with gusto; its creative culture supported many with unorthodox views, though their ideas only occasionally made it onto the screen. The studio moguls and many of the Hollywood unions, including the Ronald Reagan-led Screen Actors Guild, cooperated in trying to identify communists and bar them from work. Hollywood studios quickly rushed anti-communist films the screen, including such classic B-films as *The Red Menace*, *I Was a Communist for the FBI*, *I Married a*

Movie stars, including Danny Kaye, Sterling Hayden, Lauren Bacall, and Humphrey Bogart, return from protesting HUAC in 1947. To preserve their careers, most stars during the 1940s and 50s Red Scare soon gave up on their support of the left.

Communist, and *Kiss Me Deadly*. Looking for headlines, HUAC held widely publicized hearings in Hollywood in 1947.

When called before HUAC or less prominent investigations by the FBI, the Tenney Committee, and other bodies, witnesses were asked, "Are you now or have you ever been a member of the Communist Party?" The Communist Party and wider left argued that witnesses shouldn't answer. At first many famous Hollywood figures refused to testify or "name names" of suspected Communists. Most backed down quickly when faced with the possible end of their careers and loss of their livelihoods. Ten prominent Communist writers, directors, and actors were sentenced to serve time for contempt of Congress when they refused to testify at widely publicized HUAC hearings. Another 250 were blacklisted and unable to work openly in Hollywood. For many, it was the end of their lives in Hollywood. Some radicals on the blacklist continued to write films but were not given credit for their work. Others left the country to work in the European film industry. Writer Ring Lardner, Jr. refused most cleverly, telling the Committee "I could answer, but if I did I would hate myself in the morning."

While Hollywood blacklisting gained headlines, many more radicals and their sympathizers lost jobs on the waterfronts, in factories, and in schools. Special loyalty boards, whose findings were based on hearsay or association, investigated government employees often. In 1953, the California legislature passed the Dilworth Act, which called for the dismissal of teachers who refused to testify whether or not they were members of the Communist Party. In Los Angeles alone, the school board fired over 100 teachers. Private universities throughout the state ensured their faculties were free of subversives. For instance, despite a prank Soviet flag raising on campus in 1952, the president of Pomona College (my current employer) reported with confidence: "I do feel that we have no Communists at Pomona College." California branches of the American Legion and the Minutewomen demanded the revision of school textbooks to remove references to UNESCO or slums because, as one complainant wrote, "That's what makes Communists out of people."

The University of California and the State College system bore the brunt of the Red Scare in higher education. In 1949 the UC Regents demanded all university employees sign a loyalty oath declaring they weren't Communists. Twenty percent of the faculty refused to sign, criticizing the oath as a violation of academic freedom—though the UC faculty as a whole did vote that Communists shouldn't teach at the university. Dozens of faculty were fired and many more were denied jobs. The dismissed faculty sued and the California Supreme Court declared the oath unconstitutional in 1952. The Regents then created a new oath—still in place today—in which employees swear allegiance to the constitution of the state of California.

Containerized shipping that developed in the 1950s and 60s required enormous new ports, and grew rapidly with Asian trade. (Photo: Courtesy of the Port of Oakland)

(The vast majority of signers, of course, have no idea what actually is in the California constitution, which runs to over 100 pages. They might be surprised to realize that they are swearing to protect "against all enemies, foreign and domestic" a document requiring that grape vines under three years old be exempt from tax.)

The labor movement suffered the most from the Red Scare and subsequent purges. Several Communist-led West Coast unions, particularly the Marine Cooks and Stewards and the Mine Mill and Smelter Workers, disappeared in the 1950s as their members joined other unions and their locals were broken. Thousands of radical union members in defense-related industries lost their jobs after loyalty hearings and screenings. Only the ILWU endured. It expanded to Hawai'i and absorbed some of the weaker Communist-led unions. The Union's Communist leadership survived the powerful attacks in the 1940s and 50s because of rank-and-file loyalty and the power those workers exerted on the docks.

The Longshoremen's union, however, was severely weakened. Forced into ill-conceived strikes in 1946 and 1948 and facing rebellion from anti-communist activists within the ranks, the leadership never renounced its radical politics, though it did seek more conciliatory labor relations, culminating in the mechanization and modernization agreement. That agreement

Modernist architect Richard Neutra's plans for Chavez Ravine, a project that fell to fears of socialized housing.

marked a new stage in dockside labor relations that transformed the longshoremen from a group of tough militants led by labor radicals into highly paid entrenched powers. The new container ports also required far larger ships, cranes, and storage areas than San Francisco's port could provide. Getting rid of the port, the very reason for San Francisco's original growth, might have seemed like a self-destructive strategy. But it fit a broader plan.

The union leaders' efforts to preserve their organization contributed to a vast reorganization of California's economy. It was the beginning of a great transformation of the Bay Area and LA that redeveloped the cities and dramatically altered the industrial mix that powered the economy. While these changes fit in with the suburbanization of California society and allowed longshoremen to financially join the middle class, the reorganization in turn undercut the working-class culture that

The poor and immigrants had little power to change the course of urban renewal in the 1950s and 60s. Here Aurora Vargas resists being forced out of her home in Chavez Ravine to make way for Dodger Stadium in 1959.

had sustained the union movement. Perhaps most emblematic, Harry Bridges, the tough Aussie leader of the ILWU, became a widely respected labor statesman and political power broker in his later years—though he never openly rejected his youthful radicalism.

While California's bohemian working-class life and minority cultures survived the turmoil of the war and the conformity of the 1950s, wealthy and powerful people were making plans that would transform these ways of life. Nowhere was this felt more dramatically than in San Francisco where elites had seen

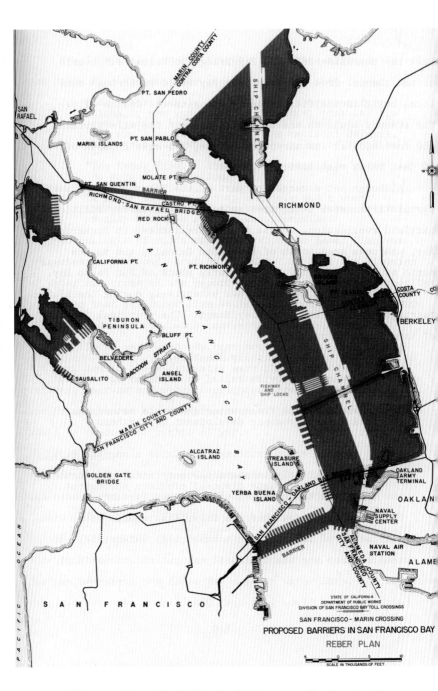

Theater producer John Reber's plan for dams across San Francisco Bay received widespread support, including from President Herbert Hoover. The Army Corps of Engineers finally rejected the plan in 1963.

their leadership role in the state continuously decline as LA rose in power, wealth, and population. Redevelopment planning boomed in the 1940s and 50s as part of a nationwide movement to rationalize urban geographies. Following the logic of the builders who had reengineered the state's landscape with dams, canals, railways, bridges, and roads, technocrats within Bay Area planning agencies received support from visionary elites who saw modernization as the way to compete with other coastal metropolises, particularly Los Angeles—though it is not clear how much their counterparts in LA paid any attention to SF's ambitions! They sought to insure their region's future prosperity and importance, not to mention their own glory and fortune.

To the urban elites, poor communities filled with "obsolescent" structures amounted to "blight." One San Francisco redevelopment agency survey made their assumptions apparent: when deciding which neighborhood needed "redevelopment," the agency considered not only the condition of the buildings, but the race of the residents and the percentage registered to vote. Larger property owners realized that block after block filled with people of color, drug addicts, and homosexuals would not put their cities in the best light. Indeed, with continual white flight and the more dramatic riots of the 1960s, urban property values plummeted and city populations declined. Urban centers suffered from a vicious cycle of declining revenues, increasing social and physical problems, and further flight and loss of services. Property values dropped. Redevelopment appeared to be a panacea to city planners and urban elites desperate to hang on to their positions of power.

In the self-confident postwar atmosphere, ambitious plans abounded. In the planners' vision, San Francisco would become a regional downtown, with glamorous shopping, financial services, and nightlife. Working-class Oakland would serve as the industrial port area. Commuters would flow in from suburban bedroom communities across the East Bay hills and the Peninsula. The planners neglected the sleepy towns of the Santa Clara Valley, thinking they would remain largely rural. The engineers imagined no limit to their ideas—the US Army Corps of Engineers even chimed in with a plan to fill the entire San Francisco Bay to provide needed territory for urban expansion. More successful plans remade the Bay Area's geographic divisions and uses. The SF Municipal Railway and the East Bay's Key Line light rail systems had made commuting easy, but planners envisioned a different sort of transport system, one based on super-highways and a modern commuter railway. The layout of the Bay Area Rapid Transit, BART, as the system became known, expressed the planners' vision: a system of trains would ring the entire bay. Funding for the train system, like so many of the other magnificent plans for the region, depended on convincing voters to pay extra taxes. Cities and neighborhoods were selected for stops based on their specialization as commercial, industrial, or residential areas.

But planners don't always get their way. Only three Bay Area counties approved the taxes. BART began construction in the 1960s as a more limited system joining San Francisco and Oakland downtowns with suburban communities in Alameda and Contra Costa counties. South Bay areas, including the future Silicon Valley and San Jose, refused to pay the sales tax required for BART. Military contracting and aerospace industries soon provided a far more lucrative development path for the peninsula and San Jose area than simple service as bedroom communities for SF commuters. South Bay growth followed the largely unplanned LA model, with developer-driven subdivision and patchwork highways. The BART system remains incomplete to this day, despite growing traffic problems throughout the region.

Redevelopment agencies grew out of the desperate postwar need for housing but soon changed character as the political winds shifted. The temporary buildings of the wartime boom proved inadequate for the state's continued population growth. The federal government, in keeping with the liberalism of the time, provided funding and legal support for the construction of hundreds of thousands of public housing units. The model of public housing was the modernist apartment tower—buildings stripped to their economical and functional essence. Inspired by the vision of the modern city, some of the most creative architects of the day joined in the effort to create new urban spaces. In the early 50s, for instance, Richard Neutra, perhaps the most important California practitioner of the International Style, designed a futuristic urban space for the urban poor to replace the haphazard neighborhood that had grown up in LA's Chavez Ravine, a mostly Mexican-American community just north of downtown. But LA's conservatism doomed the project when right-wingers, backed by real-estate developers who feared government competition, charged that public housing was a Communist conspiracy. The leftist assistant director of the city's housing agency authority, Frank Wilkinson, was fired and later served a year in jail for refusing to divulge his party affiliation. The political backlash carried conservative Mayor C. Norris Poulson to office. With the city plans stalled but the neighborhood partly destroyed, the city turned the land over to Brooklyn Dodgers owner Walter O'Malley in a sweetheart land swap. The Dodgers evicted the remaining families to make way for a new ballpark that they finished in 1962.

The reorganization of California's metropolises in the 1950s and 60s fit a larger pattern of planned growth and modernist thinking about the problems of society. Combined with a consensus in the state about the importance of public investment in schools, infrastructure, and cultural institutions, redevelopment fulfilled a vision of a society without conflict, a vision in which scientific approaches to problems, sensible planning, and intellectual leadership would create a quasi-utopia. Clark Kerr, a leading sociologist and president of the University of California, explained in 1963: "A vast transformation has taken place without a revolution, for a time almost without notice…" Similarly, scientist Edward Teller wrote a year earlier, "one is left with the strange feeling that we are on the threshold of understanding everything." Then again, maybe not.

A drive-in church designed by Richard Neutra for televangelist Robert Schuller in suburban Garden Grove, Orange County. The church had spots for 500 cars of worshippers who could feel the spirit without leaving their Fords and Buicks.

An iconic University of California, Berkeley demonstration in 1969 addressed by radical philosophers Herbert Marcuse and Angela Davis.

The Sixties

I n 1960, a group of activists, including many Berkeley students and red diaper babies, organized a protest at San Francisco City Hall against the House Un-American Activities Committee, which was on a multicity tour. Thousands of demonstrators surrounded City Hall and hundreds disrupted the hearings. SF police responded forcefully, fire-hosing students and dragging them down the stairs of the City Hall rotunda (the dome that Sunny Jim Rolph made taller than the state capitol). The unheard of actions against HUAC marked the beginning of the end of the committee's power to intimidate. The 60s had begun.

The youthful energy of the 60s broke through many old barriers in the state. The era bristled with political energy. Some young people formed new organizations, such as the Black Panthers and the American Indian Movement; others joined existing groups and radical parties. A few were drawn into sects and fanatic organizations like the Moonies, the Symbionese Liberation Army, and the People's Temple. At times, frustration with the system boiled over into riots that bordered on full-scale revolts, as in the Watts riots of 1965. Beyond the political organizations, counterculture rebels challenged social norms by using illegal drugs, dressing creatively, and living communally. From the famous Haight-Ashbury scene in San Francisco to head shops and cafés in towns around the state, a sense of community emerged that for some promised a new way of living. Alternative schools, experimental social programs, and outrageous pop music spread the ferment. To conservatives, it seemed that society was coming apart at the seams. For those open to the changes, the 60s meant creativity and excitement, despite the troubling violence, drug abuse, and political repression.

The 60s' movements for social change grew out of the African-American struggle for civil rights. While trade unions, people of color, and radicals had been involved in pickets and other efforts to force integration from the 1940s forward, most efforts had followed the legal and lobbying pattern of the main-stream movement. Californian students, galvanized by young activists in the southern states, picketed stores, restaurants, hotels, and other businesses known to discriminate. Berkeley radical Jack Weinberg recalls, "In Berkeley, the anti-Vietnam War movement was a simple extension of civil rights activism. At the start it was the same people, the same networks, the same political organizational style." Betty Denitch, an early New Left activist, explained: "the fact that all these people had already been out picketing Woolworth's [to protest its whites-only hiring policy] understood that kind of politics meant that when the call goes out 'Let's picket City Hall,' then, bang, instead of getting a couple dozen regulars out, you got thousands."

The civil rights movement directly led to the outbreak of one of the most successful student uprisings in the 60s: the Free Speech Movement at UC Berkeley. In the fall of 1964, university police arrested civil rights activists who were passing out leaflets at the entrance to campus. Students surrounded a police car holding leaflet distributor Jackie Weinberg, clambering on its roof (after carefully removing their shoes) to give speeches. Months of demonstrations, sit-ins, expulsions, and arrests ensued. The faculty and even the College Republicans sided with the demonstrators. Finally, UC President Clark Kerr convinced the UC Regents to compromise and open the campus's public spaces. It was a rare moment of political consensus. Not every-one was happy with the results: Responding to the Free Speech Movement's militancy, Ronald Reagan joked, "I'm sorry they did away with paddles in fraternities."

Universities and colleges in California were at the center of the ferment of the 60s for good reason. The student population of California had grown twice as fast as the population as a whole in the 1950s and 60s. To meet this need, California adopted a master plan for education in 1960, dramatically expanding the system, although a rapid expansion of higher education already had been underway since the 40s. Returning veterans using GI bill benefits and then baby boomers had swelled student ranks. By the 60s California had the largest student population in the country. The flagship University of California system alone grew from 44,000 students in 1958 to 100,000 in 1970. UC President Kerr, a liberal labor sociologist, managed the enormous system with creativity, wit, and an enterprising vision. As one contemporary wrote, "Clark Kerr did for higher education what Henry Ford did for the automobile: He mass produced low-cost quality education and research potential." Governor Ronald Reagan, elected in 1966, deeply disliked the liberal Kerr and worked with the FBI to smear him politically. Reagan engineered Kerr's dismissal by the University's governing board, the Regents. Kerr, unaware of the FBI involvement in sabotaging his presidency, remarked that he was leaving his job the same way he entered it, "fired with enthusiasm."

The Free Speech Movement gave rise to a diverse group of student leaders—some from Communist families, others like charismatic philosophy major Mario Savio, believers in the fundamental morality of America. Columnist Jon Carroll later described the young leader: "He was not a usual suspect. He did not come complete with buzzwords and ideology... He had been raised up by passion and circumstance. He had a moral force that almost glowed." Savio's moment soon passed as more ideologically certain and personally ambitious leaders rose to lead increasingly militant demonstrations later in the decade. Yet Savio articulated better than most the key elements of 60s' thought: resentment toward the bureaucratic institutions of modern society and an emphasis on freedom and self-assertion as much as opposition to specific policies.

Many young radicals came, like Savio, to their activism out of disappointment with the way the US failed to live up to its ideals. They began searching for more systematic explanations and ideas. Some found it in varieties of nationalism and communism—the Black Panthers, for instance, raised the money to buy their first shotgun by selling copies of Chairman Mao Ze Dong's *Little Red Book* of quotations to students at UC Berkeley in the fall of 1966. Apparently the largely middle-class students at Berkeley were thrilled to buy radical literature from tough inner-city black men. Panther Party founder Bobby Seale later admitted they sold the book without reading it, only later developing an admiration for Maoism.

Some student intellectuals embraced the western Marxist tradition, particularly the non-communist, anti-bureaucratic thought of the Frankfurt School that had been brought to the US by German émigré intellectuals in the 1930s and 1940s. Most influential was Herbert Marcuse, who taught at UC San Diego from 1965. Marcuse's critiques of bureaucratic society in *One Dimensional Man* and many other works provided a theoretical underpinning for young radicals' distrust of their seemingly self-satisfied, conformist society. Among his students was Angela Davis, who in 1969 at the age of 25 was fired by the UC Regents from her temporary assistant professor position at UCLA because of her communism. Davis soon achieved national notoriety for her support of the Soledad Brothers (George Jackson, Fleeta Drumgo, and John Clutchette), a group of radical prisoners accused of killing a guard. The state accused Davis of providing Jackson's younger brother Jonathan with weapons used in the deadly kidnapping of a Marin County judge in a failed attempt to free the Soledad Brothers in 1970. The self-educated, charismatic Jackson was killed by prison guards a year later. Davis's trial attracted international attention and widespread support among liberals and radicals. She won acquittal and returned to teaching and prison activism, later regaining a position at the University of California.

While Davis and Savio articulated a sophisticated analysis, other radicals offered more immediate and easy-to-digest slogans. The most influential radicals were the ones who mastered the sound bite. Jackie Weinberg, whose arrest for leafleting sparked the Free Speech Movement, taunted with "Never trust anyone over thirty." Timothy Leary, the proponent of drug use, created an ad tag line for a conference on LSD at Berkeley in 1966: "Turn on, Tune in, and Drop out." Black Panthers greeted each other with a clenched fist salute and the slogan "All Power to

Ronald Reagan campaigning for governor in 1966, perhaps wishing he could use a paddle on student demonstrators' behinds.

Mario Savio at a Free Speech Movement rally in 1964.
Steven Marcus photo.

We have an autocracy which runs this university....
[I]f this is a firm, and if the Board of Regents are the
board of directors, and if President Kerr in fact is the
manager, then I'll tell you something: the faculty are
a bunch of employees, and we're the raw material!
But we're a bunch of raw material[s] that don't
mean to have any process upon us, don't mean to be
made into any product, don't mean to end up being
bought by some clients of the University, be they
the government, be they industry, be they organized
labor, be they anyone! We're human beings! There is
a time when the operation of the machine becomes so
odious, makes you so sick at heart, that you can't take
part; you can't even passively take part, and you've
got to put your bodies upon the gears and upon the
wheels, upon the levers, upon all the apparatus, and
you've got to make it stop. And you've got to indicate
to the people who run it, to the people who own it,
that unless you're free, the machine will be prevented
from working at all!

—Mario Savio, speech at Sproul Plaza,
UC Berkeley (1964)

the People." Berkeley-student-turned-Yippie Jerry Rubin's silly "Rise up and abandon the creeping meatball!" failed to catch on as did the violent Symbionese Liberation Army's serious "Death to the Fascist Insect that preys on the Life of the People."

Like the rhetoric, student demonstrations turned increasingly militant as the focus of anger shifted back and forth from university administration to civil rights to the Vietnam War. Berkeley led the way, but other universities soon joined in. In 1967, police attacked protestors trying to stop draftees from being inducted at an Oakland Army recruiting station. During the Third World Strike at San Francisco State University in the fall of 1968, students demanding third world studies departments shut down the school until SFPD tactical squad officers took over the campus. Back in Berkeley, police killed one man and wounded many others when students tried to defend People's Park, an urban plot turned park. The National Guard occupied the city, dropping from helicopters tear gas that drifted over the whole town. At UCLA, police broke up an anti-war demonstration and then raided the Chicano Studies Program offices, on the other side of campus, beating students, staff, and professors in May 1970. The fighting gave credence to radicals who advocated militant self-defense, such as the Black Panthers and the Chicano Brown Berets, or who plotted violent revolutionary acts, such as the Weather Underground.

Radical violence, however ideological in origin, also drew on less clearly articulated uprisings such as the Watts riots. In August 1965—just a year after the triumphant signing of the Civil Rights Act in Washington, DC—residents of the largely black Watts area of Los Angeles rose up angrily against police harassment. The riot started when a California Highway Patrolman tried to arrest a local man for drunk driving. In the melee that followed, police beat bystanders who threw rocks and concrete blocks at them. The rioting ended after National Guard troops occupied South Central Los Angeles, but the devastation of the riot was enormous, leaving 34 dead and thousands wounded. Tommy Jacquette, who later started the Watts Summer Festival, recalled, "People keep calling it a riot, but we call it a revolt because it had a legitimate purpose. It was a response to police brutality and social exploitation of a community and of a people."

The Watts riots occurred because of frustration with daily harassment and the setbacks to civil rights, such as the repeal of the Rumford Fair Housing Act the year before. Similar frustration led to the founding of the Black Panther Party. The Panthers'

*Angela Davis complains of "fascist encroachment" after being fired
from her assistant professorship at UCLA for being a Communist, 1969.
Behind her is philosophy department chair and peace activist Donald
Kalish, who had hired Davis.*

militant self-assertion, glamorous leadership, and palatable
blend of black nationalist and Marxist ideology galvanized
inner-city black communities, first in Oakland and then around
the country. The Panthers were the creation of Huey Newton
and Bobby Seale, part of a group of talented young Oakland men
who resented the powerlessness and poverty they saw around
them. The organization's manifesto declared, in true 60s' style,
"We want freedom. We want power to determine the destiny of
our black and oppressed communities." Panthers organized free
breakfast programs in inner-city neighborhoods, started youth
organizations, and brought a radical black style—clenched fist
salutes, group chants, berets, black leather jackets, and shades—
that thrilled many in the black community and white supporters.
In their most controversial actions, Panthers carried weapons
while following police officers patrolling black neighborhoods.
With a keen sense of spectacle and US militia traditions, they
marched into the state capital armed with rifles to protest a gun
control law in May 1967.

The Panthers' assertive, often confrontational stance, their
paramilitary style, and their penchant for confrontational rhetoric alarmed conservatives. Many Panthers carried the macho
aggressiveness of their neighborhoods into Party factional fights,

beating and, on occasion, killing suspected spies. "The Black Panther Party," declared FBI Director J. Edgar Hoover in 1968, "without question, represents the greatest threat to internal security of the country." Hoover pledged to eliminate the party within a year and directed the COINTELPRO program to sabotage the Panthers. Local police agreed. Los Angeles Police Chief Thomas Reddin wanted "overkill," telling his officers, "kill the butterfly with a sledge hammer." Local and state police forces arrested, beat, and killed Panthers in raids in Oakland, Los Angeles, and other states. Within a few years the Party was in tatters, many of its leaders in exile, jail, underground, or dead. Fears of infiltration and bouts of egotism plagued the organization. A macho culture within the group had limited the role of women, but with the destruction of the male leadership, women became the majority of the Party in the 1970s. Elaine Brown led the organization, continuing its community programs and support for prisoners until its final dissolution in 1981. Newton, who had dropped out of law school in the 60s, but later earned a PhD from the University of California, Santa Cruz, could not shake the streets later in life. He died in a drug deal gone bad in Oakland in 1989. Despite the Party's and its leaders' inglorious ends, a former member recalled, the Panthers were "Black men and women willing to transform the Black community... We understood that freedom came with a price that we were willing to pay."

The new activism also reached the fields and barrios as organizers mobilized farm workers to a degree not seen since the field battles of the 1930s. The United Farm Workers of America, led by a morally driven former migrant worker, César Chávez, and a bright college-educated Chicana from Stockton, Dolores Huerta, put together the most powerful farm labor union in US history. Farm workers lacked basic protections against firing, harassment, and other malpractices by employers. Grower domination of farming towns and the racism of the surrounding communities made the countryside hostile to union drives for decades. Chávez and Huerta realized that impoverished field laborers on their own had little chance of forcing California's powerful agribusinesses to negotiate contracts. They used techniques drawn from a Mexican tradition of community mobilization, Catholic social justice theology, and pacifist civil disobedience. When Filipino workers struck at Delano grape growers in 1965, Chávez brought his largely Mexican organiza-

As part of a nationwide crackdown on militants, over 400 Los Angeles police officers raided the local Black Panther offices in December 1969.

tion to support the Filipinos in a reprise of the 1930s cross-race agricultural organizing.

With red flags emblazoned with an eagle, UFW marchers chanted "*Sí Se Puede*" (yes, it can be done) and "*Viva la causa*" (long live the cause) as they made a 340-mile pilgrimage through the state. Sit-ins, mass marches, demonstrations, hunger strikes, and boycotts turned the five-year long grape strike into a broader social movement, one that galvanized field laborers and sparked passion in urban Chicano neighborhoods. Anglo liberals joined support groups, gave up eating grapes for years, and provided financial aid. Practically an entire generation of Mexican immigrant and Chicano activists marched and worked for the UFW. The boycotts eventually forced growers to negotiate contracts in grapes and lettuce. By 1970 the UFW claimed 80,000 members. Union farm workers' lives slowly improved.

The California Agricultural Labor Relations Act, signed by liberal governor Jerry Brown in 1975, seemed to promise the union lasting success. Yet stability eluded the union. Chávez's powerful moral commitment and energy was often difficult for others to match or challenge. He moved the union headquarters to remote La Paz in the Tehachapi Mountains and demanded that union officials and organizers work extremely long days and participate in encounter groups. Many of the best and most experienced staff left. Efforts to challenge Chávez's leadership were rebuffed bitterly. Competition from the Teamsters' Union, despite a pact between the two unions in 1977, further eroded UFW membership while the ever-changing patterns of migrant labor led to high membership turnover. When Brown's successor, Republican George Deukmejian, changed the character of the California Agricultural Labor Relations Board, the union faced disaster. Membership plummeted to 20,000 by 1993, the year of Chávez's death. In the post-Chávez years, the UFW has survived and continued its organizing drives.

Outside of the fields, Mexican-American activists claimed a unique mixed identity as Chicanos. They demanded community control and power in much the same way as black activists. In LA, the Brown Berets even modeled themselves on the Black Panthers, with a multi-point party platform and free meals in the community, though they did articulate a particular Chicano militancy. Chicanos rejected the Americanizing moderation of older organizations like the Mexican American Political Association or the Mexican American Legal Defense and Education Fund. Rather, the most nationalist among them claimed that the western US was Aztlán, the mythical northern homeland of the Aztecs who had ruled central Mexico until the Spanish conquest. Organizations like the Movimiento Estudiantil de Chicanos en Aztlán (MEChA), founded at UC Santa Barbara in 1969, combined nationalism and practical organizing. "We will not assimilate into gringo society," declared one leader, "nor will we encourage others to do so."

The United Mexican American Students, which later became part of MEChA, led tens of thousands of Chicano students in school and university walkouts in 1967 and 1968. The militants' most dramatic moment was the Chicano Moratorium of August 1970, the largest Mexican-American mobilization against the Vietnam War. Thirty thousand people flooded Whittier Boulevard in East Los Angeles chanting *"Raza si! Guerra no!"* (Our people yes! The war no!). It was the largest demonstration by Chicanos until the pro-immigrant rallies of 2006. Los Angeles police attacked a rally after the march, killing three people, including *Los Angeles Times* columnist Ruben Salazar, who was sitting in a nearby bar. The police apparently killed him by accident but a US Civil Rights Commission report found "widespread misconduct" and "excessive violence" on the part of police.

Although noted for his religious nonviolence, César Chávez was also a militant activist. Here he speaks at an anti-war rally in 1971 watched over by members of the Brown Berets.

Chicano activists advocated for culturally cohesive and powerful Mexican-American and immigrant communities. Student activists forced the creation of Chicano studies programs at colleges, universities, and even some high schools throughout the state. Chicano artists, musicians, writers, and performers created politically charged works—the most visible being murals, inspired by the Mexican and 1930s New Deal muralist movements, that celebrated the culture of their community. El Teatro Campesino, which started with agitprop theater in the fields during UFW organizing drives, won over audiences around the country and spurred the career of playwright and director Luis Valdez. Chicano musicians—from Lalo Guerrero in the 1940s, Ritchie Valens in the 50s, Carlos Santana in the 60s, Malo in the 1970s, and Los Lobos in the 80s—achieved cross-over successes, but their sounds owed a great deal to a vibrant Chicano music scene. Despite these cultural successes Chicanos and Latinos continued to be largely underrepresented in media and politics.

Within the nationalist Chicano movement, as in many areas of the male-dominated new left, women found it difficult to achieve recognition. White feminists, despite their common critique of patriarchy, alienated Chicana feminists and other

Chicano/a Moratorium march against the Vietnam War in 1970.

women of color in the 1970s. Chicana writers, artists, and poets forged a distinctive style and literature in response to their multiple predicaments. Women activists within the Chicano movement demanded equal treatment as soon as the movement itself began, but with only limited success. Gloria Anzaldúa, a Texan transplant who found the queer culture of San Francisco welcoming, helped articulate a radical lesbian-of-color critique of both Chicano machismo and of dominant white feminism. Some Chicana writers, scholars, artists, and activists achieved cultural and academic success, but the radical movement remained male dominated as did the more moderate Mexican-American organizations until the 1990s.

The decline of *Chicanismo* as a dynamic movement came about partly because many of the militants achieved successes in establishing Chicano studies programs, rising in the ranks of the labor movement, and winning political office. Perhaps as important, the enormous Mexican immigration of the latter part

LA Times *columnist Ruben Salazar, one of the
few Mexican writers at the paper, was killed by
Los Angeles police during the Chicano Moratorium.*

of the 20th century brought millions of people into the community whose sense of identity and political grievance differed from the Chicanos. Radical labor activists, particularly Bert Corona and Soledad "Chole" Alatorre, tried to overcome these divisions with the organization CASA, founded in the early 1970s. CASA promoted cross-border organizing but eventually fell to factional divisions. The Chicanos had been a minority among Mexican Americans, but their militancy had won some notable victories and pushed more moderate politicians to challenge the conditions of the barrios and fields.

The spirit of activism also fueled a revival of Native-American militancy. Economic desperation, heightened by a federal "termination" policy that stripped tribal rights, had pushed native people in California into the cities. By the 1960s, Oakland and Los Angeles had some of the largest urban Indian populations in the country. Indeed, fewer than 10 percent of the natives in the state lived on reservations. Reservation and rancheria termination laws enacted in 1956 and 1958 in California had been designed to allow Americanized native people to stand on their own without the crutch of government aid. Dillon Meyer, the same person who had run the Japanese internment camps in World War II, administered the termination process. By mid-century, Indians had begun building their own organizations, from tribal governments to the Native-American Church. Native-American World War II veterans began demanding greater control over reservation life and fairer treatment. A few tribes managed the natural resources of their reservation lands so well that they achieved prosperity close to that of their white neighbors. The Klamath Reservation, home to California's Modoc tribe, was one of these, and as a result the federal government terminated the reservation, selling off "surplus" land and effectively destroying the economic gains the tribes there had made. Another mid-century reform, a 1964 settlement of Indian claims for lands taken from them in the 1850s and 1860s, offered tribal people a mere 47 cents an acre. Many tribes, including the Pit River and Feather River Nations, rejected the settlement as paltry. The overall result of mid-century Indian policy in California was continued frustration, poverty, and underdevelopment on the reservations and greater migration to the cities, where Indians fared little better.

The intermixing of Indian peoples from different tribes in the cities fostered a greater sense of pan-tribal identity and grievance. It inspired Indian student activists at Berkeley to demand and win the creation of a Native American studies department in 1968, the first of its kind in the country. More spectacularly, Indian students organized Indians of All Tribes to take over Alcatraz Island and reclaim it for native people. Alcatraz, which had been the site of one of the grimmest prisons in the US, had been effectively abandoned by the federal government after the closure of the prison in 1963. Ironically, people from non-California tribes spearheaded the occupation. Led by the charismatic Richard Oakes, a student at San Francisco State, and LaNada Boyer, a UC student who had helped organize the movement for a Native American studies department at Berkeley, the occupiers proved themselves committed and media savvy. They held regular press conferences and broadcast a weekly radio program on Berkeley's KPFA. The takeover received national coverage and brought renewed attention to the predicaments of native peoples. The occupation lasted two years until factional conflicts among the occupiers and the students' return to school reduced their numbers. In June 1971, Federal Marshals and FBI agents took the island back. The occupiers did win some of their demands—the government turned over a former Air Force command center near Davis for the creation of D-Q University, one of the first tribal colleges in the country. The school prospered for years, reaching a peak enrollment of 500 in the 1990s, but declining numbers of students led to it losing accreditation and closing in 2005 after years of mismanagement and internal conflict.

> Fellow citizens, we are asking you to join with us in our attempt to better the lives of all Indian people.... We, the native Americans, reclaim the land known as Alcatraz Island in the name of all American Indians by right of discovery.... We will purchase said Alcatraz Island for twenty-four dollars in glass beads and red cloth... We know that $24 in trade goods for these 16 acres is more than was paid when Manhattan Island was sold, but we know that land values have risen over the years.... Since the San Francisco Indian Center burned down, there is no place for Indians to assemble and carry on tribal life here in the white man's city.... We feel this claim is just and proper, and that this land should rightfully be granted to us for as long as the rivers run and the sun shall shine. We hold the rock!
>
> —Indians of All Nations, "The Alcatraz Proclamation to the Great White Father and His People" (1969)

The mobilization of communities of color in the 60s profoundly challenged the racial divisions that had so long structured California politics and society. One lasting change was the rise of a generation of politicians of color, from Willie Brown in the Bay Area to Antonio Villaraigosa in Los Angeles, who gained their start in the activism of the era. The shift also included more moderate politicians like Norman Mineta of San José, who became the first Asian-American mayor of a major city in 1971 and, although a Democrat, served as secretary of transportation for President George W. Bush. Newly assertive neighborhood and political groups demanded political representation and greater proportions of government money. The polarization of state politics in the last quarter of the century limited the success of these demands as conservatives mobilized voters in greater numbers. Nonetheless, as California moved toward becoming a state without a racial majority, the power of Latino politicians in particular and people of color in general grew to levels unseen since the American conquest.

In the fall of 1966, a group of street actors and radicals, the Diggers, began giving out fruit, vegetables, and stew in San Francisco's Panhandle Park. "It's free," the Diggers proclaimed, "because it is yours." Named after an English radical agrarian group from the 17th century, the young activists sought to transform society through direct actions that challenged fundamental market and social relations with humor and irony. Emmett Grogan, a creative but troubled working-class Irish American, inspired the group with his high spirits and irreverent in-your-face style. Grogan's own struggles with addiction and the law as well as his tough background provided a connection to the Beats and the blue-collar counterculture of mid-century San Francisco. Grogan could not, however, be called a leader. "Do your own thing," the Diggers admonished, "Be what you are. If you don't know what you are, find out. Fuck leaders."

The Diggers lived communally in a large house open to anyone who wanted to stay—a group that included runaways and members of the Hells Angels motorcycle club. San Francisco politicians pressed the city's health department to close down this prototypical commune. Raids and inspections along with their street happenings, marches, free food giveaways, and concerts brought the Diggers publicity, good and bad. By the spring of 1967, tens of thousands of young people flooded the Diggers' Haight-Ashbury neighborhood looking for an alternative to the dominant conservative culture. News reports of wild hippies dancing in the streets or confronting city authorities spread a sense of radical cultural change. The Diggers provided free food, social services, and concerts. Rock bands, particularly the Grateful Dead, and concert promoters funded the events since these free things did actually cost something. Communes sprouted in low-rent buildings; street people panhandled for spare change; drugs were shared.

The Diggers, fed up with both the flood of apolitical young people and the repressive San Francisco police response, advised the hippies to go back to the land and dig. Groups of hippies moved to rural areas of California, particularly to Santa Cruz, Humboldt, and Mendocino counties, as well as the canyons surrounding LA. One of the most charismatic leaders of the back-to-the-land trend, Korean War vet and San Francisco State University instructor Stephen Gaskin in 1970 led a caravan of 90 vehicles from San Francisco to settle "The Farm" in Tennessee. The Farm found coherence in Gaskin's spiritual teaching. "Going to the land," Gaskin wrote later, "seemed like the natural progression of the whole hippy movement."

The utopian back-to-the-land retreat was a reaction in part to the commercialization of the counterculture. Some of the participants, such as LSD apostle Timothy Leary, appeared more interested in self-promotion and self-indulgence than in social transformation. Rock concert promoters like Bill Graham were able to turn a free movement into one that paid quite well. Others understood the wider appeal of the counterculture. Stewart Brand, army vet and former member of the Merry Pranksters, hippie apostles of pyschedelia, recalled years later: "So we became small business people, and technology enjoyers, appreciators, users, and inventors. That's why the 60s had a lasting impact and effect." Brand claimed that the hippies learned from Native-American elders "as a source of inspiration and possible alliance." Perhaps equally influential was the Sears Roebuck catalog: Brand's biggest impact came with the *Whole Earth Catalog*, a compendium of gadgets, books, wisdom, and other items for back-to-the-landers that sold millions of copies from 1968 to 1974. But unlike Sears, Brand and the Whole Earth Company gave away their profits from the catalog.

Gaskin's Farm was typical of the gaggle of quasi-cult religious groups that pioneered "New Age" ideas and techniques. Among these were the Ananda Community, the Tassajara Zen Center, and the Esalen Institute. Esalen, spectacularly sited on the ocean at Big Sur, started in the early 60s as "an educational center for the exploration of unrealized human capacities." Its combination of East-West mysticism, appropriation of Native-American religion, hot tubbing, massage, and sexual exploration set the model for a widespread popularization of mysticism and bodywork among the middle class and elite. Farther out groups abounded. The One World Family ran one of the first vegetarian restaurants in the state from their communal home in Berkeley. Inspired by Michael Allen, "The New World Comforter," the group was pretty harmless unless you liked flavorful food. Allen explained to his followers and anyone else who would listen that galactic beings flying UFOs watched over the earth and wanted people to eat natural foods at the Messiah's World Café in San

Love-in, Griffith Park, 1967: The hippie movement quickly spread from San Francisco.

Francisco and Berkeley. "All food is psychedelic!" he wrote. "The cause of all mental and physical illnesses, aches and pains, is in the food people eat and the bad mental karma they are attached to." The One World Family was rumored to practice ritualized group sex, but it was their advocacy of natural, vegetarian food that fit into the growing health food movement.

Left-leaning Berkeley grad Alice Waters dramatically improved the generally bland, heavy hippie food with French-inspired sophistication when she started a deceptively casual restaurant in Berkeley in 1971. Her Chez Panisse, with its reliance on organic, locally-raised produce and meat, started a food trend far removed from the radical milieu in which it started. "It's not just food," Waters explained, echoing the New World Comforter, "but a way of life." The demand for organic food spread to Southern California in the 1970s and then much of the rest of the country as hip Hollywood actors and wealthy foodies gave it wide publicity. Californians became the first to regulate organic food, first privately in 1973 through the California Certified Organic Farmers and then by the state in 1990. The nation's largest organic grower, Earthbound Farms, started by UC grads

Drew and Myra Goodman, sold $450 million worth of organic produce in 2006 by marrying alternative farming techniques to California agribusiness—a rather different "way of life" than the hand-crafted emphasis of Alice Waters and the gourmets or the back-to-the-land hippies from whence they came. The natural food movement succeeded ultimately because it appealed to health- and environmentally-conscious consumers, not because of its fundamental challenge to the industrial agriculture of the state or because it carried out instructions from UFOs.

In the more conservative years after the 60s, the rise of cults and radical splinter parties like the Revolutionary Communist Party or the Weather Underground appeared to prove the dangers inherent in throwing off conventional authority. Indeed, many groups formed around unscrupulous but charismatic men who manipulated those seeking spiritual or political guidance. Bob Avakian in the Revolutionary Communist Party and Lyndon La Rouche in the National Council of Labor Committees, originally New Left radicals, used psychological manipulation to control supporters in their national and California organizations. Similar manipulation came with groups like Synanon and Scientology. Synanon had begun in the 1950s as an effective drug treatment program, which used emotionally confrontational techniques and occasional violence to manipulate and control people desperate to overcome addiction. By the mid-70s, Synanon had become a substantial countercultural institution with 16,000 people who had renounced society living at its facilities on Tomales Bay, north of San Francisco. Founder Chuck Dederich was the man responsible for the phrase "today is the first day of the rest of your life," but unfortunately he himself became increasingly dictatorial and erratic, probably returning to alcohol abuse. At one time he demanded all pregnant Synanon residents get abortions, then forced many couples in the group to change partners. Synanon members even attempted to assassinate an attorney who was suing the organization in 1978 by putting rattlesnakes in his mailbox.

Religious cults drew even more people in, most horribly in the case of the People's Temple. Charismatic minister Jim Jones had built a popular, activist, and multiracial church in San Francisco. His devoted adherents provided political muscle for progressive political campaigns in the 1970s, while Jones became more and more paranoid and exploitative. Jones convinced his followers to found a series of utopian communities, ultimately moving hundreds of people from the Bay Area to a rural Guyana settlement they called Jonestown. In November 1978, Congressman Leo Ryan of South San Francisco brought a delegation to Guyana to investigate reports that Jones was holding people against their will. Jonestown guards killed Ryan at the airstrip near the settlement, while in the camp, Jones exhorted his followers to drink cyanide-laced kool aid. Over 900 died or were killed.

Although the Jonestown massacre took place in the 70s, it provided a tragic coda to the shortlived cultural utopianism of the 60s. It was a brief time from the Diggers' free store of 1966 to the 1969 rock concert at Altamont Speedway near Livermore, where Hells Angels hired to provide security beat a man to death. It didn't seem to take long for idealistic political activists to become sectarian fanatics or guerrilla fighters, ending up in prison, isolated, or dead. Social experimentation and openness drew some people further from society into cults. Mind-expanding exploration with drugs unlocked new paths to addiction and delusion. Rock and soul became options on the radio dial. The back-to-the-land and natural food movement isolated many hippies and turned others into gourmet yuppies. In the 1970s, a revitalized right stalemated both creative reforms and outrageous behavior, linking sensible dissent and blind opposition. Factional fighting doomed the activist organizations that managed to withstand government sabotage. With the end of the Vietnam War and the collapse of the militant movements of people of color, political activism disappeared from the streets. As the optimism of the 60s faded, so did the state's economy in a post-Vietnam War retrenchment. Given this rapid demise, it is easy to look on the spirit of the era as simply an outburst of misplaced youthful enthusiasm. It is easy, but it is wrong.

Countercultural openness, for so many years a barely tolerated eccentricity, achieved a widespread, if at times patronizing, acceptance. The political calculus of the state no longer hid the racial order at the root of so much inequity. Black, Chicano, and Asian people, while hardly free of the weight of decades of discrimination and exclusion, exercised far greater power over their own communities and participated far more fully in the political life of the state. The changes of the 60s and early 70s also paved the way culturally and socially for a fundamental reorganization of the urban California economy, away from heavy industry and toward services and technology. The ferment of those years profoundly changed California, the US, and much of the world.

Hippies, like Tony and Ellen Russo with their son Jesse in Mendocino County in 1972, built alternatives to the dominant culture by living a self-sufficient, communal life. (Photo: 1972 Nicholas Wilson)

*Howard Jarvis surrounded by supporters after the victory of anti-tax,
anti-government Proposition 13 in 1978.*

18

Return of the Right

The youthful counterculture, the anti-war movement, and the assertiveness of people of color raised fears among many that liberal coddling of dissent was causing the disintegration of the social order. California's conservatives articulated these fears first in the fight against neighborhood and school integration. The movement soon spread to support for anti-tax initiatives, cuts in government services, and harsh penalties for criminal activity.

The witty yet hard-nosed Ronald Reagan embodied the conservative movement. Reagan won the governorship in 1966, defeating Pat Brown, who was seeking a third term. Reagan's stunning electoral victory depended on white resentment of Brown's support for civil rights and his inability to control the turmoil in the ghettos and campuses of the state. Reagan declared that he was "sick of the sit-ins, the teach-ins, the walkouts" and promised voters that he would get a handle on the demonstrations in Berkeley. Reagan's campaign blended an informal, rustic style with hopeful patriotism and moralistic outrage at big government for its interference in business prerogatives, its excessive taxation for unapproved purposes, and its support of social and cultural change.

The integration of housing and schools enraged many white voters in the 1960s and 70s because it violated longstanding practices of geographic segregation. The Spanish and Mexicans had maintained strict rules controlling where Indians could live. In the Constitution of 1879, the state formalized municipal power to force Chinese to live and work within Chinatowns. In 1888, the US Supreme Court struck down this provision, declaring it in violation of the 14th amendment and "a naked and arbitrary power"—a remarkable ruling given that the same court severely limited the Reconstruction-era Civil Rights Act. Nonetheless, while the court restricted government-enacted segregation, it still allowed individuals to discriminate and California realtors and developers to create a new system of racially restrictive covenants. In 1948, during the more tolerant post-World War

11 years, the California Supreme Court ruled racially restrictive covenants unconstitutional. However, racial exclusion remained a common practice throughout the state.

In 1963 California's first black assembly member, Byron Rumford, who represented largely black districts of Berkeley and Oakland, pushed through legislation outlawing housing discrimination. The Rumford Act provoked outrage among segregationist whites and the California Real Estate Association launched an initiative, Proposition 14, to overturn it. Even though Californians overwhelmingly supported pro-integration Democratic President Johnson in the 1964 election, they voted in a landslide for Proposition 14. Reagan, who had opposed the 1964 federal Civil Rights Act, began his campaign for governor on a platform of overturning the court decision and the Rumford Act. The former actor swept to victory. Reagan condemned bigotry, but said efforts to undo intolerance by a "big brother sitting in Sacramento" actually increased resentment. Anti-discrimination law, he thundered in his stump speech (echoing Tenney's argument of 14 years before), "invaded one of our most basic and cherished rights." Unlike hardline southern segregationists who spoke openly of their dislike of blacks, Reagan's California right pioneered a coded language for racial fears, one couched in anti-government rhetoric. Using an argument that became essential to the growth of conservative outrage at efforts to undo centuries of inequity, Reagan accused liberals like Governor Brown of giving "one segment of our population rights at the expense of the basic rights of all our citizens."

Reagan's New Right appealed to the white working-class constituencies in California who feared for their homes and families. Security for many was tied up in their houses—it was often a working-class family's only wealth. Imagined and real threats to property values had an enormous impact. Nothing revealed these sentiments more graphically than the residents of the white towns surrounding Watts, who stood guard on their roofs and streets armed with rifles and shotguns during the 1965 riots. Similarly, when Reagan condemned liberal tolerance of a supposedly drug-addled UC Berkeley where "the campus has become a rallying point for Communism and a center of sexual misconduct," he expressed a popular discomfort at difference and a fear that children would be seduced by drugs and debauchery. Reagan's particular gift was his ability to acknowledge and articulate these fears and resentments while conveying a sunny optimism about the future. His political talents also extended to an ability to make up fabulous tales of vicious immoral behavior that jibed perfectly with widely accepted prejudices, as when he concocted an incongruous story about a group of "Negroes" who wielded switchblades to force a university administrator to enroll them in classes.

Despite a moral certainty buoyed by a slim majority in the legislature, Reagan failed to roll back many of the racial advances of the era. The Rumford Act remained law. State and federal courts continued to order the integration of schools. His anti-tax rhetoric program turned out to be harder to implement than promise. He actually agreed to raise taxes—though claimed he was dragged kicking and screaming to the desk to sign. Instead of shrinking, the California state budget doubled during his years in office. (Somehow Reagan's reputation as a budget hawk continues even though he repeated this performance while president, when federal spending increased by 50 percent.) Still, he cut funding to the University of California and the California State University systems, forcing the formerly free schools to charge tuition. He also pushed through major cuts in mental health programs. His muscular response to campus disorders and his rhetorical lashing of the liberals who coddled criminals and radicals won him the undying affection of conservatives. By the time he left the capital in 1974, he was positioned for national office.

The rebirth of the right in the 1960s in California appeared to be a reversal of the consensus years of the 1940s and 50s. Yet it actually built on longstanding conservative tradition. Fear of disorder, minorities, radicalism, crime, and government interference in business prerogatives had repeatedly motivated conservative movements in the state.

Lynching and other forms of terrorism had long been part of systems establishing community power and reinforcing a dominant group's sense of order. The word "vigilante" came to English from Spanish to describe members of a "junta to defend the public security." Vigilantes operated in Mexican Los Angeles where, in 1836, a mob shot a woman accused of killing her husband. In gold rush California, gangs of self-styled "vigilancers" from differing class backgrounds fought for domination over San Francisco and Mother Lode communities. The Hounds, Anglo Mexican-American war veterans, teamed with Australian immigrants, the Sydney Ducks, to attack minority communities. In 1849 the two gangs, "under inspiriting stimulants," burned San Francisco's Chilean tent settlement next to

*Outside the 1964 Republican Convention in San Francisco, where
southern California's New Right helped win Barry Goldwater the
Presidential nomination. Though it never regained its 1920s power in
California, the Ku Klux Klan violently expressed the racial fears of
many whites.*

Telegraph Hill, forcing thousands to flee. "Not knowing what
might next follow," 19th-century chronicler Hubert Howe
Bancroft wrote, elite San Franciscans responded with charitable
donations for the Chileans and the city's first tax. "The first available money," Bancroft continued, "was applied to the purchase
of a prison brig and shackles for chain gangs." But these weren't
enough to control the unruly city. Two years later ex-Mormon
merchant Sam Brannan led a "Committee of Vigilance" that
retaliated against the Ducks, the Hounds (by then known as the
Regulators), and any other people who displeased them—the
first victim of their lynching was a petty thief. Rebranded the
Law and Order Party by the media-savvy Brannan, the vigilantes drew on merchants and government officials in the town.
Not limited to the cities, vigilantes throughout the state attacked
people of color, Indians, and Mexicans, as well as white people
accused of crimes.

In the mid-1850s, San Francisco again experienced "a business man's Revolution," to quote philosopher and political commentator Josiah Royce. This "revolution" pioneered the most effective organizing strategy for the right—using the fear of crime and working-class violence in order to consolidate power and slash taxes. While most lynch mobs and vigilante committees were ad hoc organizations, thrown together on a moment's notice, the San Francisco Vigilance Committee of 1856—a direct descendant of Brannan's Law and Order Party—seized the city's entire government after the shooting of an anti-Catholic newspaper publisher. Thousands of vigilantes took over the county jail and defied the State Supreme Court and Governor's demands to disband. The Governor declared the city to be in insurrection against the state and ordered the state militia to take over. The commander of the federal arsenal at Benicia, however, refused to arm the militia and the general in charge resigned. In the midst of the crisis, a State Supreme Court justice stabbed one of the vigilantes with a bowie knife in a courtroom scuffle. The vigilantes soon disbanded their junta; instead they swept the next municipal elections, bringing into office some of the city's leading tax evaders. Once in power, they cut taxes so low that several of the booming town's schools had to close and the fire department had to make do without hoses.

Later movements echoed the 1850s vigilante campaigns against working-class immorality, against crime, and against government regulation. Political repression in response to seeming social disorder led to recurring constitutional tinkering. Californians remade the state's basic documents and political system repeatedly in a cycle of political outrage, uprising, and reform. The state had two distinctly different constitutions, the first from the gold rush year 1849, which Californians threw away a mere 30 years later. Such constitutional upheaval didn't continue into the 20th and 21st centuries only because after 1911 Californians transformed their constitution simply by adding to it.

California's political upheavals often centered on race, but the state's wealthiest people had often pushed for greater ethnic diversity and immigration. Elites opposed white working-class attacks on Chinese workers and supported immigration from Mexico and the Philippines. Brannan's San Francisco vigilantes, for instance, had come to power after outrage over anti-Chilean violence. As working-class power grew in the late 19th and early 20th centuries, elite right-wingers learned they could use racial antagonisms to win elections. For instance, San Francisco's anti-labor ex-mayor James Phelan, a patrician banker and real-estate developer, won a US Senate seat in the 1920s with the populist slogan "Save Our State From Oriental Aggression: Keep California White."

Conservatives viewed labor militancy as the product of alien ideas and foreign agitators, combining anti-foreign and anti-union sentiment in an effective package. From the French Revolution forward, radicalism had appeared to have a foreign tinge in the US, yet elite interests in immigration had kept xenophobia somewhat in check. But the rise in labor radicalism coupled with huge waves of immigration at the turn of the century brought a new synthesis for the right. In 1919 conservatives fearful of foreign revolutionary ideas pushed through a broad criminal syndicalism law banning the advocacy of violence for political or economic change. The state first targeted the IWW, but the law had its greatest effect against union organizing drives in agriculture in the 1920s and 30s. Courts repeatedly imprisoned union activists for encouraging strikers to defend themselves against vigilantes. The cause of order and control received enormous impetus from World War II as the previously controversial impulse toward state planning, regulation, and management gained further legitimacy in the national emergency. Control over society required large increases in police patrols at the same time that efforts to root out enemy spies and saboteurs led to wholesale civil rights violations and the growth of a national security apparatus run by the federal government. Like their precursors the vigilantes, most right-wing politicians in California have used the fear of crime and the disorder of the lower orders to catapult them into power. Fears of immorality and of a government seemingly out of tune with the true interests of the people and the state also motivated these movements.

The rebirth of the right during Reagan's years and the economic crisis of the early 1970s changed the basis of California politics for decades. Yet these changes continued earlier ideologies. The Reagan right mobilized new constituencies for conservatism, cutting deeply into the Democrats' white working-class base and creating a profound polarization in state politics. Some Democrats attempted to adjust to the new reality, none more openly than Edmund "Jerry" Brown, son of the earlier Governor Edmund "Pat" Brown. Declaring "an era of limits," the younger Brown, a former theology student, took office as governor after decisively winning election in 1974. Brown tried to adjust California political ideas to the seismic shifts in the US economy

The Governor's Mansion

Governor Reagan's wife Nancy hated the gimcrackery of the Victorian 1877 governor's mansion. She convinced some wealthy benefactors to donate a modernist ranch home to replace it. Journalist Jeff Kearns described the new mansion as having "the unmistakable feel of California living, like something from an old *Sunset* magazine except on a grander scale." As part of his rejection of the trappings of traditional power, Governor Jerry Brown refused to live in the modern mansion designed for his predecessor Ronald Reagan. The old mansion is now a museum and the new one was sold by the state. Governors since then have lived in apartments or their own homes in Sacramento.

brought on by the economic fallout of the end of the Vietnam War, a sudden rise in gasoline prices, and increased overseas economic competition. He drove a modest car and refused to move into the grandiose governor's mansion built to the exacting standards of Nancy Reagan, the previous governor's wife. But then came Proposition 13.

Two wealthy businessmen, Howard Jarvis and Paul Gann, authored 1978's Proposition 13, which dramatically reduced property tax rates and restricted the state and local government' ability to raise taxes. The initiative passed by almost 2 to 1, sparked similar efforts around the country, and provided some relief to homeowners who had seen their property taxes rise dramatically as the 1970s' real-estate boom increased property values. Large landowners reaped the most benefits. The new law, for instance, saved Standard Oil of California almost $50 million a year and Southern Pacific $20 million. Landlords got a $4 billion tax reduction, the lion's share of the benefits. Property tax money had been the lifeblood of local government, but Prop 13 drastically restricted the ability of towns and cities to raise other taxes to replace the lost revenue. The results were dramatic and immediate. Throughout the state, school funding plummeted. Streets went unpaved, parks untended, and social services cut. Municipal life and standards of living, never that strong, entered a period of crisis that continues to this day.

Although Brown had originally opposed Prop 13, after the measure's overwhelming victory he changed his tune, endorsing strict limits on government spending and taxing. Brown's cautious policies had left the state with substantial budget surpluses that the government used to help bail out local governments devastated by Prop 13 and to build up the size of the state budget, in contradiction to the intention of the initiative's backers. Soon other voter initiatives further restricted the government's flexibility. Proposition 4 in 1979 limited the growth of all state taxes and ordered rebates of surpluses. The drastic effects of tax cutting on schools led voters to support Prop 98 in 1988, which guaranteed schools and community colleges a fixed portion of state revenues. Several other propositions sidestepped the legislative budget process, dictating how sale taxes, cigarette taxes, and other revenues should be spent for a variety of purposes.

By the end of Brown's second term in 1982 the surpluses were long gone, as revenues plummeted in the midst of a national recession. Republicans attributed the economic crisis to Brown's mismanagement, but as with later governors accused of incompetence, the political situation in the state made sensible budgeting practically impossible. Brown had indeed combined a moderate fiscal policy with liberal appointments throughout state government, infuriating conservatives. He broke with previous governors in supporting environmentally inspired limitations on water projects. He also backed significant reforms for farm labor, appointed more women and minorities to office than any previous governor, and supported the development of high-tech industries in the state. While many of his policies were popular, Brown's anti-capital punishment stance and his appointment of Rose Bird, who also opposed putting criminals to death, as chief justice of the Supreme Court, played into conservative anger over crime. Brown tried to follow Reagan into national office, but failed as opponents and the national press branded him "Governor Moonbeam," deriding the former seminarian for his innovative ideas, liberal sympathies, and countercultural openness.

It seemed during the Brown years that California's move to the left would continue strongly. Nothing revealed this trend more clearly than the rise of gay militancy in San Francisco. The 1960s had been a turning point in San Francisco's queer activism. With the help of liberal churches, homophile organizations won greater prominence in the city. A New Year's drag ball at California Hall was sponsored by a clerical and homophile group in 1965, but the police nonetheless raided the event. Unlike victims of earlier raids the arrestees found widespread sympathy. The following year, drag queens and street hustlers fought

Howard Jarvis

Anti-tax activist Howard Jarvis found the key to transforming the loony anti-government thinking of the 1950s and 60s into the basic principles of national politics of the last decades of the century. He galvanized the old elite of the GOP and new suburbanites and seniors with plans to drastically cut real-estate taxes. "I've been called a right-wing extremist, a gadfly, a tax advocate, a demagogue, an anarchist and a populist," Jarvis said proudly, "They're all true in a way." Jarvis, however, was more of a typical elite western Republican, refreshingly disdainful of the stiff formality of the eastern rich but no less defensive of the prerogatives of wealth. While he claimed to be a self-made man, he had been born to an elite Mormon family; his father had been a Utah Supreme Court Justice whose connections helped the younger Jarvis start a small newspaper chain. His family ties also won him a job with Herbert Hoover's election campaign. He moved to Northern California in the early 1930s after making friends with up-and-coming Alameda County politician Earl Warren, who later became governor and US Supreme Court Justice. After working for oil magnate J. Paul Getty, he sold his newspapers and bought some manufacturing companies. Although he resented the federal government's heavy-handed control over his business in World War II, his anti-tax philosophy did not extend to refusing to get paid with tax money for government contracts. Moving to Southern California, he and his corporation, Femco, joined the fifties military-industrial boom by manufacturing missile and airplane parts for the government. He lived the good life in Los Angeles: "I'm what you call a Jack Mormon. That means I'm no goddam good. I drink vodka, smoke a pipe and play a little golf on Sunday." Jarvis' anti-tax ideology and dramatic style drew him back to politics. For years he labored unsuccessfully on the lunatic fringe of the Republican Party. He was too cantankerous to achieve elective office—when a junior high schooler wrote accurately in his school newspaper that Jarvis was a real-estate magnate, he threatened him with a lawsuit. He had a hard time making a speech without swearing. Eventually, however, his right-wing ideas found the right moment.

back against a police raid at Compton's Cafeteria, an all-night hangout in the tough Tenderloin neighborhood. The 1966 riot was the first example of transgender militancy in US history—three years before the more famous riots at the Stonewall in New

York City. As rioter Amanda St. Jaymes later explained, "we got tired of being harassed." Gay militancy from groups such as the Lavender Panthers and the Gay Liberation Front continued into the next decade, while social service organizations and political groups proliferated amid the city's growing tolerance. At the same time, a great migration of gays, lesbians, and transgender people filled the old gay neighborhoods with clubs, bars, bath-houses, and stores. They spilled out into new areas, particu-larly the Castro. Castro businessman Harvey Milk became the country's first openly gay elected official, winning office as a city supervisor in 1977. Statewide efforts to force gays back in the closet, particularly a 1978 initiative sponsored by State Senator John Briggs to ban gay and lesbian teachers, faltered. Even Reagan opposed the initiative. But just after Briggs's defeat, a disgruntled former supervisor, Dan White, killed Milk and progressive Mayor George Moscone. The angry reaction to White's acquittal led to riots, and gay power in San Francisco did not recede despite the toll of AIDS in the 1980s.

The distinctiveness of San Francisco's left politics was shown by another Brown, a state assemblyman who authored the 1975 law legalizing sex between consenting adults (thus making gay and lesbian sex a personal rather than legal act). Willie Brown's tolerance was smart politics for a San Francisco representative; his long career showed him to be among the smartest. Brown, a Democrat and no relation to the governor, presided as speaker of the state assembly for fifteen years—even when Republicans held the majority. He later served two terms as mayor of San Francisco, the first and only African American to win that post in a city where blacks were a small minority of the electorate. Mayor Brown had a personal style that was diametrically opposed to Governor Brown's asceticism. The mayor dressed stylishly—he was rarely seen without an expensive suit and dapper hat. He loved fast cars, boasting that every California Highway patrol-man knew his black Porsche and allowed him to "establish the land speed records" between San Francisco and Sacramento. But Brown dominated state politics in ways that went beyond style. His skills at deal-making kept the legislature firmly in the liberal camp despite years of Republican ascendancy in top state offices. Brown also compromised his principles in ways that alarmed many supporters, by making deals with developers and other big businesses as well as enriching himself through his law practice. His political skills infuriated his opponents, who used him as the symbol of all that was wrong with state politics in 1990 to pass an

Drag queens and an escort arrive at a ball in San Francisco in the early 1960s. The San Francisco drag scene, replete with its own elaborate social hierarchy of courts, aristocracy, and parties, owed its institutionalization to the efforts of entertainer and early gay rights activist José Sarria. In 1961, Sarria, dubbed the "Nightingale of Montgomery Street" for his shows at the Black Cat Café, became the first openly gay person to run for public office in the US.

initiative setting limits on the number of terms legislators could stay in office.

Republicans faced many challenges in addition to Willie Brown in the 1980s and 90s as the state's Latino population grew and the political landscape shifted back to the left. Within the Republican Party, moderates lost control to the right, leading

George Deukmejian made killing criminals the center of his political career. As a young state senator, he authored a bill, signed by Governor Reagan, with him in 1973, to reinstate the death penalty.

to increasingly conservative nominees for office. Yet despite the state's Democratic majority the Republicans maintained a hold on California politics throughout the 80s and 90s. To win elections they pushed "wedge issues"—particularly crime, immigration, and homosexuality—that tended to split the Democratic vote. Governors George Deukmejian and Pete Wilson won two terms each and led their party to control over the state legislature using these techniques. Deukmejian, the state's most prominent Armenian-American politician, had championed a series of anti-crime laws in the late 1970s and was the author of the state's new capital punishment law. He defeated LA's first black mayor, Tom Bradley, in the gubernatorial race in 1982 after labeling Bradley soft on crime. Bradley was a former LAPD officer. In that election, race certainly played a role though not necessarily in the way we would expect: 5 percent said they would vote against a black candidate, but 15 percent said they would vote against an Armenian.

As governor, Deukmejian benefited from the recovery from the 70s economic crises. He further stimulated the state's economy and paid back his Central Valley supporters by pushing through a vast increase in prison construction with new facilities to be built in small rural towns. But his political masterstroke was to turn his reelection bid in 1986 into a referendum on State Supreme Court Justice Rose Bird and two other justices who opposed the death penalty (and whose acceptance of limitations on corporate power upset wealthy Californian backers of the "no" vote). The recall succeeded and Deukmejian appointed new justices in favor of the death penalty. In his second term, Deukmejian slashed the state's consumer watchdog agencies and gutted labor protections for agricultural workers. Deukmejian also began the practice of borrowing money to pay the state's bills—a practice ostensibly forbidden by the state constitution but made necessary by his refusal to raise taxes. The result was a state government teetering on the brink of collapse. California's shortage of public revenue eventually led to declines in vital social services such as road maintenance and levee reinforcement in the Sacramento delta.

Pete Wilson, Deukmejian's Republican successor, lacked Deukmejian's charismatic appeal and came to office in the midst of a recession in 1990. The deindustrialization of Southern California contributed to the state's enormous deficits and to the bankruptcy of school districts, cities, and counties. Revenue-starved Orange County could not turn to residents to replace lost funding after the collapse of the local aerospace industry. Instead, county supervisors, trusting in the inevitable beneficence of markets, gambled county money on short-term interest rates in the bond market. They bet wrong; the wealthy county declared bankruptcy in 1994. Similar predicaments faced other conservative bastions of fiscal probity, particularly the state's second largest city, San Diego, which almost went under in the first years of the new millennium. San Diego, labeled "Enron by the Sea," belied its fiscally conservative reputation by financing the city with money raided from pension funds and then trying to sell practically fraudulent bonds to cover the pension deficit. A whistleblowing pension trustee described the city: "It's reckless, it spends wildly and lavishly, it saves nothing and it hides the truth."

Governor Wilson followed the Reagan-Deukmejian formula of blaming illegal immigrants, criminals, and "Big Government" for the state's problems. His first solution to the state's problems was to back a 1990 initiative limiting legislators to a few terms in office. The Democrats could offer little in the way of opposition, given their fractured constituencies in the state, fear of crime, and widespread support of tax cutting. They followed the conservative Democratic leadership of Diane Feinstein, former mayor of San Francisco, into embracing

Republican policies against immigrants, crime, social services, and taxes. Wilson faced intense problems in trying to win reelection in 1994. He was the most unpopular governor in decades—yet sailed to victory over his opponent Kathleen Brown, daughter of Governor Pat Brown and sister of Jerry. Wilson won by championing two vicious Propositions: 184, the "Three Strikes" initiative, and 187, the anti-immigrant "Save Our State" plan. The initiatives galvanized his supporters and disheartened liberals. Both passed overwhelmingly. The baseball phrase "three strikes and you're out" provided a clever marketing package for a law that set mandatory minimum sentences for a variety of crimes and forced judges to send people convicted of a third felony, even a relatively minor one, to prison for 25 years to life. Prop 187, which would have denied medical care, education, and social services to undocumented immigrants and their children, was immediately declared unconstitutional.

The use of wedge-issue initiatives to mobilize supporters and deal with complex policy decisions through the simplified language of the political campaign proved a powerful technique for the right that liberals were slow to take up. Ironically, the California Republican Party had long refused to take positions on state propositions—for instance, it had taken no position on Prop 14, which repealed the 1963 Fair Housing Act—Republicans in those days saw initiatives in true progressive fashion as democratic instruments outside of partisan politics. The Jarvis-Gann strategy won over the GOP after 1979. It embraced wedge propositions as key to splitting the white vote in an increasingly Democratic state. Left-leaning activists eventually jumped into initiative politics. Harvey Rosenfeld and a savvy group of activists based in Los Angeles did succeed in passing initiatives that reformed the state's auto insurance industry, insured school funding, and taxed cigarettes highly in 1988. But other leftist efforts, particularly on healthcare, fell far far short. Nonetheless, the number of initiatives on the ballot increased every election cycle. Only nine voter-qualified initiatives appeared in the entire decade of the 1960s and just ten in the 70s. But then forty-six made it to the ballot in the 1980s, sixty-one in the 90s, and over a hundred in the first decade of the new century. The propositions may not have always expanded democracy but they certainly swelled election information pamphlets practically to the size of phone books.

Few initiatives had a greater impact than Prop 184, the three strikes initiative that further fed the prison construction boom

Rebuilt as a maximum security prison during the construction boom of the 1980s, the California Correctional Institution soon held 5,700 prisoners—twice the number it was designed for—in the remote Tehachapi mountains southeast of Bakersfield.

that had begun under Deukmejian. The prison boom enriched contractors and real-estate speculators especially in perennially depressed Central Valley towns and desert areas. The boom actually failed to generate widespread prosperity in these poor communities, but rather brought in new residents who took the prison jobs. Nonetheless, with prisons located in so many remote areas, families of prisoners spent days traveling to visit incarcerated parents, spouses, and children. The small towns, along with the prison guards' unions, prison construction companies, and other contractors forged a potent political alliance that protected prison budgets even during periods of fiscal crisis.

The effect of the anti-crime efforts on people of color, especially African Americans, was quite revealing. Racism certainly lay behind this dismal trend but so did class and politics—African Americans suffered disproportionately in the deindustrialization waves of the late twentieth century; as poverty rates rose, so did criminal activities. Police caught poor drug users—by far the largest group of prisoners—more easily than those with the money to use in posh neighborhoods and exclusive clubs. The poor could not afford expensive lawyers to fight their cases and instead relied on an overburdened system of public defenders, who were often as interested in moving through cases quickly as in winning verdicts. Juries proved more likely to convict blacks than whites. By 2003, 29 percent of the jail population was black—in a state with an African-American population of less than 10 percent. Blacks were sent to prison at four times the rate for Latinos and seven times the rate for whites.

California led a boom in prison construction that soon turned the United States into the world's largest jailer—surpassing China in the early years of the new millennium. Dozens of new prisons were built at a cost of many billions of dollars and the numbers of prisoners increased enormously, from 25,000 in 1980 to 93,000 in 1991. Fear of crime continued to be a potent political force, even for middle-of-the-road Democrats like Gray Davis, a former Jerry Brown staffer who won election as governor in 1998 and reelection in 2002. Unlike Brown, Davis supported the death penalty and the three strikes law. At the turn of the millennium, California had a massive "correctional" system with 32 state prisons, 37 wilderness work camps, and 5 "prisoner mother facilities." While the crime rate dropped in the 1980s and 90s, the prisons continued filling with people serving longer and longer terms, often for non-violent drug offenses. Along with county jails, the state population of prisoners hit record highs, with over 160,000 incarcerated in 2000. Convicts filled the new prisons as soon as they were built, resulting in dismal overcrowding in a system designed to hold only half the number of prisoners now inside. Californians had built, in the phrase of geographer and activist Ruth Gilmore, a "Golden Gulag."

Tehachapi Loop

Our plan is to stop at the Astroburger for lunch and then head backwards through transportational history (via Highway 58) from Edwards Air Force Base to the Tehachapi Loop, from where the sound barrier was broken and the space shuttle lands to where 4,000-foot long trains cross over their own back ends as they spiral up the steep Tehachapi grade. The desert reclines in all directions. A recumbent landscape. A drawing of it would consist of a series of straight lines across the very bottom of a sheet of paper; the rest of the unfilled paper would be sky.

The dashboard clock reads 11:46 am when the Astroburger signs loom into view, decorated with what could be taken to be either swooping missile bombers or space shuttles. But another era has dawned in Kramer Junction: the diner itself is draped with "El Torito" banners. We stand aimless in the parking lot. A plastic Subway bag tumbles by. To the north, acres of solar panels gleam.

We cross the highway to investigate a derelict motel. Minutes later, we are visited by a woman named Diane in a large white sedan with Edwards AFB decals on the windscreen. She wants to make sure we are not from the county building department. She is friendlier when we are not. She has lived in the nearby town of Boron for the last ten years. It's a place "where kids can be kids," she says, and when they visit her mom "down the hill," the kids want to know "What's that smell? Why does the air look like that?" She tells us about the people she knows who live "up here" and commute "down the hill" daily.

While she is chatting, another sedan pulls up several hundred yards from us. An old man emerges slowly while his small black terrier dashes around. Both simultaneously take a bowlegged pee.

Diane is still on about the county. "Before you can build a house in the area, they come out and count every one of your Joshua trees," she tells us, "and every single one had better be there when you're finished!"

In 1882, Southern Pacific (SP) began construction of a railroad line from Mojave to Needles, presumably paying no attention to the number of Joshua trees. Originally, the federal government, looking to create a second transcontinental railroad, in 1867 granted a franchise to the Atlantic & Pacific Railroad, which was affiliated with (and later became part of) the Santa Fe Railroad. But in true robber baron tradition, despite the fact that it was involved in building its own transcontinental line, the Sunset Route, from New Orleans to LA, SP jumped in and built the Mojave-Needles segment to prevent

A train climbs the Tehachapi loop, a major engineering achievement, which allows mile-long freight trains to spiral up the steep mountain range not far from the California Correctional Institution.

the Atlantic & Pacific, that is, the Santa Fe Railroad, from entering California. In an elaborate swap involving other routes, Santa Fe ended up with the line anyway, along with an agreement to run its trains on the SP line from Mojave to Bakersfield through the Tehachapi Loop.

One of the water stops along this line, near the lakebed, was called "the Rod," short for Rodriguez, then the dry lake's name. The air base was first established out here because the vast hard playa called Rogers Dry Lake Bed provided an ideal landing surface. "Rogers" is a shortened version of "Rodgers," which is itself an anglicized version of Rodriguez. The base was originally Muroc Army Air Base, named for the word carved into the playa to point pilots to the landing area. In other words, the army named the base after its own markings.

Signs in the town of Boron: Arabian RV Oasis, River of Life Church, Desert Lake Apartments. The hope of water a predominant theme. Then "Visit Boron Again." No lunch.

On a ridge to the south, the buildings of the Rocket Propulsion Lab are as close as we'll get to Edwards AFB, because the Department of Homeland Security has closed the base to visitors. So, we miss the historic 10-by-20-foot mural, "Golden Age of Flight Test," and the displays on Chuck Yeager's sound-barrier-breaking flight and the first Columbia space shuttle landing. We won't see the commemoration of the life of Glen Edwards, the base's namesake, who survived missions against the Germans over Tunisia only to die testing a flying wing bomber over this desert.

But the boron mine is open, once owned by Borax of 20-mule-team fame, now "a member of the Rio Tinto Group." We pass the ILWU

Local 30 Headquarters. To survive the post-World War II Red Scare, the Western Federation of Miners, once a radical part of the IWW that had turned Communist, merged with the International Longshoremen's and Warehousemen's Union (ILWU). So the union has a local here, though there isn't a shore in sight.

We can see tailings piled along the horizon. As we approach, the piles become all we can see, become a line of hills, and then the mine pit itself inverts the landscape.

"This is big," one of us says into stunned silence.

We see no movement at first, then make out a small truck crossing one of the lower terraces: a flea in the rings of a flea circus. The desert silence is unbroken. A half hour later, the truck appears again, having lumbered out of the pit at last, huge, its engine now a roar, its wheels twice the height of a man: a 789 Cat, carrying who knows how many tons of ore. I count seventeen terraces; we estimate that each one is two stories high (or deep, depending on how you look at it). We enter the mine museum; a docent points out a dark, tiny hole in the lower depths of the pit: the entrance to the old, underground mine, converted in the 1950s to a bomb shelter extensive enough to hold 12,000 people: all the military personnel on Edwards AFB and all the mine employees, including the ones in the formerly Communist union.

The glossy brochure we are given in the mine museum assures us that "boron is part of the natural world." We are allowed to take samples from piles of six-sided crystals dumped on the edge of the parking lot. Mine is three inches long, its translucence shot with striations, in which mysterious, black, fernlike structures are suspended. Victor takes several, one for each son and a handful for his wife's second-grade classroom.

But we still have had no lunch, so dive into a taqueria on the edges of Tehachapi where chains of freight cars lumber by: hoppers coded BORX linked to red Hanjin containers and auto-carriers masquerading as cattle cars. All of this freight is routed at Tehachapi, up the highway from the Loop. After a detour to take a look at a "California Correctional Institution" marked on the map that we never manage to see, we arrive at the Loop's vista point as the light is fading. From what we can see, the track at the base of the steep slope below simply runs straight into the hillside. We wait until full dark, straining our ears for the rumble of freight. On the map, the Loop looks like a dropped piece of string. Despite the fact that two railroad companies run tons and tons of freight through here, not one train arrives, from either direction. Abandoning all hope, we descend into Bakersfield.

The California Aqueduct in the San Joaquin Valley moves water from Northern California to the south, but the political and environmental effects flow in all directions.

19

You Can't Step in the Same River Even Once

The environmental cost of California's historic and ongoing growth has been enormous—agriculture, industry, and the presence of tens of millions of people have transformed ecosystems throughout the state. While the rich abundance of the state had seemed inexhaustible to all but a few in the first half of the twentieth century, by the 1970s, environmental devastation was obvious: massive oil spills, water shortages, toxic dumps, clear-cut forests, unburied nuclear waste, dried up rivers and lakes, collapsing fisheries, and choking smog. These multiple calamities spurred a new activism.

Bodies of water revealed some of the most far-reaching environmental changes. Draining, filling, and diversion had devastated San Francisco Bay and the Great Valley's complex ecosystems of rivers, marshes, and ponds. By the mid-twentieth century less than 10 percent of the Central Valley's original wetlands remained intact. Between 1920 and 1950, because of the use of powerful pumps for wells, the water table in parts of the Central Valley dropped by 200 feet. Increasing salinity rendered irrigated fields sterile or required massive amounts of water to flush salts. Spectacular and highly visible collapses of bird and salmon populations alarmed the public—in the 19th century an estimated 60 million ducks and geese had used the valley; a hundred years later, there were little more than 2 million. Salmon had once been so numerous during their spawning runs that farmers scooped them out of rivers by the ton to use as fertilizer. Then the massive water projects of mid-century decreased flows or blocked the fishes' passage. Clear-cut mountainsides dumped eroded soil into the rivers and, by the 1990s, combined with pollution and climate change to drive the fish to near extinction in the Sacramento and San Joaquin rivers.

Industrial and experimental processes in the aerospace and high-tech industries spread toxic pollution in the air, water, and land. In addition to contributing to smog, solvents used in the factories and labs saturated the ground, often poisoning under-

The McColl toxic dump for oil industry waste in Orange County was capped by the EPA as a Superfund project and is now part of the lovely Los Coyotes Country Club golf course.

ground aquifers for miles around. Polluted water from one of the largest toxic sites in the country, the Stringfellow Acid Pits in Riverside County, poured into the nearby community of Glen Avon during a storm in 1978. Toxic waste spills also spoiled the soil and groundwater in the Santa Clara Valley in Northern California. Once "the Valley of Heart's Delight," Santa Clara County eventually had 23 Superfund toxic sites, more than any other county in the country. The sites came courtesy of such clean industry pioneers as Hewlett Packard, Fairchild Semiconductor, Intel, Teledyne, Westinghouse, and Applied Materials. California as a whole has more than 2,600 toxic waste sites identified by the EPA.

Modern environmental activism combined earlier conservationist tactics with more militant 60s-style demonstrations and even occasional acts of sabotage by a few of the most dogmatic. One of the people who made the change from conservationist to environmentalist was climber and photographer David Brower, who took control of the venerable Sierra Club in the early 1950s. Brower and his staff steadily built the organization from a small regional group of little more than 1,000 to a national institution of 77,000 by 1969. Frustrated at the moderation of the Sierra Club, Brower left in 1969 to found the more activist Friends of the Earth. Brower, though from an earlier generation, supported the militancy of younger environmentalists, explaining: "Polite conservationists leave no mark save the scars upon the Earth that could have been prevented had they stood their ground."

Fish and fowl crises in the valley and along the coasts, the disappearance of birds of prey due to the effects of the pesticide DDT, and water-quality problems sparked a new political coalition of environmentalists, conservationists, scientists, and hunters to fight for the preservation and protection of the remaining wetlands. At the same time community anti-pollution efforts drew in people motivated by fear of the effects of toxic pollution on their communities and families. Local activists, including suburban moms such as Penny Newman, fought to clean up Stringfellow. Working-class, poor, and native communities began mobilizing as well. By the 1980s, environmentalists had achieved widespread legitimacy, and California pioneered a series of environmental agreements and regulations that set the standard nationwide.

Renewed fights over water marked the beginning of a significant shift in state water and environmental politics. Despite the *Gold Run* decision, early efforts to limit water use and diversion for environmental reasons rarely succeeded. That began to change in the 1960s with renewed opposition to dam building and river diversions. Voters bitterly divided along north-south lines, barely approving water bonds in 1960. The acrimony of the dispute renewed bluster about the state splitting in two. From Shasta Dam at the north end of the Great Valley to the Friant Dam 300 miles to the south, the Bureau of Reclamation had built 147 dams. Even with Central Valley Project and the poetically-named State Water Project, there still wasn't enough water. Today the State Water Project carries water 444 miles through the state, bringing Northern California water south in the California Aqueduct, which can be seen running alongside Interstate 5 through the Central Valley. The water is pumped over the Tehachapi Mountains and into the LA region. The San Joaquin River used to flow north to the delta, but now its water flows southwards, away from the delta (where it was "wasted"), uphill. The result is that the San Joaquin riverbed is dry for 60 miles.

As dams were built to redirect Sierra water over the last 150 years, less and less fresh water made it in to the delta. The tides pulled salty seawater farther and farther upstream into the delta as the decades passed. Salinity problems had been apparent early in the 20th century. Contra Costa County farmers in Pittsburg and Antioch, for instance, had to stop using irrigation water from

Kesterson Mutations

In the early 1980s, scientists discovered hundreds of bizarrely deformed bird chicks in the Kesterson Wildlife Refuge, west of Modesto. The cause was not pesticides but naturally occurring selenium (the poison in locoweed that makes cows act, well, loco): evaporation concentrated the element in the water to toxic levels. Selenium may have been natural, but how it got to toxic levels was anything but.

Diminished river flows in the valley increased the naturally occurring salts and trace elements in irrigation water. Since increased salt concentrations hurt crops, "family farmers" Southern Pacific, Standard Oil, JG Boswell, and others on the west side of the valley flushed their enormous but poorly drained fields into a canal—more properly, a drain—designed to carry the over-salinated water into Suisun Bay. Except that the drain was never completed; instead, when construction stopped in 1973, agricultural runoff flowed into a reservoir in the Refuge.

In the ensuing political uproar, the Department of the Interior's Fish and Wildlife Service tried to stop delivery of irrigation water to the farms—perhaps the only cardinal sin in California water politics. That failed, but they did succeed in closing the drain. It took more than a million yards of dirt to fill in the polluted reservoir and surrounding pools. The Kesterson Refuge has largely recovered, though in rainy years selenium rises to the surface, causing renewed deformities.

Suisun Bay, the inland extension of San Francisco Bay, as early as 1926. The Army Corps of engineers had modestly proposed damming the entire north bay but abandoned the plan in the 1950s as a bit too complicated. Engineers with the State Water Project proposed a peripheral canal that would keep fresh water separate from the brackish delta water. The canal was to start just north of the capital and carry the water from the Sacramento River into the California Aqueduct. Engineers designed the canal large enough to swallow the entire summertime flow of the river. It seemed like water business as usual in 1977 when a Southern California legislator introduced a bill to build the canal and thereby finish the State Water Project.

But agribusinesses, particularly JG Boswell, the nation's largest cotton grower, actually supported environmentalists opposed to the peripheral canal, funding opposition with $1.2

Salt laden fields in the San Joaquin Valley reveal the mineral cost of irrigating the area's heavy clay soils. (Photo: Scott Bauer, USDA)

million. Agribusiness hadn't suddenly become conservationist but ironically feared environmental protections inserted in the bill as a sweetener, which would have protected the delta and North Coastal rivers had the canal been built. Voters in 1982 overwhelmingly rejected the canal in a statewide referendum— the first time a major water project had been defeated at the polls. Since then battles over delta water have increased, with the listing of delta fish as endangered, the collapse of levees in winter storms, and declines in drinking water quality.

The peripheral canal defeat heralded a series of reversals for water engineering. Having successfully diverted all of the Owens River water by 1913, LA's appropriately named Department of Water and Power (LADWP) further diverted almost all the snow-fed streams that flowed into Mono Lake, which lies at the base of the Sierra Nevada Mountains, downhill from Yosemite Park, on the eastern edge of the Great Basin. The lake is an alkali "sea whose flowerless shores seem scarcely to belong to the habitable earth," as 19th-century geologist Israel Russell described it. Yet the lake supports tens of thousands of birds, particularly sea gulls, which feed on lake brine shrimp and breed on the islands in the center of the lake. As a result of LAWDP diversions, the lake's level dropped nearly forty-five feet by 1979, allowing predators to get to the island bird colonies.

When biologists from the University of California discovered that the gull populations at Mono Lake were on the verge of collapse, a group of dedicated graduate students teamed with the bird-loving Audubon Society to save the Lake. In 1983 the California Supreme Court handed down one of the most far-reaching environmental decisions of the era. The creeks feeding the lake could not be diverted, the court found, without taking into account the "human and environmental uses of Mono Lake—uses protected by the public trust doctrine." The idea of a "public trust" in navigable rivers and streams had been used a century before in the *Gold Run* case. But now places like Mono Lake, the court found, had value as places of beauty and recreation whether or not they were navigable. The Court ruled that while LA was entitled to take some of the water, this right had to be balanced with the "condition" of the streams.

The 1983 defeats of the overweening LADWP, the largest municipal utility in the country, and of the peripheral canal, were part of a larger shift in the balance of power in state water politics. Conflicts over water quality and preservation of wild rivers flowed turbulently through the 1980s and 90s. On the western slope of the Sierra, a group of river rafters and environmentalists launched a campaign in 1973 to stop the New Melones Dam on the Stanislaus River, part of the federal Central Valley Project. The campaign against the dam failed, but river activists succeeded in getting fifteen other California rivers protected from further alteration. Other local advocacy groups used the Mono Lake cases to insist on restrictions on property rights to protect the environment. Starting in the 1950s, increased urban development around once pristine Lake Tahoe spurred activists to fight for growth limits. The movement grew substantially in the 80s with declines in the astounding clarity of the lake—it was once possible to see objects 100 feet below the water's surface. The lake had lost a third of its clarity since the 1960s. Conservationists won court decisions, including one in 1984 that temporarily froze all development around the lake. In 2007, water even began to flow again in the Owens River. Most recently, the same legal doctrine led to an agreement to put some water back into the San Joaquin River.

Environmental crises similarly led to changes in resource extraction, particularly mining and oil drilling. In 1969 a Union

Oil offshore well blew out, spilling almost a hundred thousand barrels of thick gooey petroleum along the Santa Barbara coast in an oil slick covering 800 square miles. Thousands of birds, fish, and sea mammals died as volunteers struggled to save them. Union Oil President Fred Hartley, showing a lack of public relations savvy, was "impressed at the publicity that death of birds receives versus the loss of people in our country in this day and age." Santa Barbara activists created the cleverly named GOO, Get Oil Out, to campaign against coastal drilling, one of the most successful environmental movements in the state. In response, Governor Brown pushed for a California Coastal Commission in 1976. The Commission managed to stop some large developments, but also drove property values to stratospheric levels, further reinforcing the exclusive character of many coastal towns. Today federal and state laws restrict drilling on the petroleum-rich California coast, though 21 offshore rigs in the Santa Barbara Channel continue to produce oil and natural gas.

Energy development also led to one of the largest left-wing movements of the 1970s and 80s. Energy monopoly Pacific Gas and Electric had begun developing a nuclear power plant at Diablo Canyon on the coast in San Luis Obispo County in the mid-60s. Activists with Mothers for Peace, a local anti-Vietnam War organization, saw a connection between nuclear power and nuclear weapons and began protesting the plant. The Sierra Club had supported the use of supposedly clean energy nuclear power, but more militant environmentalists flocked to the cause. The discovery of an earthquake fault near the plant and multiple defects in its construction inspired further opposition. The movement against nuclear power had national connections—substantial protests against a nuclear power plant in New Hampshire by the Clamshell Alliance had inspired Californians to form their own group. Expressing solidarity with their bivalve brothers, they called their organization the Abalone Alliance. The Abalone Alliance drew thousands to anti-nuke protests, including a 1981 action in which 2,000 people committed civil disobedience. Despite this concerted opposition, the power plant began operation in 1985. Nonetheless, the anti-nuke movement raised sufficient concern about the safety of nuclear power, particularly after the Three Mile Island and Chernobyl disasters, that voters shut down the Rancho San Seco nuclear power plant near Sacramento.

The counterculture connections of the new environmental activists proved a mixed blessing for the movement, particu-

California's waterfowl population began recovering in the 1980s and 1990s but has declined again in recent years. (Photo: Gary Cramer, NFWS)

larly in battles over logging. Conflicts in remote logging towns between back-to-the-land hippies and locals that had begun in the 1960s and 70s worsened as the logging industry declined and environmental laws, such as the Endangered Species Act of 1973, restricted logging. Most famously, the federal government listed the Northern Spotted Owl as endangered in 1990. The owls lived in old growth coniferous forests, including the iconic redwoods of the Pacific Coast. Few old growth forests, areas with massive trees that had never been logged, survived into the late twentieth century. Radical environmentalists associated with the group Earth First! camped in trees marked for logging. A few even spiked trunks to prevent sawing or engaged in other forms of sabotage. Loggers viewed the young, longhaired militants as an alien threat to the survival of their communities. Worse, some logging companies had been bought up by speculators who demanded immediate profits from the forests, leading to increasingly destructive logging practices, most notoriously in the Headwaters Forest owned by stock speculator Charles Hurwitz's Maxxam Corporation. Earth First! leaders Judy Bari, a former carpenter, and Darryl Cherney, a folksinger, had tried to reach out to loggers and even helped found a branch of a nouveau IWW in Humboldt County, but these minimal efforts failed to overcome the deep social divisions of the North Coast. At the peak of the conflict in 1990, someone bombed the car of Cherney and Bari as they drove through Oakland. The Oakland police, acting on false information from the FBI, arrested the pair for "ecoterrorism." They were acquitted and won substantial judgments against the city and the FBI. In the mid-1990s, more mainstream environmentalists brokered a compromise preserving some old growth stands in Headwaters. Bari died of cancer in 1997, but her legacy lives on in an activist foundation and among countercultural environmental activists around the state.

Environmental regulation and the historic preservation of cities had dramatically reduced pollution in coastal areas and saved much of California's most beautiful and interesting places from destruction by the early years of the new millennium. Yet these victories also further emphasized California's economic polarities. Anti-development rules have indeed protected much of the coast, but they also drove up property values in coastal towns to stratospheric levels and prevented the construction of less expensive multi-family housing. Restrictions on urban infill development and increased density, a result of community mobilization against the aggressive urban renewal of the 1950s and 60s, has preserved the architectural but not the economic or social character of center-city areas. Minimum acreage requirements for new construction in outlying areas—intended to limit sprawl—made many rural areas similarly unaffordable. Budget cuts forced the state and localities to charge for many previously free public services, such as camping in state parks or using park picnic areas, which limits access for the poor. Wealthy urbanites enjoy consuming lovingly cultivated organic fruits and vegetables produced by charming characters at picturesque farmers' markets or served in casually hip restaurants, while many of their poorer neighbors live in areas without even a nearby supermarket.

Ian Parker, Evanescent Light

Tulare Lake

In a year of heavy rain, Tulare Lake will reappear. In the spring of 2006, the internet showed aerial images of water in the lakebed. We decide to sidetrack on a drive from the Bay Area to Los Angeles, to see if we can get find it. In the middle of the Central Valley, Interstate 5 is called the "Westside Freeway." On either side, miles of mechanically squared-off orchard trees, hills corrugated by cows' hooves. Swallows dart out from mud nests plastered below the parapet of every overpass. Highway 33, also known as Derrick Road, comes in at an acute angle from the north, merges with 5 for five or six miles, then heads west through the Anticline Hills towards Coalinga. From there it will run parallel to 5 through a moonscape of oil wells—on the maps, hundreds of small blue circles on the tidy grid of thin red quartersection lines. We see none of them; we are on the lookout for Highway 198 east, our first planned sweep across the midsection of the valley. The road runs next to the barbed wire fencing and high walls of the Lemoore Naval Air Station and its peeling, wind-chapped barracks. At the forlorn junction of 198 and 41, we turn south again.

The ambitiously named town of Stratford is equally forlorn and peeling. Storefronts remain, none occupado. Anyone who still lives here is working somewhere else: in the fields, on the derricks, or driving mowers over scruffy golf course lawns.

A little way past the town, we see a sign for the Kings River. What we see when we turn on the dirt drive is the place where the Kings River is reduced at last to a canal. A man is fishing from the concrete dam. Victor talks with him while I crunch along the muddy bank in the opposite direction to get closer to a pack of birds shrieking in a wedge of sycamores. They are as large as magpies but lack the dramatic white-and-black tuxedo coloration. They spread long brown tails into diamond-shaped fans as they swoop from tree to tree. Grackles.

The man says he knows nothing about a lake in this vicinity, and if there was one, he boasts, he would know. Yet the map shows us the lakebed begins more or less right where we are. From the small dam that a man can walk across in fifteen strides, the Blakely Canal curves to the west, Highway 41 beside it, and the Tulare Lake Canal curves to the east, two long arms embracing the blank space where a lake used to be. The Kings River, now itself a canal, runs in a straight line toward the middle, where it meets the Tule River, channelized into an equally straight line, to form a perfect right angle.

We continue south on 41. The afternoon shadows are growing long, we are hungry. In Kettleman City near a major toxic dump site, a Mexican grocery advertises *comidas*. I eat too much of the best burrito I can ever remember eating: the meat slow-cooked over smoke before being slow-cooked again in *chili colorado*. Fair compensation for failed casting about for phantom lakes. After Kettleman City, Kettleman Junction, gas stations and fast-food chains clustered around the interstate's on-off ramps. Resigned to our failure, we have begun to discuss how many hours of driving we have left when Victor yells, "THERE IT IS!" "Where? Where?!" "Over there!" But it's only visible from the high point of the overpass; I've missed it.

The next off-ramp is five miles down. We get off, get back on heading north, get off again. At the top of the ramp we pull over. In the far distance, beyond the rooftops of the Taco Bell and the Chevron, beyond the spectrum of several rows of spring-green fields lies a long, long, dark blue line. Lake waters, once again gathering in their ancient bed.

The largest power plant in the state shares the coastal waters with a fishing fleet at Moss Landing on Monterey Bay. The plant warms the Bay, attracting fish to the area.

20

To Live and Work in CA

On a warm May Day in 2006, millions of people left their jobs and classrooms to take to the streets in protest of restrictive immigration laws. It was one of the largest days of mass mobilization in US history. Coming on the heels of a similarly enormous demonstration a few weeks before, the marchers expressed a widely shared commitment of the Mexican- and Central-American communities in California and throughout the US to counter negative policies toward immigrants. The marchers also made clear that the great wave of post-World War II immigration to California had fundamentally transformed the make up of the state. Soon, many believed, political power would shift as well. Or would it?

By marching on May Day, the crowds harkened back to a long tradition of working-class activism, but the largely Latino demonstrators wore white tee shirts, not Socialist red, and focused their common demands not on calls for workers' power but for greater respect for the rights of newcomers to the US. This moderation expressed the character of the main organizers: unions, the Catholic Church, and Spanish language media. Yet rather than bringing broad social change, the result was a strengthening of the ethnic and economic divisions that had long split California.

How did this great lack of change happen—or, rather, not happen? It began with the collapse of the state's heavy industry and military economy. Rather than respond with political or social activism, Californians took a series of economic gambles, joining speculative booms in high tech and housing. Rapid economic growth after deindustrialization increased inequality in the state. Broad growth had been key to the state's political economy—without it the state's politicians could no longer create compromises to win support for budgets and programs. While the state voted overwhelmingly Democratic, a cohesive minority of conservative ideologues held legislative veto power. As California's economic base fractured, political stalemate ensued.

By the early 1980s, deindustrialization hit the older cities in California hard. Unionized blue-collar jobs disappeared as plants closed or modernized. Steel, auto, tire, aluminum, and other heavy industries closed down, putting thousands out of work and devastating nearby towns. By the mid-80s the state had only one auto plant, a joint venture between GM and Toyota in Fremont, and no integrated steel manufacturer. Worse, the end of the Cold War led to a massive military retrenchment—forty bases closed and contracts were cut. This post-Cold War downturn hit Southern California hardest. Factories shut down, tax revenues fell, schools faltered, and cities emptied out. Aerospace employment dropped by 75 percent, and overall the state lost approximately 300,000 high-paying jobs in the decade. Defense spending, which had provided half of the state's economic growth in the 1940s and 50s, now led the state to the brink of disaster.

Political solutions appeared few and far between for the defense industries. Senator Barbara Boxer suggested to the industry "you can build the best buses in the world," but defense contractors never got on that bus. The profound shift in California's economy appeared most clearly in 1995 when the number of jobs in the growing entertainment industry exceeded the number in aerospace. For people on the lower end of society's income hierarchy, the decline in heavy industry and slowdown in construction created increasing hardship. Unemployment rates for people of color other than Asians increased at a far faster rate than for whites. Poor and minority neighborhoods bore the brunt of the economic restructuring as blue-collar jobs became harder to find.

Homeless rates began to increase in the state in the late 1970s as redevelopment cleared the city centers of SRO hotels while policy changes in the state legislature and in Washington reduced affordability requirements for new construction. By the 1980s the problem began to make headlines, as the sight of homeless people living on the streets and parks became commonplace. By the late 1990s, the number of homeless hit over 300,000—more than 1 in every 100 people in the state.

Homeless figures do not include the substantial migrant farm worker population of the state, nearly a million people, including many thousands of children. Fieldworker housing has suffered—in 1976 farmers and agribusinesses provided temporary shelter for 45,000 people; by 2000, that number had dropped to 23,000. The migrants, who travel from field to field following the crops—as migrants have done for more than 100 years—

sometimes can afford temporary housing in nearby towns but more often camp out in canyons, forests, and fields.

The economy in California, unlike in many rustbelt states, survived the industrial retrenchment. The diversity of the economy, the strength of its agricultural sector, and the growth of the high tech and entertainment industries kept the state growing. California's economy was further strengthened by its connection to expanding global trade. The computer and telecommunications revolution spurred a record-setting boom in the 1990s, though the heavy manufacturing sector continued to suffer even as the economy grew. Service jobs on the low end and high-tech design, programming, and commercial jobs on the high end did grow.

Silicon Valley entrepreneurs had made fortunes from the development of the semi-conductor and mainframe computers, but it was not until the mass marketing of the personal computer in the 1980s that the valley became a national symbol of techno-commercial savvy. With the rapid development of the Internet in the 1990s, a high-tech boom shifted the center of gravity of the state's economy to the north, first to Santa Clara and San Mateo counties where computer hardware was developed and

Homelessness in California, already twice the national rate, increased as the economic crisis deepened after 2007. The number of encampments such as this one in Fresno multiplied in 2010. (Photo: Kelly Borkert)

then to San Francisco, where the dot-com industry fed a new youth culture. The dot-commers often drew their informal personal style from earlier countercultures, but this boom had more in common with the Gold Rush than the Summer of Love. In the six years starting in 1994, high-tech employment more than doubled to 340,000 workers. Thousands of ambitious young people flooded into the region, hoping to strike it rich with new forms of enterprise. Housing prices skyrocketed and traffic worsened, but prosperity enlivened the cities and suburbs.

The success of the tech industry, both hardware and software, spawned a feverish optimism. Promoters spoke of an end to the business cycle, of a "new economy" that would put an end to brick-and-mortar businesses as virtual companies would supplant them. A few entrepreneurs struck it rich as start-up companies received massive infusions of cash for ideas ranging from the brilliant to the absurd. Some of the best developed an entire new industry and generated unbelievable fortunes for people such as the youthful founders of Google and Yahoo: Sergey Brin, Larry Page, Jerry Yang, and David Filo.

Others dot-coms are memorable only for their stupidity, like Ismell, which promised to add scents to your web browser, or Cyberrebate, which provided 100 percent rebates on all the overpriced goods it sold. At the peak of the boom, tiny software and web companies were worth more than major industrial firms. For instance, internet portal Yahoo's stock was worth $115 billion in early 2000, making the company's stock larger than the combined value of Boeing, H.J. Heinz, and General Motors.

Despite the economic boom of the late 1990s, economic inequality increased dramatically. Computer manufacturers took advantage of globalization to send hundreds of thousands of lower-level jobs overseas, dramatically cutting industrial employment in Silicon Valley. Many enterprising young people made decent wages working extremely long hours in the high-tech industry; a few made incredible fortunes. But far more people toiled in low-wage jobs—the gap between the top income earners and the bottom grew at a faster rate than any other state—the rich got richer faster and the poor stayed poor.

The new economy turned out to not be exempt from the boom-and-bust cycle after all—in 2000, dot-com retailers began to fail, and increasing interest rates tipped the stock market into free fall. Trillions of imaginary dollars disappeared from companies' stock values. Accounting scandals in Internet, telecommunications, and finance companies further shattered confidence.

Enormous numbers of migrant workers, including families like the Villas, in Gilroy in 1983, continue to provide the muscle behind California's modern economy.

One of the most spectacular collapses of the dot-com era was Webvan, a food delivery service. The company leadership had no experience with the grocery business but raised billions selling stock. It lost $1.5 billion in 1.5 years. (Photo: Mark Coggins)

Real-world effects soon followed—young entrepreneurs gave up on their ambitions and moved out of the Bay Area. Santa Clara County's population fell by 75,000 in just three years. The number of 25–34 year olds living in San Francisco dropped by 25 percent. Trendy restaurants closed as companies cut back on expense accounts. Unemployment in Santa Clara County shot up from little over 1 percent in 2001 to more than 9 percent in 2002. Still, a strong tech sector survived the bust—and Silicon Valley remains a global center of the industry.

While the crash devastated the Bay Area's economy for years, the state as a whole survived because of the diversity of its industries. Imports and exports continued to grow, sustaining the state's ports. Businesses connected directly to the global market flourished and jobs in the export sector paid better than in many other areas of the economy. California boosters liked to boast that the state's economy made it the world's sixth largest economy, accounting for nearly 15 percent of all US economic activity in 2002. Despite the shock of the crash and the economic crisis following the September 11th attacks, the state remained a massive industrial, agricultural, and service producer.

The US took California from Mexico in the 19th century in pursuit of an older vision of globalization. The strategy succeeded beyond the most extravagant dreams of President Polk. The state has played a key role in making the US a great military and economic power in both hemispheres of the globe. Its strategic position and its export-oriented economy, from the otter pelts of the early 19th century to the agricultural produce of the 20th to the microchips and software of the 21st, have made California the country's most successful expression of globalization. California's docks have become the main location for the import of foreign manufactures, particularly Chinese and Japanese goods. Its ports hum with business. Commerce, however, is not the only cross-border movement in an increasingly interdependent world.

From the 1980s through the first decade of the 21st century, the US, particularly California, experienced its largest immigration wave in history. Many of the immigrants had been displaced by economic changes at home brought on by the same global forces that increased world commerce. Others were refugees from civil wars and the collapse of the Communist bloc.

It is easy to see why this great wave of immigration raised expectations of a big shift in the state's racial politics. California was home to nearly 4.5 million Mexican-born people, far more than any other state. The Mexican/Latino population, immi-

Immigration officers arrest a man during a round-up of undocumented and criminal immigrants in South Gate near Los Angeles in 2009. Deportations of immigrants rose substantially under Presidents Bush and Obama. (Photo: Courtesy of ICE)

grant and American-born, increased ten times from 1950 to 1990, growing from approximately 7 percent of the state's population to more than 25 percent. Other immigrants also swelled the non-Anglo populations—Central and South Americans, particularly Guatemalans, Salvadorans, and Nicaraguans. The 2000 census counted more than 2 million non-Mexican Latinos in the state. Substantial Asian migration also contributed to the state's ethnic complexity. The percentage of Asian-born or descended people shot up from less than 2 percent of the population in 1950 to nearly 10 percent in 1990, making a greater portion of California's population of Asian origin than at any other time in the state's history, even more than in the 1840s and 1850s when Chinese immigrants sought "Gold Mountain." In 2000 the state population became a majority of minorities—with no single racial/ethnic group predominating.

Asian educational achievements led to increasing enrollment in the state's universities. Admissions officers at the University of California system met rising Asian enrollment in the 1980s with a counter-affirmative action program that penalized Asian students. After a federal investigation revealed the program at the flagship UC Berkeley campus, the university chancellor publicly apologized. Asian, South Asian, and Pacific Islander enrollment jumped from 20 percent in 1986 to more than 27 percent in 1990 and 40 percent in 2000. But these figures for Asian-American successes in school and in the burgeoning high-tech and technical fields hid stark differences in achievement within this group of people. Southeast Asians and many Chinese immigrants lacked the skills and education to succeed in their new country. Nothing so starkly demonstrated the dangers for immigrant workers as the discovery of dozens of undocumented Thai garment workers who had been imprisoned in a garment factory in El Monte near LA in 1995.

The El Monte scandal brought to light the deplorable conditions in California's garment manufacturing industry. During the 1970s, the unionized garment industry had collapsed. LA nonetheless retained thousands of small factories sewing garments in competition with overseas companies. By the mid-90s nearly 100,000 people, mostly Asian and Latina women immigrants, labored in sweatshop conditions. The passage of NAFTA shifted jobs to Mexico and the entry of China into the World Trade Organization brought Chinese-made goods into the US at ever cheaper prices, pushing US employers in the needle trades to ever more brutal practices. The El Monte slave labor case brought increased inspection and a revitalized popular movement against sweatshops. Yet trade union efforts to start cooperative apparel manufacturing in LA in 2002 failed quickly despite backing from ice cream tycoon Ben Cohen.

Mexican immigrants moved from the fields and into jobs formerly held by Anglo workers. The building trades, once a whites-only domain, become overwhelmingly Mexican, first in Southern California but by the end of the millennium in the entire state. In 1980, 40 percent of Mexican-born men in California worked in construction, mining, or transportation—compared to 20 percent for the population as a whole. In the fields, Mixtec, Zapotec, and other indigenous Mexican people, many of whom didn't speak Spanish, replaced the mestizos who were able to move into higher-paying urban jobs.

Some union-minded immigrants revitalized the labor movement, which had been devastated by the defense and heavy industry cuts of the 1980s and 90s. The percentage of workers in unions had plummeted from more than 40 percent in the 1950s to little more than 15 percent at the end of the millennium. Mexican and Latino workers often had experience in the militant trade unions or radical politics in their homelands and proved open to organizing drives. Chicano and Latino organizers, some veterans of the United Farm Workers, led strikes by sheetrock hangers

By 1998, Native Americans had regained their pre-contact population of 300,000. Pow wows, like this one at UC Davis in 2003, blend many traditions but help pass on Indian culture.

and hotel workers in Los Angeles in the early 90s, ushering in a new era of labor militancy. Over the next fifteen years janitors, hotel workers, home healthcare workers, and even graduate students in the University of California joined unions.

Some of the most effective labor organizations came in the booming healthcare industry, where nurses in particular waged successful strikes against hospitals and HMOs throughout the state yet maintained public sympathy. The California Nurses Association and the state's two teachers' unions, all led by women, successfully countered efforts to weaken their organizations through the initiative process. As a consequence of the new service union militancy and the influx of people of color and highly educated workers into the labor movement, California bucked the national trend with the percentage of union members in the workforce actually increasing in the new millennium. Nurses Association leader Rose Ann DeMoro explained the reasons for their success: "We are a genuine social union. We believe the interests of our members and the public interest are identical." Indeed, the CNA requires its officers to continue working at patients' bedsides. It championed popular issues that also helped unions' needs, such as a law that limits the number of patients assigned to hospital nurses. Yet the CNA and DeMoro, once called "Mother Teresa in brass knuckles," fought bitter conflicts with other unions, particularly with the Service Employees International Union.

Beyond the workplace, immigrant diversity has transformed cities around the state, but particularly Los Angeles and Long Beach, which are today among the most diverse places in the country. LA residents speak 113 languages, from Africaans to Marathi to Yiddish. Many of the suburbs of the big cities also experienced growing immigration, mostly Mexican and Asian. Anaheim, in formerly uniform Orange County, has speakers of 29 different languages—though 95 percent speak Spanish or English. Greater diversity has brought challenges to the school systems as more and more students need time to develop English-language skills. From the 1980s on, California's chronically underfunded public schools saw language-proficiency skills drop at the same time that their budgets suffered.

Efforts to help Spanish-speaking students, and to a smaller degree, Chinese speakers through bilingual classes, brought a powerful reaction from politicians. A neoconservative entrepreneur, Ron Unz, playing on and responding to Anglo fears of submersion in a polyglot society or of potential civil strife because of ethno-linguistic division, in 1998 pushed Proposition 227, which promised to end bilingual education in the state. Voters endorsed it overwhelmingly. Convinced that bilingual education actually helped kids learn English better and succeed in school, educators found ways to work around the intention of the law by allowing parents to choose to put their kids in bilingual classes. Raised by a single mom in LA who subsisted on welfare (he later opposed welfare, claiming recipients should find minimum wage jobs), Unz tried but failed to turn his success at initiatives into higher office.

Inequality in California grew from the 1970s on, even increasing between people with middle and upper incomes. The enormous immigration of poor and less-skilled people along with the decline of heavy industry increased the mass of low-wage workers in California. At the same time, demand for highly trained and highly skilled people in tech, commerce, and the professions swelled the burgeoning upper middle class. Over the twenty years from 1986–2006, all of the US experienced a growing disparity between the top 20 percent of earners and the bottom—but California's was one of the worst. The Golden State had never had an egalitarian economy, but the shrinking economic gaps of the postwar boom were a thing of the past.

Meanwhile, the environmental and anti-redevelopment movements of the 1960s and 70s succeeded in limiting urban growth, forcing the construction of new housing farther and farther from city centers that were themselves less and less affordable for poor and even middle-income people. Housing prices throughout the urban areas of the state picked up from their postwar slump in the mid-70s. House values more than tripled between 1970 and 1980, doubled between 1980 and 1990, and doubled again between 1990 and 2005. In the craziest years of the boom, 2002 to 2005, house prices increased by about 20 percent a year. House prices peaked in early 2007 at a stratospheric $484,000-median statewide and much, much higher in the coastal areas. Housing construction grew quickly and thousands of people earned a living in the business. In 2006, 15 percent of people in the state worked in construction and real estate, a much larger share of total employment than just ten years before. And these figures don't include the millions of people who bored their friends at parties with obsessive talk of markets, remodels, equity, and sales.

The huge price rise meant that less than one in four Californian families could afford to buy a middle-priced house in the state (compared to almost two in three nationwide). At the worst of the housing bubble, fewer than 15 percent of San Franciscans and 11 percent of Santa Barbara residents could afford to buy a home. California had the second lowest rate of homeownership in the country. The newest suburbs are among the most racially diverse, but housing segregation is determined more by income and wealth. Worst for poor people, rental housing failed to grow with the state's population. The vast majority of lower-income renters paid more than 60 percent of their income for rent. The poor lived in overcrowded apartments and their adult children stayed home longer, the specter of homelessness lurking outside their doors. Restrictions on new construction and plummeting rates of rental property and apartment construction forced lower-income people to move farther and farther from their jobs and to take advantage of risky loans to buy homes. People in the inner cities lucky enough to own property saw their wealth shoot up. Some used the funds to compensate for the wide disparity in incomes between working-class and upper middle-class jobs. Black and Latino families with the means moved quickly out of redlined cities and neighborhoods just as rising rental costs pushed their poorer neighbors to the edge of desperation. Debt skyrocketed. The entire housing-market edifice, which accounted for an enormous portion of economic activity in the state, was built on the widely accepted belief that real-estate values, like the stock market, would only go up.

Then in 2006 the bubble burst. Interest rates rose and the romantically named "sub-prime" mortgages, loans used by poorer homebuyers and speculators, devolved from clever financial instruments into economic millstones. The market froze, and housing prices tumbled. Thousands who had bought homes as speculative investments or borrowed staggering amounts, counting on ever-rising prices in an ever-improving economy, found themselves in dire straights. Foreclosures shot up, particularly in the outlying sprawl areas where working-class people had hoped to live middle class lives. Homebuyers in Stockton, formerly a sleepy delta port in between San Francisco and Sacramento, had eagerly signed on to the speculative craziness, hoping to get their piece of real property in the growing corridor between the cities. But the crash hit Stockton hard; it had the highest foreclosure rate in the country in 2008. California as a whole led the nation in foreclosures—entire neighborhoods sprouted for-sale signs, particularly in the worst hit towns of the delta, the Central Valley, and the Inland Empire east of LA. People simply walked away from their homes, leaving appliances and clothing behind—or wrecked the place, taking even the plumbing to sell for scrap, in what realtors called a "trash out."

Soon the real-estate crisis spread to the entire financial industry and then to the rest of the economy. The US slid into the worst economic downturn since the Great Depression. California had among the highest unemployment rates in the country. The fallout from this economic crisis has spread across society in ways that we don't quite understand yet.

California's many cultural groups, regions, and economies had fostered an astounding diversity for hundreds of years—a complexity that only grew in the latter part of the twentieth century. One of the biggest issues in California's growing social diversity and economic polarization was the political fragmentation of the state. Los Angeles County and the Bay Area voted for liberal Democrats, while the Central Valley, San Diego, and most of the far suburbs and rural areas returned conservative

"McMansions," like this modest spread in Salinas, democratized the ostentatious taste of the robber barons. The percentage of new homes larger than 4,000 square feet doubled between between 1999 and 2009. (Photo: Brendel)

Republicans. Politically, California seemed more clearly to be two states—a culturally and politically liberal place centered on the major population centers of LA and the San Francisco Bay Area and a more conservative state everywhere else. Liberal and moderate Republicans found themselves isolated in the party of Earl Warren while savvy, sometimes corrupt politicos controlled the Democrats. Voting patterns in national, state, and local elections bore out these divisions with Republicans and religious conservatives winning offices from school boards to Congress in the 'burbs and the countryside and Democrats winning the big cities. With the state balanced between the far right and the moderate left, elections came to be decided by whichever side could turn out more of its core constituency to vote.

Despite slipping in the polls from the 1990s onward, conservatives were able to mobilize significant voter turnout on cultural issues, particularly same-sex marriage, immigration, and crime. The Republican Party tried to reproduce the victories of the Deukmejian-Wilson years. While the right was unable to regain control in the legislature, it did mobilize voters in large numbers. A significant victory came in 2008 when Democrats swept the state for Barack Obama but conservatives rallied older, religious voters to overturn the California Supreme Court's approval of same-sex marriage.

At the same time that liberal Democrats solidified their majority in state politics, Republicans became more and more deeply committed to conservative ideology, particularly on taxes and spending for social services. The state constitution requires a two-thirds majority in the legislature to raise taxes and until 2010 even pass a budget. Republicans holding on to a solid minority of seats would not go along with Democratic budget proposals, even when they did not raise taxes. Little shows the political character of the stalemate better than the rise of Arnold Schwarzenegger.

In 2003 voters recalled Governor Gray Davis, a Jerry Brown protégé who had originally run on a platform touting his bland character as proof of his administrative competence. In office, his bland character appeared to be political incompetence. He quickly alienated the labor movement and other core Democratic Party constituencies. Although reelected in 2002 over a weak Republican, he soon outraged anti-immigrant groups with his support for driver's licenses for undocumented immigrants. His poor handling of corporate-manipulated electrical shortages in the wake of utility deregulation further undercut his authority. When the state's perennial fiscal crisis forced him to propose sell-

Properties flooded the market as the housing bubble collapsed in 2007 and 2008. (Photo: The Truth About)

ing bonds and raising the vehicle registration fee to balance the state budget, conservatives launched a recall to marshal populist resentments against the unpopular governor.

Champion bodybuilder and movie star Arnold Schwarzenegger swept into office after the recall, easily defeating an unusually broad field of candidates that included Davis's lieutenant governor and a former porn star. Promising to "cut up the credit card," the new governor set out to reform the budget process. In office he proved to be a moderate, backing environmental protections and refusing to support a constitutional amendment against same-sex marriage. Soon, however, he resorted to the exact same deficit funding mechanisms that he excoriated Davis for—selling long-term bonds to fund short-term budget gaps. Blaming unions for his problems, he backed a series of anti-labor initiatives in a special 2005 election, but effective organizing by the Nurses Association and the Service Employees Union blocked his plans. The combination of anti-immigrant sentiment, the continuing binders imposed on state budgets by anti-tax restrictions, and the demagogic appeal against entrenched politicians indicated that, despite the turmoil of the recall election and Schwarzenegger's charisma,

The "Governator," Arnold Schwarzenegger, pictured here with his wife Maria Shriver at his swearing in ceremony in November 2003. Elected to two terms in office, Schwarzenegger proved to be as good an executive as he was an actor. (Steven Hallon, Office of the Governor)

California's political stalemate would continue. Indeed, each successive budget required more and more accounting gimmicks and "temporary" emergency borrowing as well as "revenue increases"—a euphemism for tax increases. At the same time, Republicans attacked their former hero for even considering raising taxes and their representatives voted as a bloc in the legislature against their governor's budgets. The stalemate has meant that California, the wealthiest state in the US, has a cobbled-together budget, unpredictable funding for local and state agencies, and a terrible bond rating.

The viciousness and divisiveness of California politics from the 1960s into the new millennium were expressed through partisan politics and cultural/ethnic conflict. These divisions had their roots in the shifting economic and demographic sands of the state. The great demographic transformation of California at the turn of the millennium coincided with economic upheavals and continued stalemates in state government. Just as non-whites began to gain in blue-collar jobs, those jobs became devalued in the economy. Just as immigrant and black leaders gained control of cities and inner-ring suburbs, the population of the state shifted further inland. The top 20 percent of the state did very well in those years, the bottom 20 percent did poorly, and those in middle could never be sure on which side they would end up. For many, the state's uneven growth could no longer assure them a better future, a promise that been key to political consensus. Society changed in alarming ways around Californians; they doubted the security of their homes and their futures. The politics of the Golden State in the new millennium embodied these multiple insecurities.

Despite the economic crisis, the burgeoning Latino political culture revealed in the 2006 demonstrations may be having a larger political effect. In the 2010 gubernatorial election, eBay executive Meg Whitman, "eMeg," spent more than $140 million of her own money to succeed Schwarzenegger. Despite this record sum, she lost the race to former Governor Jerry Brown. Her overspending and callous treatment of undocumented immigrant Nicky Diaz, the Whitman family nanny, alienated many Latino voters. They overwhelmingly supported Democrats up and down the ballot, allowing California to resist the "Red Tide" of Republican victories that year. The racial divisions that fracture California still exist, but the sentiment behind these votes may point to a less bitter, more egalitarian politics.

Hunted almost to extinction for their blubber, northern elephant seals have made a remarkable recovery. These two at Monterey Bay, however, don't participate in politics.

Hundreds of thousands of marchers in Los Angeles on May 1, 2006 reclaimed the May Day tradition as they demanded better treatment for immigrants. (Photo: Jonathan McIntosh)

21

What California Is

> History, history! We fools, what do we know or care?
> History begins for us with murder and enslavement,
> not with discovery. No, we are not Indians, but we
> are men of their world. The blood means nothing; the
> spirit, the ghost of the land moves in the blood, moves
> the blood.
>   —William Carlos Williams, *In the American Grain*

While the underside of California's past may make for disturbing reading, no history of California can or should ignore what William Carlos Williams named "the spirit, the ghost of the land." This spirit still haunts the state's phenomenal growth and prosperity. Droughts, earthquakes, fires, floods, mudslides reappear like spirits made restless by the changes people have wrought. The state's transformations proved calamitous for native peoples above all, a destruction that was explained alternately as the work of a powerful God or inevitable progress. Of course, it was neither. All too often later observers reported this history with a resigned sense of its inevitability and without considering what it meant for one society to be based on the ruins of another. Many peoples suffered greatly: victims of race riots and lynching, people who lost their homes and lands, Japanese internees, those excluded from decent lives, peons laboring in near slavery, migrants stooped in the fields, all those relegated to the margins of their communities, or locked away in endless prisons. It has been easy for subsequent society, politically safer for historians and public intellectuals to ignore or downplay society's deep-rooted dependence on war, inequity, and destruction. One constant in the history of the Golden State is the yawning gap between what people like to imagine they are doing—saving souls, building an empire for liberty, or just living the good life on the left coast—and what they actually accomplish.

Yet to portray California's past as unrelentingly grim or singularly hypocritical is as mistaken as to ignore its brutal heritage. Today California has the largest Indian population of any US state. Given the devastation of the 18th and 19th centuries, mere survival is a victory in itself. Indian communities thrive throughout the state, underwritten, of course, by casino earnings. Asians, blacks, and Mexicans—excluded, marginalized, interned, deported—have rebounded with growing populations and political power. California's environmental regulations, however perverse some of their outcomes, set the standard for US regulations as a whole. The state's labor movement defied a forty-year long trend by actually growing in the last decade. Openly queer elected officials and enormous GLBT communities thrive despite setbacks such as the overturning of same-sex marriage by voters. Far more than at any time in its history, California is open to diverse subcultures, allowing widespread cultural creativity. It is a state justly proud of the diversity that its official institutions once tried to prevent.

How do we put together these multiple Californias, these varied inventions and contending histories? Ultimately, the place cannot be summed up, its fractured histories tied up in a neat package of easily digested conclusions. It can, however, be understood. California's past, like its sprawling countryside, can be toured through. It is a tour best taken without the expectation that what you see out of the window of your car or through the pages of this book is all there has been. There is so much more to discover about our past.

The peoples of the state have transformed themselves and their land in the last 250 years. We have changed much of the face of California, covering it with roads and buildings, draining swamps and redirecting rivers, flooding some valleys and drying up others. The world Californians found themselves in has, in turn, changed them. California was born as the outgrowth of two imperial trajectories, the Spanish and American. It first found its place in the world as a screen on which outsiders could project their global ambitions. The state has largely fulfilled these dreams of imperial greatness. The opportunity for wealth, power, or simply a life of relative prosperity drew successive waves of outsiders. Once in California, the reality of the state's strained resources and bitter politics required of its residents social and political adjustments as great as the environmental manipulations that made the state's growth possible.

Even after the invention of California, however, subterranean forces still push up the mountains; ocean currents still flow mostly southward. The coastal fog still blows in on summer evenings. Most Californians will tell you that California is not what it used to be. It has changed, they say, from what it was like when they were young or when they first arrived. But they are mostly wrong. California remains both what it once was and also what it has become.

California after a winter storm in 2004. From space, human history is difficult to see.

Mono Lake on the eastern side of the Sierra Nevada.

Bibliography

General Sources

McWilliams, Carey. *California: The Great Exception.* Reprint ed. Berkeley: University of California Press, 1999.

Rawls, James & Walton Bean. *California: An Interpretive History.* New York: McGraw Hill, 2008.

Rice, Richard, William Bullough & Richard Orsi. *The Elusive Eden: A New History of California.* New York: McGraw Hill, 2001.

"Five Views: A History of Mexican Americans in California" www.cr.nps.gov/history/online_books/5views/5views5h.htm

Starr, Kevin. *California: A History.* New York: Modern Library, 2005.

WPA Federal Writers Project. *California: A Guide to the Golden State.* New York: Hastings House, 1929. www.archive.org/details/californiaguidet-00federich

18th and 19th Centuries

Almaguer, Tomas. *Racial Fault Lines: The Historical Origins of White Supremacy in California.* Berkeley: University of California Press, 1994.

Bancroft, Hubert Howe et. al. *History of California.* San Francisco: The History Company, 1890. books.google.com

California State Parks. California Indian Heritage Center. www.parks. ca.gov/?page_id=22628

Chan, Sucheng. *This Bittersweet Soil: The Chinese in California Agriculture, 1860–1910.* Berkeley: University of California Press, 1986.

Cornford, Daniel, ed. *Working People of California.* Berkeley: University of California Press, 1995.

Deverell, William. *Railroad Crossing: Californians and the Railroad.* Berkeley: University of California Press, 1994.

Fogelson, Robert M. *The Fragmented Metropolis: Los Angeles, 1850–1930.* Berkeley: University of California Press, 1993.

Fradkin, Philip. *The Seven States of California: A Natural and Human History.* Berkeley: University of California Press, 1995.

Griswold del Castillo, Richard. *The Treaty of Guadalupe Hidalgo: A Legacy of Conflict.* Norman: University of Oklahoma Press, 1992.

Haas, Lisbeth. *Conquests and Historical Identities in California, 1769–1936.* Berkeley: University of California Press, 1995.

Hurtado, Albert. *Indian Survival on the California Frontier.* New Haven, CT: Yale University Press, 1988.

Johnson, Kristin. ed. *"Unfortunate Emigrants": Narratives of the Donner Party.* Logan: Utah State University Press, 1996.

Levy, Jo Ann. *They Saw the Elephant: Women in the California Gold Rush.* Norman: University of Oklahoma Press, 1992.

Library of Congress. *California as I Saw It: First-Person Narratives of California's Early Years, 1849–1900.* rs6.loc.gov/ammem/cbhtml/cbhome.html

McPhee, John. *Assembling California.* New York: Farrar, Straus and Giroux, 1993.

Margolin, Malcolm. ed. *The Way We Lived: California Indian Reminiscences, Stories, and Songs.* Berkeley: Heyday Books, 1981.

Monroy, Douglas. *Thrown Among Strangers: The Making of Mexican Culture in Frontier California.* Berkeley: University of California Press, 1993.

Pisani, Donald. *Water, Land, and Law in the West: The Limits of Public Policy, 1850–1920.* Lawrence: University Press of Kansas, 1996.

Pitt, Leonard. *Decline of the Californios: A Social History of the Spanish-Speaking Californians, 1846–1890*. Berkeley, CA: University of California Press, 1966.

20TH AND 21ST CENTURIES

Banham, Reyner. *Los Angeles: The Architecture of Four Ecologies*. Berkeley: University of California Press, 2009.

Bérubé, Allan. *Coming Out Under Fire*. New York: Free Press, 1992.

Boyd, Nan. *Wide-Open Town: A History of Queer San Francisco to 1965*. Berkeley: University of California Press, 2003.

Davis, Clark. *White-Collar Life & Corporate Culture in Los Angeles, 1892–1941*. Baltimore: Johns Hopkins University Press, 2000.

Davis, Mike. *Ecology of Fear: Los Angeles and Imagination of Disaster*. New York: Henry Holt & Co, 1998.

Davis, Mike & Robert Morrow. *City of Quartz: Excavating the Future in Los Angeles*. New York: Verso, 1990.

Gioia, Ted. *West Coast Jazz: Modern Jazz in California, 1945–1960*. Berkeley: University of California Press, 1998.

Guerin-Gonzales, Camille. *Mexican Workers and American Dreams: Immigration, Repatriation, and California Farm Labor, 1900–1939*. New Brunswick, NJ: Rutgers University Press, 1994.

Gilmore, Ruth. *Prisons, Surplus, Crisis, and Opposition in Globalizing California*. Berkeley: University of California Press, 2007.

Gregory, James N. *American Exodus: The Dust Bowl Migration and Okie Culture in California*. New York: Oxford University Press, 1989.

Gutierrez, David. *Walls & Mirrors: Mexican Americans, Mexican Immigrants, and the Politics of Ethnicity*. Berkeley: University of California Press, 1995.

Hart, John. *Storm Over Mono: The Mono Lake Battle and the California Water Future*. Berkeley: University of California Press, 1996.

Hine, Robert. *California's Utopian Colonies*. Berkeley: University of California Press, 1983.

Johnson, Marilynn S. *The Second Gold Rush: Oakland and the East Bay in World War II*. Berkeley: University of California Press, 1994.

Nee, Victor & Brett de Bary Nee. *Longtime Californ': A Documentary Study of an American Chinatown*. New York: Pantheon Books, 1972.

Pepin, Elizabeth & Lewis Watts. *Harlem of the West: The San Francisco Fillmore Jazz Era*. San Francisco: Chronicle Books, 2005.

Reisner, Marc. *Cadillac Desert: The American West and Its Disappearing Water*. New York: Penguin Books. 1986.

Sanchez, George J. *Becoming Mexican American: Ethnicity, Culture and Identity in Chicano Los Angeles, 1900–1945*. New York: Oxford University Press, 1993.

Stryker, Susan & Jim Van Buskirk. *Gay by the Bay: A History of Queer Culture in the San Francisco Bay Area*. San Francisco: Chronicle Books, 1996.

Tygiel, Jules. *The Great Los Angeles Swindle: Oil, Stocks, and Scandal During the Roaring Twenties*. Berkeley: University of California Press, 1996.

Ullman, Sharon. *Sex Seen: The Emergence of Modern Sexuality in America*. Berkeley, CA: University of California Press, 1998.

Walker, Richard. *The Conquest of Bread: 150 Years of California Agribusiness*. New York: The New Press, 2004.

Weber, Devra. *Dark Sweat, White Gold: California Farm Workers, Cotton, and the New Deal*. Berkeley: University of California Press, 1994.

A Very Abbreviated List of Great California Movies

Feature Films

1920 *The Mark of Zorro*
The masked champion fights the Spanish and courts the lovely Lolita; Dir.: Fred Niblo; Writer: Johnston McCulley; Starring: Douglas Fairbanks, Noah Beery, Claire McDowell, Marguerite de la Motte

1934 *Our Daily Bread*
Depression era city dwellers create a socialist utopian colony against the odds; Dir./Writer: King Vidor; Writers: Elizabeth Hill, Joseph Mankiewicz; Starring: Karen Morley, Tom Keene, Barbara Pepper

1936 *Ramona*
Hunt Jackson's story of forbidden love in old California; Dir.: Henry King; Writers: Helen Hunt Jackson, Lamar Trotti; Starring: Loretta Young, Don Ameche

1936 *San Francisco*
A saloon keeper and socialite compete for the love of a singer during the 1906 earthquake; Dir: W.S. Van Dyke; Writers: Robert Hopkins, Anita Loos; Starring: Clark Gable, Jeanette MacDonald, Spencer Tracy

1940 *The Grapes of Wrath*
The Joads' epic journey from the Dustbowl to California's fields; Dir.: John Ford; Writers: Nunnally Johnson, John Steinbeck; Starring: Henry Fonda, Jane Darwell, John Carradine, Charley Grapewin, Dorris Bowdon

1941 *The Maltese Falcon*
Hard boiled detective outsmarts an international group of crooks after a legendary treasure; Dir.: John Huston; Writers: Dashiell Hammett, Huston; Starring: Humphrey Bogart; Mary Astor; Gladys George; Peter Lorre; Sydney Greenstreet

1941 *Citizen Kane*
Newsman builds an empire but misses Rosebud; Dir.: Orson Welles; Writers: Welles, Herman J. Mankiewicz; Starring: Orson Welles, Agnes Moorehead, Joseph Cotton, Ruth Warrick, Ray Collins

1950 *DOA*
Poisoned man searches for answers in LA and SF; Dir.: Rudolph Maté; Writers: Russell Rouse, Clarence Greene; Starring: Edmond O'Brien, Pamela Britton, Luther Adler

1955 *Seven Cities of Gold*
De Portola and Serra conquer California's Indians for God and Glory; Dir.: Robert D. Webb; Writers: Isabelle Gibson Ziegler, Richard L. Breen, John C. Higgins, Joseph Petracca; Starring: Richard Egan; Anthony Quinn, Michael Rennie, Jeffrey Hunter, Rita Moreno

1958 *Vertigo*
Acrophobic detective is obsessed with a friend's wife who is obsessed with her California ancestor; Dir.: Alfred Hitchcock; Writers: Alec Coppel, Samuel Taylor, Pierre Boileau; Starring: James Stewart, Kim Novak, Barbara Bel Geddes

1958 *Kiss Me Deadly*
Hard-boiled detective pursues a radioactive package and even hotter women in Cold War LA; Dir.: Robert Aldrich; Writers: Mickey Spillane, A.I. Bezzerides; Starring: Ralph Meeker, Albert Dekker, Paul Stewart, Cloris Leachman

1967   *The Graduate*
Recent grad sleeps with the mom, loves the daughter, but should go into plastics in the Bay Area. Dir.: Mike Nichols; Writers: Calder Willingham, Buck Henry, Charles Webb; Starring: Anne Bancroft, Dustin Hoffman, Katherine Ross

1968   *Bullit*
Tough cop roots out a killer and corruption with breakneck driving through SF; Dir: Peter Yates; Writers: Alan R. Trustman, Harry Kleiner, Robert L. Pike; Starring: Steve McQueen, Robert Vaughn, Jacqueline Bisset

1969   *They Shoot Horses Don't They?*
Dancers join a Santa Monica dance marathon to fight the Depression; Dir.: Sydney Pollack; Writers: Horace McCoy, James Poe, Robert E. Thompson; Starring: Jane Fonda, Michael Sarrazin, Susannah York, Gig Young, Red Buttons

1971   *Play Misty for Me*
An obsessed fan stalks a DJ in Carmel; Dir.: Clint Eastwood; Writers: Jo Heims, Dean Riesner; Starring: Clint Eastwood, Jessica Walter, Donna Mills

1972   *Blacula*
African vampire stalks LA; Dir.: William Crain; Writers: Raymond Koenig, Joan Torres; Starring: William Marshall, Vonetta McGee, Denise Nicholas

1973   *American Graffiti*
Modesto teens in the 60s face the future after high school;   Dir./ Writer: George Lucas; Writers: Gloria Katz, Willard Huyck, Francis Ford Coppola; Starring: Richard Dreyfuss, Ron Howard, Paul Le Mat, Cindy Williams, Kathy Quinlan, Candy Clark, Harrison Ford

1974   *Chinatown*
Hard-boiled detective gets in over his head in LA elite's love and water wars; Dir.: Roman Polanski; Writer: Robert Towne; Starring: Jack Nicholson; Faye Dunaway, John Huston

1975   *Shampoo*
Which is harder in Beverly Hills: Love or hairdressing? Dir.: Hal Ashby; Writers: Robert Towne, Warren Beatty; Starring: Warren Beatty, Julie Christie, Goldie Hawn, Lee Grant

1977   *Killer Of Sheep*
A man in Watts tries to maintain his humanity while working in a slaughterhouse; Dir./Writer: Charles Burnett; Starring: Henry Gayle Sanders, Kaycee Moore

1982   *Blade Runner*
Hard-boiled detective gets in over his head in LA's diverse future; Dir.: Ridley Scott; Writers: Hampton Fancher, David Peoples, Philip K. Dick; Starring: Harrison Ford, Rutger Hauer, Sean Young, Edward James Olmos, Daryl Hannah

1987   *The Lost Boys*
Vampires bikers prowl the Santa Cruz boardwalk; Dir.: Joel Schumacher; Writers: Janice Fischer, James Jeremias, Jeffrey Boam; Starring: Jason Patric, Corey Haim, Dianne Wiest, Kiefer Sutherland

1991   *Boyz n the Hood*
Three friends face their futures in South Central LA; Dir./Writer: John Singleton; Starring: Ice Cube, Cuba Gooding, Jr., Lawrence Fishburne, Nia Long, Tyra Ferrell, Angela Bassett

1995   *Mi Familia*
Three generations of a family in East LA experience trials but triumph;

Dir./Writer: Gregory Nava; Writer: Anna Thomas; Starring: Edward James Olmos, Rafael Cortes, Ivette Reina, Amelia Zapata

1997 *LA Confidential*
Corrupt cops drawn into the Hollywood underworld; Dir./Writer: Curtis Hanson; Writers: James Ellroy, Brian Helgeland; Starring: Kevin Spacey, Russell Crowe, Guy Pearce, James Cromwell, Kim Basinger, Danny DeVito

2005 *Crash*
The many sides of LA intertwined through racial conflict and crime; Dir./Writer: Paul Haggis; Writer: Bobby Moresco; Starring: Sandra Bullock, Don Cheadle, Michael Peña, Matt Dillon, Terrence Howard, Thandie Newton

DOCUMENTARY FILMS

1970 *Gimme Shelter*
The Rolling Stones concert at Altamount Pass ends the 60s. Dir: Albert Maysle, David Maysles, Charlotte Zwerin

1980 *The Life and Times of Rosie the Riveter*
Working women fight for their rights in WWII Shipyards; Dir.: Connie Field

1984 *The Times of Harvey Milk*
Moving and gripping: Better than the fiction film!; Dir.: Rob Epstein

1985 *A Dollar a Day, Ten Cents a Dance*
Filipino immigrant lives in California in the 20s and 30s; Dir.: Geoffrey Dunn & Mark Schwartz

1988 *Yosemite: The Fate of Heaven*
Beautifully filmed history and prospects of the Park; Dir.: Jon Else

1989 *Tongues Untied*
Black gay life in the Castro of San Francisco; Dir.: Marlon Riggs

1990 *Berkeley in the Sixties*
Berkeley's turbulent era; Dir.: Mark Kitchell

1992 *The Donner Party*
The ill-fated pioneer journey; Dir.: Ric Burns

1995 *We Have a Plan*
EPIC stirs up Depression-bound California; Dir.: Lyn Goldfarb

1997 *The Fight in the Fields*
Struggles of Chavez and the UFW; Dir.: Rick Tejada-Flores & Ray Telles

1999 *Rabbit in the Moon*
Reflects on lingering effects of the Japanese internment; Dir.: Emiko Omori

2001 *Alcatraz is Not an Island*
Native activists seize the former prison; Dir.: James M. Fortier

2001 *Dogtown and Z-Boys*
Surfers invent skateboarding; Dir.: Stacy Peralta

2005 *Screaming Queens*
Rioters start SF's transgender movement; Dir.: Victor Silverman and Susan Stryker

2005 *Zoot Suit Riots*
Zoot Suiters and GIs recall the riots; Dir.: Joseph Tovares

2007 *Bastards of the Party*
LA gangs origins in Black Panther militancy; Dir.: Cle "Bone" Sloan

Some Great California Writing

María Amparo Ruiz De Burton	*The Squatter and the Don*
Mary Austin	*The Ford*
Carlos Bulosan	*America is in the Heart*
Raymond Chandler	*Lady in the Lake*
Ina Coolbrith	*Songs from the Golden Gate*
Joan Didion	*Slouching Towards Bethlehem*
Ernesto Galarza	*Barrio Boy*
Dashiell Hammet	*The Maltese Falcoln*
Bret Harte	*Tales of the Argonauts*
Maxine Hong Kingston	*China Men*
Helen Hunt Jackson	*Ramona*
Jack London	*The Sea Wolf*
Cherrie Moraga & Gloria Anzaldúa	*This Bridge Called My Back*
Toshio Mori	*Yokohama, California*
David Mas Masumoto	*Epitaph for a Peach*
Walter Mosley	*Red Death*
John Muir	*My First Summer in the Sierra*
Frank Norris	*McTeague*
William Saroyan	*The Human Comedy*
Upton Sinclair	*Oil*
Gary Snyder	*The Practice of the Wild: Essays*
John Steinbeck	*Tortilla Flat*, *Of Mice and Men*, etc.
Michelle Tea	*Valencia*
Karen Tei Yamashita	*I Hotel*
Mark Twain	*Roughing It*
Yoshiko Uchida	*Desert Exile*
Nathanael West	*Day of the Locust*
Oscar Zeta Acosta	*Revolt of the Cockroach People*

California History Websites

Online archive of California www.oac.cdlib.org

California Geography, Geology, Hazards, and Natural History Information
 www.education.usgs.gov/california/resources

California Historical Landmarks www.ohp.parks.ca.gov

Five Views: An Ethnic Historic Site Survey for California
 www.nps.gov/history/history/online_books/5views/5views6

California Historical Society www.californiahistoricalsociety.org

LearnCalifornia.org www.learncalifornia.org

San Diego Historical Society www.sandiegohistory.org

Public Policy Institute www.ppic.org

H-California www.h-net.org~cal

Blogs on California politics today   www.sacbee.com/783/story/95704

California Historian   www.californiahistorian.com

California's Living New Deal Project   www.livingnewdeal.berkeley.edu

Rough & Tumble: News on California politics and policy   www.rtumble.com

California-Focused Museums & Centers

Agua Caliente Cultural Museum
219 South Palm Canyon Drive, Palm Springs   www.accmuseum.org

Autry National Center
4700 Western Heritage Way, Los Angeles   www.autrynationalcenter.org

California Military Museum
1119 2nd Street, Sacramento   www.militarymuseum.org

Crocker Art Museum
216 O Street, Sacramento   www.crockerartmuseum.org

Eastern California Museum
155 N. Grant Street, Independence   www.countyofinyo.org/ecmuseum

Manzanar National Historic Site
U.S. Highway 395, 9 miles north of Lone Pine   www.nps.gov/manz

Merced County Courthouse Museum
21st & N Streets, Merced   www.mercedmuseum.org

Oakland Museum of California
1000 Oak @ 10th Street, Oakland   www.museumca.org

San Diego History Center
Casa de Balboa Building, Balboa Park
1649 El Prado, San Diego   www.sandiegohistory.org

Santa Barbara Museum of Natural History
2559 Puerta del Sol, Santa Barbara   www.sbnature.org

Sherman Indian Museum
9010 Magnolia Avenue, Riverside   www.shermanindianmuseum.org

Turtle Bay Museum
840 Auditorium Drive, Redding   www.turtlebay.org

A Sampling of Murals

For a good list of murals in Los Angeles   www.amurals.org

Coit Tower Murals by various artists
1 Telegraph Hill Boulevard, San Francisco

A History of our Struggle
by Goez Art Studio, 3640 East First Street, East Los Angeles

History of San Francisco
by Anton Refreigier, Rincon Annex, 101 Spear Street, San Francisco

Incidents in California History
by Suzanne Scheuer, Berkeley Main Post Office, 2000 Allston Way,
Berkeley

Land of Irrigation
by Norman Chamberlain, Selma Post Office, 2058 High Street, Selma

Maestrapeace
by various artists, Women's Building, 3543 18th Street, San Francisco

Pan American Unity
by Diego Rivera, Diego Rivera Theater, City College of San Francisco
50 Phelan Avenue, San Francisco

Prometheus
by José Clemente Orozco, Frary Hall, Pomona College, 6th Street,
Claremont

Quetzalcóatl
by Toltecas en Aztlán & El Congreso de Artistas Chicanos en Aztlán and
"Coatlicue" by Susan Yamagata

Chicano Park
Logan Avenue & Cesar E. Chavez Parkway,
San Diego

Ramona Gardens Murals by Mechicano Arts Center muralists, Lancaster
Avenue & Murchison Street, Los Angeles

Recreation in Santa Monica
by Stanton Macdonald-Wright, Santa Monica City Hall, 1685 Main
Street, Santa Monica

Women and the Labor Movement in California
by Eva Cockcroft, Southern California Library for Social Studies and
Research, 6120 South Vermont Avenue, Los Angeles

Cultural Festivals, Rodeos, & Parades

JANUARY

Indian Storytellers Festival—San Leandro
Dodge California Circuit Finals Rodeo—Norco

FEBRUARY

Chinese New Year Parade—San Francisco
Tet Festival—San Jose
Monterey Park Chinese New Year Lantern Festival—Monterey Park
Queen Mary Scottish Festival & Games—Long Beach
Latino Cultural Arts Festival—Monterey Park

MARCH

St. Patrick's Day Parade—various cities
Desert Pro PRCA Rodeo—Indio
Needles Rodeo (GCPRA)—Needles

APRIL

César Chávez commemorations—various locations
Cherry Blossom Festival—Japantown SF
Pasadena Cherry Blossom Festival—Pasadena
Lao Festival—San Francisco
Children's Faerie Festival—Cambria
Sherman Indian School Pow Wow—Riverside
Chumash Pow Wow—Malibu
Grand National Rodeo, Horse, and Stock Show—Daly City
Auburn Wild West Stampede—Auburn
La Grange CCPRA Rodeo—La Grange

MAY

Children's Fantasy Faire—Los Gatos
Stanford Pow Wow—Palo Alto
Kinderfest—Anaheim
Himalayan Fair—Berkeley
Cinco de Mayo Celebrations—various cities
Carnaval—San Francisco
Israel Independence Day Festival—LA
Holland Festival—Long Beach
Aloha Expo—Santa Fe Springs
Conejo Valley Days Rodeo—Thousand Oaks
Etna California Cowboys Pro Rodeo Association (CCPRA) Rodeo—Etna
Kern County Sheriff Reserve Stampede Days—Bakersfield
Mother Lode Round-Up Profesional Rodeo Cowboys Association (PCRA) Rodeo—Sonora
Chico CCPRA Rodeo—Chico

JUNE

Juneteenth Festival & Carnival—various cities
Campbell Highland Games and Celtic Gathering—Campbell
Dia de Portugal—San Jose
Yuba Pow Wow—Marysville
Da Show (Hawai'ian)—Manhattan Beach
Ventura County Greek Festival—Camarillo
Polish Spring Festival: "Proud to be Polish"—Yorba Linda
Ho'olaule'a Pacific Island Festival from Hawai'i—Northridge
Fiesta Filipina—San Francisco
SF LGBT Pride—San Francisco
Jurupa Rodeo—Jurupa
Livermore Rodeo—Livermore
Stanislaus County Sheriff's Posse Rodeo—Turlock
Eureka CCPRA Rodeo—Eureka

JULY

Lotus Festival—Silverlake, LA
Obon Festival—Mountain View
Mariachi Festival—San José
    Mexican Heritage Plaza
Japantown Bon Festival—San
    Francisco Japantown
Mariachi Festival—San José
    Mexican Heritage Plaza
Oxnard Salsa Festival—Oxnard
California Rodeo Salinas—Salinas
Marysville Stampede—Marysville

AUGUST

Nisei Week Japanese Festival—
    Downtown LA
Watts Summer Festival—LA
Pistahan (Filipino)—San Francisco
Sri Lanka Day—Santa Monica
Tofu Festival (Japanese)—
    downtown LA
Scottish Games & Celtic
    Festival—Toro
Filipino Heritage Festival—San Jose
Ruth CCPRA Rodeo—Ruth
Old Spanish Days—Santa Barbara
Truckee Rodeo—Truckee
Hoopa CCPRA Rodeo—Hoopa

SEPTEMBER

Native American Day celebra-
    tions—various cities
Los Angeles Korean Festival—
    Mid-City LA
The Moon Festival of Silicon
    Valley—Cupertino
Scottish Gathering and
    Games—Pleasanton
Brazilian Street Carnival—Long
    Beach
Cabrillo Festival—San Diego
Aloha Days Longboard Surf Contest
    and Hawai'ian Festival—
    Hermosa Beach
Arab Cultural Festival—San
    Francisco
Hellenic Festival—Pasadena
Danish Days—Solvang
Festival of Philippine Arts and
    Culture—San Pedro
Bishop CCPRA Rodeo—Bishop
Barstow Stampede—Barstow

Poway Original Coors
    Rodeo—Poway

OCTOBER

Columbus Day Parade—San
    Francisco
Indigenous People's Day—Berkeley
Seaside Highland Games—Ventura
Banning Stagecoach
    Days—Banning
Industry Hills Charity PRCA
    Rodeo—Industry

NOVEMBER

Island Creation Christmas
    Bazaar—Gardena
Mid-Autumn Festival (Hong
    Kong)—Universal City
Tamale Festival—Los Angeles
Un-Thanksgiving Day—Alcatraz
    Island
Dia de los Muertos—Downtown
    LA
Southwest Museum Intertribal
    Marketplace—Los Angeles
Brawley Cattle Call PCRA Rodeo—
    Brawley, Imperial County

DECEMBER

Winter Gathering Pow Wow—29
    Palms

County Fairs & Festivals
by region, north to south

Far North Coast: Del Norte, Humboldt

Del Norte County Fair (Early August; Crescent City)
Humboldt County Fair (Mid-August; Ferndale)
Redwood Acres Fair (Late June; Eureka)

Far North Mountains: Trinity, Siskiyou, Shasta, Lassen, Modoc

Inter-Mountain Fair of Shasta County (Late August-Early September; McArthur)
Shasta District Fair (Mid-June; Anderson)
Siskiyou Golden Fair (Mid-August; Yreka)
Trinity County Fair (Late August; Hayfork)
Lassen County Fair (Mid-Late July; Susanville)
Modoc District Fair (Mid-August; Cedarville)

Upper Central Valley: Tehama, Glenn, Butte, Colusa, Sutter,Yuba

Butte County Fair (Late August; Gridley)
Colusa County Fair (Early-Mid-June; Colusa)
Colusa Farm Show (Early February; Colusa)
Glenn County Fair (Mid-May; Orland)
Tehama District Fair (Late September; Red Bluff)
Tulelake-Butte County Fair (Early September; Tulelake)

Northern Sierra: Plumas, Sierra, Nevada, Placer, El Dorado, Amador, Calaveras

Amador County Fair (Late July; Plymouth)
Calaveras County Fair & Jumping Frog Jubilee (Mid-May; Angel's Camp)
El Dorado County Fair (Mid-June; Placerville)
Gold Country Fair (Mid-September; Auburn)
Nevada County Fair (Mid-August; Grass Valley)
Placer County Fair (Mid-June; Roseville)
Plumas-Sierra County Fair (Mid-August; Quincy)
Yuba-Sutter Fair (Early August; Yuba City)

Sierra: Alpine, Tuolumne, Mono, Inyo

Bishop Mule Days Celebration (Memorial Day; Bishop)
Eastern Sierra Tri-County Fair (Late August-Early September; Bishop)
Motherlode Fair (Early July, Sonora)

DELTA: YOLO, SACRAMENTO, SOLANO, SAN JOAQUIN

California Exposition & State Fair (Mid-August-Early September; Sacramento)
Sacramento County Fair (Late May; Sacramento)
San Joaquin County Fair (Mid-Late June; Stockton)
Solano County Fair (Mid-Late July; Vallejo)
Dixon May Fair (Mid-May; Dixon)
Yolo County Fair (Mid-August; Woodland)
Lodi Grape Festival & Harvest Fair (Mid-September; Lodi)
Lodi Spring Wine Show (Late March; Lodi)
Western States Horse Expo (Early June; Sacramento)

NORTH COAST AND WINE COUNTRY: MENDOCINO, LAKE, SONOMA, NAPA

Cloverdale Citrus Fair (Mid-February; Cloverdale)
Mendocino County Fair & Apple Show (Mid-September; Boonville)
Napa County Fair (Early July; Calistoga)
Napa Town and Country Fair (Mid-August; Napa)
Lake County Fair (Late August-Early September; Lakeport)
Sonoma County Fair & Exposition (Late July-Early August; Santa Rosa)
Sonoma-Marin Fair (Late June; Petaluma)
Redwood Empire Fair (Mid-August; Ukiah)

BAY AREA: MARIN, CONTRA COSTA, ALAMEDA, SAN FRANCISCO, SANTA CLARA, SAN MATEO

Contra Costa County Fair (Early June; Antioch)
Marin County Fair & Exposition (Late June-Early July; San Rafael)
San Mateo County Exposition & Fair (Mid-August; San Mateo)
Santa Clara County Fair (Early August; San Jose)

CENTRAL VALLEY AND SOUTHERN SIERRA: SAN JOAQUIN, MARIPOSA, MADERA, STANISLAUS, FRESNO, KINGS, TULARE, KERN

Desert Empire Fair (Mid-October; Ridgecrest)
Big Fresno Fair (Early & Mid-October, Fresno)
Kern County Fair (Late September-Early October; Bakersfield)
Kings Fair (Early July; Hanford)
Madera District Fair (Early September; Madera)
Mariposa County Fair & Homecoming (Early September; Mariposa)
Merced County Spring Fair (Early May; Los Banos)
Porterville Fair (Mid-Late May; Porterville)
San Joaquin Fair (December; Stockton)
Stanislaus County Fair (Late July-Early August; Turlock)
Tulare County Fair (Mid-September; Tulare)

CENTRAL COAST: SANTA CRUZ, MONTEREY, SAN BENITO, SAN LUIS OBISPO

Santa Cruz County Fair (Mid September; Watsonville)
California Mid-State Fair (Late July-Early August; Paso Robles)
Salinas Valley Fair (Mid-May; King City)
San Benito County Fair (Late September-Early October; Tres Pinos)
Monterey County Fair (Mid-August; Monterey)

California Indian Market and Peace Pow Wow (May; San Juan Bautista)

SOUTHERN COAST: SANTA BARBARA, VENTURA, LOS ANGELES, ORANGE, SAN DIEGO

Antelope Valley Fair (Late August-Early September; Lancaster)
Los Angeles County Fair (Early September-Early October; Pomona)
Orange County Fair (Early-Late July; Costa Mesa)
San Diego County Fair (Mid-June-Early July; Del Mar)
San Fernando Valley Fair (Early June; Sherman Oaks)
Santa Barbara Fair and Exposition (Late April; Santa Barbara)
Santa María Fair Park (Mid-July; Santa Maria)
Schools Involvement Fair (Mid-May; Walnut)
Southern California Fair (Early-Mid-October; Perris)
Ventura County Fair (Early-Mid-August; Ventura)

SOUTHERN INLAND AND DESERT: SAN BERNARDINO, RIVERSIDE, IMPERIAL

California Mid-Winter Fair & Fiesta (Early-Mid-March; Imperial)
Chowchilla-Madera County Fair (Mid-May; Chowchilla)
Colorado River Fair (Late March-Early April; Blythe)
National Orange Show (Late May; San Bernardino)
Riverside County Fair & National Date Festival (Mid-Late February; Indio)
San Bernardino County Fair (Early-Mid-May; Victorville)

STATE PARK EVENTS

The California State Parks website has an exhaustive list of parks. www.parks.ca.gov/parkindex. Check out this website for a listing of events across the state, from the August Blackberry Festival at Anderson Marsh State Historic Park in Kelseyville to the traditional ground-blessing ceremony in the fall at the Antelope Valley Indian Museum State Historic Park.

FOUR SEASONS OF FOOD

WINTER

Apple Butter Festival—Yucaipa—November
San José Harvest Festival—November
Fungus Fair—Oakland—December
Zinfandel Festival—San Francisco—January
Date Festival—Indio—January
Crab Festival—San Francisco—February

SPRING

Grunion Night—Doheny State Beach—March
Asparagus Festival—Stockton—April
Beer Festival—San Francisco—April
Grapefruit Festival—Borrego Springs—April

Halibut Derby—Marina del Rey—April
Lemon Festival—Upland—April
Orange Festival—Fillmore—April
Oyster and Beer Festival—Fort Mason, San Francisco—April
Strawberry Festival—Santa María—April
Apple Blossom Festival—Sebastopol—April
International Food Festival—Berkeley—Late April
Artichoke Festival—Castroville—May
Strawberry Festival—Oxnard—May
Fruit & Nut Festival—Hughson—May
Mushroom Mardi Gras—Morgan Hill—May
ZinFest—Lodi—May
Wine Festival—Tiburon—May
Uncorked! The San Francisco Wine Festival—San Francisco—May
Great Monterey Squid Festival—Monterey—May
Strawberry Festival—Arroyo Grande—May
Strawberry Festival—Garden Grove--May
Strawberry Festival—Oxnard—May
Cherry Festival—San Leandro—June
Cherry Festival—Beaumont—June

SUMMER

Peach Festival—Marysville—July
Garlic Festival—Gilroy—July
Strawberry Festival—Watsonville—July
Blackberry Festival—Lower Lake—August
Downriver Blackberry Festival—Big Flat—August
Dry Bean Festival—Tracy—August
Onion Festival—Vacaville—August
Gravenstein Apple Fair—Sebastopol—August
International Tomato Festival—Yuba City—August
Tomato Festival & West Coast BBQ Championship—Fairfield—August
Almond Festival—Oakley—September
Lemon Fest—Ventura—September
TomatoFest—Carmel—September
Tomato and Olive Oil Festival—San Francisco—September
Lobster Festival—Port of Los Angeles, San Pedro—September
Dried Plum Festival—Yuba City—September
Chocolate Festival—Ghiradelli Square, San Francisco—September
Zucchini Festival—Angels Camp—September
Eggplant Festival—Loomis—September/October

FALL

Calabasas Pumpkin Festival—Calabasas—October
Clam Festival—Pismo Beach—October
Alpine Village Oktoberfest—Torrance—October
Big Bear Lake Oktoberfest—Big Bear Lake—October
OktoberFest by the Bay—San Francisco, Fort Mason—October
Oktoberfest—Campbell—October
Avocado Festival—Carpinteria—October
Spice of Life Festival—Berkeley—October
Pumpkin Festival—Half Moon Bay—October
Ferry Building Marketplace Harvest Festival—San Francisco—October
Return of the Salmon Festival—Redding—October

HISTORIC NATIVE AMERICAN SITES

ALAMEDA COUNTY

Hilltop Tavern
> 3411 MacArthur Boulevard, Oakland. Where Indians met to plan the
> 1969 takeover of Alcatraz.

AMADOR COUNTY

Chaw'se/Indian Grinding Rock State Historic Park
> Highway 88 east of Jackson on the Pine Grove-Volcano Road. Bedrock
> mortars in marbleized limestone outcroppings, used by Miwok people.
> Indian families gather on the weekend after the fourth Friday in
> September for annual acorn gathering ceremonies.

The Place Where They Burnt the Digger
> Old Stockton Road east of Highway 88 near Ione. In this place in 1922,
> a straw dummy was burned as an effigy for the name "Digger," the
> derogatory name for Miwok Indians.

BUTTE COUNTY

Ishi's Hiding Place
> Two miles east of Oroville at Oak Avenue and Quincy Road (site of the
> old Ward Slaughterhouse). An oak tree stands where Ishi was first seen
> in 1911.

Mechoopda Indian Rancheria
> Chico. Mechoopda was a village 3.5 miles outside of what is now the
> town of Chico on Little Butte Creek. One of the last remaining buildings
> of the historic rancheria, is at 620 Sacramento Avenue. Further info:
> www.mechoopda-nsn.gov.

CONTRA COSTA COUNTY

Mount Diablo
> Two Highway 680 exits—Diablo Road to South Gate or Ygnacio Valley
> Road to North Gate. Both wind up at Summit Road to the museum. The
> mountain is said to be the place of origin of the Miwok people. The two
> peaks were surrounded by water; from them, Coyote and Eagle made the
> world and the First People.

DEL NORTE COUNTY

Re-kwoi
> One-and-one-half miles off Highway 101 on a gravel road at the mouth
> of the Klamath River. Re-kwoi, once a large village, is now a single
> reconstructed redwood plank house, 150 years old. Jump dance, brush
> dance, white deerskin dance, and ghost dance are still performed there.

Smith River Shaker Church, Del Norte County
> Town of Smith River, 12 miles north of Crescent City on Highway 101.
> The Hoopa people received federal land to build this Indian Shaker
> church, still active today, on the Smith River Rancheria in 1931.

Humboldt County

Gunther Island (also called Indian Island)
> Samoa Bridge (Highway 255) from Highway 101. Woodley Island exit.
> The site of the 1860 Indian Island Massacre. The Wiyot Tribe returned
> to the island in 2000. Special Event: A candlelight memorial is held in
> February each year. Contact info: www.redwoods.info.

Fort Gaston
> Route 96, Hoopa. The fort, built within the Hoopa Valley Indian
> Reservation, from which the US military put down the rebellions arising
> from massacres such as Indian Island.

Inyo County

Fish Slough, Chidago, Red Canyon, and Chalfant Petroglyphs
> Off of Highway 395 on LADWP land. Directions can be obtained from
> the BLM office, Cottonwood Plaza, 785 North Main Street, Suite E,
> Bishop. Paiute rock engravings.

Titus Canyon Petroglyphs
> Death Valley. Trail off of Titus Canyon Road, a dirt road between
> California Highway 190 and Nevada Highway 374 north of Stovepipe
> Wells. Shoshone/Paiute rock art site.

Kern County

Coso Range Petroglyphs
> Ridgecrest, within the China Lake Naval Weapons Center lands.
> Shoshone, Northern and Southern Paiute, and Kawaiisu peoples traveled
> from as far away as Utah to this site. Accessible only by guided tours in
> spring and fall. Tours take an entire day; reservations fill up months in
> advance. Maturango Museum: (760) 375-6900 or www.maturango.org.

Squaw Springs Petroglyphs (also called Steam Wells)
> Johannesburg. US Highway 395 to Trona Road northeast to a dirt road
> east, BLM 1444, 100 yards in to fenced area labeled "Squaw Spring
> Archeological District." The Kawaiisu created these rock engravings.

Tomo-Kahni State Park Pictographs
> East of Tehachapi on Sand Canyon Road. Visits by guided tour held two
> Saturdays per month. Contact: Lancaster office of the California State
> Parks, (805) 942-0662.

Kings County

Santa Rosa Rancheria
> Location of Tribal office: 16835 Alkali Drive, Lemoore. Home of the
> Tachi, a Yokuts people whose village historically lay on the Kings River
> on Douglas Avenue. The tribal cemetery is on 19th Avenue. Special
> permission is required from the tribal office to enter.

LAKE COUNTY

Anderson Marsh
> This State Historic Park is on Highway 53, one half hour north of
> Calistoga. Once home to one of the largest groups of Native Californians,
> the Southeastern Pomo, the descendants of whom still live throughout
> the area.

Bloody Island (also called Bo-no-po-ti)
> Highway 20 one mile east of the Highway 29/20 junction, south on
> Reclamation Road. Monument marks the site of the massacre of 135
> Indians in retribution for the killing of 2 white men.

LOS ANGELES COUNTY

El Escorpión Ranch
> El Escorpión Park. At the west end of the San Fernando Valley at the
> intersection of Vanowen Street and Sunset Ridge Court. The Scorpion
> Ranch was granted to three Indians in the 1830s. About 25 years later,
> a Basque immigrant acquired the ranch by his marriage to an Indian
> heiress. The location of the village of Huwam, a village where Chumash,
> Tongva, and Tataviam peoples lived.

Rogerio's Rancho
> In the San Fernando Heritage Park at the corner of Hubbard and Fourth
> Street. The land was once owned and occupied by Rogerio Rocha, the
> leader of a small group of Fernandeño Tataviam Indians evicted from
> their San Fernando homes in 1885.

MARIN COUNTY

Angel Island
> San Francisco Bay. Access via ferry. Miwok Indians fished and hunted
> deer, seals, sea lions, and sea otters on Angel Island. They had camps
> at what are now known as Ayala Cove, Camp Reynolds, and Fort
> McDowell. Displays relating to Miwok occupation can be found at the
> Immigration Center.

MARIPOSA COUNTY

Ahwahnee
> Half-mile west of Yosemite Village in Yosemite Valley. The site where
> the National Park Service built 15 cabins to house the Yosemite Miwok.
> The cabins are razed, but remnants can be seen, as well as grinding holes.

MENDOCINO COUNTY

Round Valley Indian Reservation
> Covelo. The Round Valley Indian Reservation was in the Yuki home-
> land, but other Indians, some of whom were enemies, were forced onto
> the reservation. The descendants of Yuki, Maidu, Pomo, Nomlaki,
> Cahto, Wailaki, and Pit River peoples eventually formed a new tribe on
> the reservation, the Covelo Indian Community.

Modoc County

Captain Jack's Stronghold
> Lava Beds National Monument. The site where Kintpuash, also known as Captain Jack, made his last stand in the Modoc Wars in 1873.

Monterey County

La Cueva Pintada (The Painted Cave)
> Fort Hunter Liggett, 25 miles southwest of King City. An ancient pictograph site of the Salinin Esselen people. Further info: www.esselen.com/hands1.

Plumas county

Mankins Ranch (Janesville Bear Dance site)
> Janesville, southeast of Highway 395 north of Honey Lake. A privately held ranch where the Maidu have been performing their Spring Bear Dance for many years.

Riverside County

Malki Museum
> Morongo Indian Reservation, Banning. Constructed by the Cahuilla Indians to preserve and enhance their way of life. They sponsor a Fiesta on Memorial Day, an Agave Harvest and Roast in April, and a Fall Gathering in late October.

Andreas Canyon Pictographs
> Palm Springs. Interstate 10 to Highway 111 (Palm Canyon Drive). Turn off on South Canyon Drive. Enter Indian Canyons, south to Andreas Canyon turn. For information on visitation times, contact the Tribal Office of the Agua Caliente Band of Cahuilla Indians. www.aguacaliente.org.

Idyllwild Pictographs
> Highway 243 south, just short of the town of Idyllwild, turn west on Riverside County Playground Road leading into a campground. Riverside County Parks, (909) 275-4310. Site of Cahuilla girls' puberty initiations.

San Bernardino County

Black Canyon and Inscription Canyon Petroglyphs
> Highway 58 between Boron and Barstow. Hinkley Road, about 8 miles north to unpaved Brown Ranch Road west. After Brown Ranch Road turns north, Jackrabbit Road east 2.4 miles to another, unnamed road north. 2.6 miles to a right branch into Black Canyon, another 7.8 to Inscription Canyon. (Note: High ground clearance vehicle needed.) These sites fall within what was Kawaiisu territory.

San Diego County

Cupa (also called Warner Springs Ranch or Agua Caliente Village)
> State Highway 79, north of Interstate 8 and east of Lake Henshaw. The site of a 200-acre Cupeño village, then a Mexican rancho. The Indians were evicted in 1903 and sent to Pala on the Quechal/San Luis Rey River.

Quechla/San Luis Rey River
> The 80-mile river begins in the Cleveland National Forest, flows along Highway 79 and enters the Pacific near Oceanside. In 1922 a dam was built, but in 1950 46 Indian bands initiated proceedings for damages from the government for failure to protect their land and water rights. This legal battle continues.

Viejas VFW Hall
> Viejas Indian Reservation, Alpine, northeast of Interstate 8 on Brown's Road. The first all-Indian VFW post, now abandoned. Many of the veterans who met there weren't citizens of the US at the time they served in its military.

San Francisco County

Alcatraz Island
> San Francisco Bay. Though Alcatraz was not inhabited by the coast people when the Spanish first arrived, it was the site of a protest organized by Indians from 1969 to 1971.

Santa Barbara County

Mescalitan Island
> Just east of the Santa Barbara Airport. An important archeological site and location of a Chumash village where Juan Rodriguez Cabrillo may be buried. It used to be an island within the Goleta Slough.

Painted Cave Pictographs
> Santa Barbara. State Street exit off of Highway 101 to Highway 154 to Painted Cave Road.

Sonoma County

Ya-Ka-Ama
> 6215 Eastside Rd., Santa Rosa. Ya-Ka-Ama ("our land" in the Kashaya Pomo language) has hosted courses ranging from heavy equipment to electronic assembly. The Ya-Ka-Ama Nursery in nearby Forrestville specializes in native plants.

Stanislaus County

Stanislaus River
> Originally the border between Sierra foothills Miwok and Central Valley Yokuts, the river was renamed in honor of rebel leader Estanislao (Cucunuchi).

Knights Ferry
> Just west of the junction of Highways 108 and 120, on Sonora Road. Where Estanislao fought Californios through the 1830s. Settlers of Knights Ferry report him living among them in the 1840s.

Tehama County

Nome Lackee Indian Reservation
> Highway 99 to Road A9, through Corning past Flournoy, north on
> Osborn Road. Thousands of native people were moved here in the 1850s.
> Corrupt administrators outraged the Indians and a group of fighters
> burned the reservation buildings. The Indians were moved to the Nome
> Cult farm.

Tulare County

Hospital Rock Pictographs
> Sequoia National Park. Adjacent to California Highway 198 between
> Three Rivers and Giant Forest Villages, six miles inside of the Ash
> Mountain entrance to the park.

Tulare Painted Rock Pictographs
> Tule River Indian Reservation. Ten miles east of California Highway
> 190. For access, contact Tulare River Indian Res.,
> www.tulerivertribe-nsn.gov

Tuolumne County

Pate Valley
> In the Grand Canyon of the Tuolomne River, a half-mile northeast of
> White Wolf, below Muir Gorge. The site of pictographs made by Mono
> Lake Paiute, who traveled along all the Mono trails.

Ventura County

Rancho Cañada Larga
> 234 Cañada Larga Road near the Ojai Freeway. The most significant
> remaining section the San Buenaventura Mission Aqueduct, built of
> stone and mortar in 1780–90 by Chumash neophytes.

Shisholop
> Directly on the beach at the foot of Figueroa Street in Ventura. A coastal
> Chumash village, believed to have been a kind of provincial capital,
> thriving at the time of Cabrillo's arrival in 1542. Archeologists excavated
> the site in the 1960s.

Oakbrook Park Pictographs
> Thousand Oaks. Westlake Boulevard north from Highway 101, east
> on Lang Ranch Parkway to the Chumash Interpretive Center, 3290
> Lang Ranch Parkway. Visit only during guided walks on Saturdays and
> Sundays. Contact: (805) 492-8076.

Yolo County

D-Q University
> Road 31 west of Davis. Deganawidah-Quetzalcoatl University was a fully
> accredited two-year college situated on acreage deeded to Indian people
> after they left Alcatraz. D-Q lost its accreditation in 2005.

CHRONOLOGY OF MAJOR EVENTS

400 million years ago
  California emerges piecemeal from the ocean
5 million years ago
  Sierra Nevada, Mt. Shasta, and Mt. Lassen created
15,000–12,000 years ago
  First People migrate to the coast
11,000–4,000 years ago
  Droughts and animal extinctions push more people to the coast.
  Increasing linguistic diversity; population reaches about 4,000
4,000–500 years ago
  Major migrations; growing linguistic complexity; larger settled
  villages and extensive trade networks between different groups;
  elaborate public rituals; bow and arrow arrives; indigenous population reaches 300,000

1542	Juan Cabrillo expedition
1579	Sir Francis Drake expedition
1768	Baja and Alta California administratively separated
1769	Gaspar de Portolá and Padre Junipero Serra's sacred expedition founds Mission San Diego; Kumeyaay rebel against Mission San Diego
1770	Monterey founded
1776	San Francisco founded
1781	Los Angeles founded; Yuma defeat Spanish at the Colorado; Mohave destroy two inland missions
1784	Padre Junipero Serra dies; Dominguez land grant
1785	Toyipurna lead San Gabriel rebellion
1796	*USS Otter* visits California
1806	Measles epidemic kills thousands
1812	Russians found Fort Ross
1820s	Epidemics sweep through the missions; Indian population: 150,000; Mexican population: 5,000
1821	Mexico gains independence; Indians made citizens
1824	Narciso leads revolt at Santa Ynes
1826	Jebediah Smith party arrives
1829	Estanlislao and Miwok battle Mexicans
1831–4	Secularization of the missions
1833	Malaria epidemic kills thousands in Central Valley
1836	California gains autonomy under Alvarado
1840	Johann Sutter founds New Helvetia
1841	Bartleson-Bidwell party sets out west
1842	Commodore Jones seizes Monterey
1846	Donner Party; Bear Flag revolt; US invades Mexico
1847	Californios defeated at Cahuenga
1848	Gold discovered at Sutter's Mill; Treaty of Guadalupe Hidalgo
1849	Gold rush; Clear Lake massacre
1850	California admitted to statehood
1851	Land Act challenges Californio land claims; Congress rejects Indian treaties
1852	San Quentin Prison established
1856	Vigilance Committee insurrection in San Francisco
1860	Indian Island massacre; Indian population: 50,000
1862–64	Multi-year drought bankrupts Southern Californios
1866	Wheat boom

1869	Transcontinental Railroad completed
1871	LA anti-Chinese rioters lynch 19 people
1872–73	Modoc War
1877	William Chapman creates first subdivision near Fresno; Workingmen's Party formed; railway strike; anti-Chinese riots
1882	Chinese Exclusion act signed
1884	*Gold Run* case bans dumping in rivers
1885	Entire Chinese community cleansed from Eureka
1887–88	San Diego land bubble; 8-hour work day law; population passes 1 million
1892	Sierra Club founded; oil discovered in Los Angeles
1898	Eastern Bankers take over California rail monopoly
1900	First Peoples population: 22,000; state total population: 1,485,053
1902	Reclamation Act for western water projects
1903	Oxnard Beet Workers strike by Japanese and Mexican laborers
1905	Salton Sea created; Union Labor Party controls San Francisco
1906	3,000 people die in San Francisco earthquake and fire
1907	Japanese immigration restricted
1908	Great White Fleet arrives
1910	*LA Times* building bombed by McNamara brothers; Hiram Johnson elected governor
1911	Progressive victories: women's suffrage, initiative, referendum, and recall
1911–12	IWW free speech demonstrations; Socialist loses LA mayoral race; Navy base established in San Diego
1913	Alien Land Act; Wheatland Riot at Durst Ranch
1914	Kelley's Army marches on Sacramento
1916	Tom Mooney and Warren Billings convicted of SF Preparedness Day bombing
1918	Criminal Syndicalism Act; first women elected to the State Assembly
1921	Fatty Arbuckle acquitted of murder
1923	Douglass begins airplane production in LA
1924	Edward Doheny admits bribery in Teapot Dome scandal; Owens Valley farmers dynamite aqueduct
1926	Oil fire in Brea
1930	LA population reaches 1.2 million
1931	Mexican repatriation
1935	Central Valley Project begins; initiative requires 2/3 vote for new taxes
1934	Upton Sinclair loses governor's race; San Francisco general strike
1937	Golden Gate Bridge opens
1938	Democrat Culbert Olsen wins governorship
1939	Tom Mooney pardoned; Hewlett Packard founded
1940	Arroyo Seco freeway opens
1942	Japanese internment begins
1943	First smog in LA; zoot suit riot
1946	Oakland general strike
1948	RAND Corporation founded
1951	HUAC Hollywood Hearings
1952	Alien Land law overturned; Livermore Labs open
1955	Disneyland opens
1957	Allen Ginsberg's *Howl* ruled not obscene
1960	Mechanization and Modernization agreement on the docks
1963	Rumford Fair Housing Act; California now the most populous state

1964	Free Speech Movement at Berkeley
1965	Watts Riots; Delano grape strike begins
1966	Compton's Cafeteria Riot; Ronald Reagan wins governorship
1967	Summer of Love
1969	Alcatraz occupation by Indians of All Nations; Santa Barbara Oil spill
1972	BART begins running—late
1975	Agricultural Labor Relations Act
1976	Apple Computer launched
1978	Prop 13 passes; Harvey Milk and George Moscone killed
1981	AIDS epidemic begins
1982	Last LA auto plant closes; peripheral canal defeated
1983	California Supreme Court rules for Mono Lake
1992	Los Angeles uprising/riots after Rodney King case verdict
1993	César Chávez dies
1994	"Three Strikes" initiative passes
1995	Entertainment employment surpasses aerospace industry
1998	Native-American population reaches pre-conquest size: 309,000
2000	Dot-com crash; no racial majority in population of 33 million
2003	Governor Gray Davis recalled
2005	Antonio Villaraigosa elected, first Latino mayor of LA since 1872
2006	Millions march for immigrant rights
2007	Housing bubble bursts
2008	Proposition 8 bans same-sex marriage
2009	State furloughs workers in fiscal stalemate
2010	Federal judge overturns ban on same-sex marriage; Jerry Brown wins third term as governor.

Schooners were key to coastal shipping. This rare photochrom print shows one sailing past Alcatraz Island in San Francisco Bay in the 1890s.

INDEX OF PLACES

Death Valley hasn't changed much since the 1960s.

PHOTO CREDITS

Front Cover: La Jolla Coast, California, with red succulents © Jay Beiler, Dreamstime.com; Golden Gate Bridge, San Francisco, California © Linda Bair, Dreamstime.com; Man in Car, Dorothea Lange, Library of Congress, LC-USF34- 019645-C

Back cover: Big Pine Hotel, Archives and Special Collections, William H. Hannon Library, Loyola Marymount University

Ch. 01: Bar scene, Public Domain; Map, U.S. Geological Survey; Forest, Courtesy California Department of Transportation

Ch. 02: Channel Islands, National Park Service; Woman, San Diego History Center; Grinding rock, Laurie Glover; Tabuce, Yosemite NPS Library; Basketweaver, Courtesy Frasher's Fotos and Pomona Public Library; Mohaves, Courtesy of The Bancroft Library, University of California, Berkeley; Map, public domain; Ohlones, Courtesy of The Bancroft Library, University of California, Berkeley; Roundhouse, Laurie Glover; Petroglyph, Laurie Glover

Ch. 03: Mission San Diego, Library of Congress, LOT 13923, no. 404; Map, Library of Congress, G4410 1720 .F42 TIL Vault; Monk, Special Collections, Honnold/Mudd Library of The Claremont Colleges; Felipa Yorba, Courtesy Anaheim Public Library; L. Meza, Special Collections, Honnold/ Mudd Library of The Claremont Colleges; Headstone, Laurie Glover; Gracia de Cruz portrait, Special Collections, Honnold/ Mudd Library of The Claremont Colleges; Firefighter, Cal Fire San Diego County Fire Authority

Ch. 04: Fort Ross, Library of Congress, HABS CAL, 49-FORO,1-5; Sutter, Courtesy of The Bancroft Library, University of California, Berkeley; Pico, Courtesy Anaheim Public Library; Lola Pacheco, Santa Clara University, de Saisset Museum, Leonardo Barbieri, 1852-53, Gift of Monserrat Roca; Mariano Malarin, Santa Clara University, de Saisset Museum, Leonardo Barbieri, 1852-53, Gift of Monserrat Roca; Perez, Courtesy California Historical society; Vaquero, Courtesy of The Bancroft Library, University of California, Berkeley; Mission Play, Special Collections, Honnold/Mudd Library of The Claremont Colleges

Ch. 05: Woodcut, Public Domain; SF 1849, Courtesy of The Bancroft Library, University of California, Berkeley; SF 1850, Courtesy of The Bancroft Library, University of California, Berkeley; Frémont, Harper's Weekly—Public Domain; Mining print, Library of Congress, LC-USZC2-1755; Mining Photo, Library of Congress, LC-USZ62-7122; Vallejo, Courtesy of The Bancroft Library, University of California, Berkeley; *Westward*, Architect of the Capitol; Freeway, Victor Silverman

Ch. 06: Lula Loof and child, Eastman Collection, Special Collections, University of California Library, Davis; Pio Pico house, Whittier Public Library; Oatman, Courtesy History San Jose; Schoolchildren, Special Collections, Honnold/Mudd Library of The Claremont Colleges; Espinoza, Special

Collections, Honnold/Mudd Library of The Claremont Colleges; Ft. Bidwell, Eastman Collection, Special Collections, University of California Library, Davis

Ch. 07: Baseball card, Library of Congress, LOT 13163-09, no. 2; Worker, Courtesy of The Bancroft Library, University of California, Berkeley; Crocker mansion, Courtesy of The Bancroft Library, University of California, Berkeley; 6-in-1 citrus, Courtesy Frasher's Fotos and Pomona Public Library; Crate label, Courtesy Orange Public Library; Packinghouse, Whittier Public Library; Tree, Annie R. Mitchell History Room, Tulare County Library, Visalia, California

Ch. 08: Union hall, Courtesy Labor Archives and Research Center, San Francisco State University; Cartoon, Puck—Public Domain; Store, Courtesy of The Bancroft Library, University of California, Berkeley; Boxcar, Palmquist Collection, Humboldt State University Library; Grange Hall, Eastman Collection, Special Collections, University of California Library, Davis; Orchard, Courtesy of The Bancroft Library, University of California, Berkeley; Explosion, Security Pacific National Bank Collection/Los Angeles Public Library

Ch. 09: Post-earthquake, Library of Congress, LC-G4085- 0201; Soldier in SF, Special Collections, Honnold/Mudd Library of The Claremont Colleges; Postcard, Special Collections, Honnold/Mudd Library of The Claremont Colleges; Johnson, Library of Congress, LC-USZ62-110240; Vallejo Haraszthy, Courtesy of The Bancroft Library, University of California, Berkeley; Stump, Courtesy of The Bancroft Library, University of California, Berkeley; Log Roller, Eastman Collection, Special Collections, University of California Library, Davis; Yosemite Valley, Yosemite NPS Library; Ramona poster, Special Collections, Honnold/Mudd Library of The Claremont Colleges

Ch. 10: *Allegory of California*, The Empire Group/Stock Exchange Tower Associates; Field, Victor Silverman; PCH, Courtesy California Department of Transportation ; Crowe, Tulare Public Library; Salton Sea, Courtesy Frasher's Fotos and Pomona Public Library; Aqueduct gates, Water Resources Center Archives, University of California, Riverside; Crowd, Archives and Special Collections, William H. Hannon Library, Loyola Marymount University; Orchard, Archives and Special Collections, William H. Hannon Library, Loyola Marymount University; Shasta Dam, Russell Lee, Library of Congress, LC-USF35-574; Yolo Bypass, Victor Silverman

Ch. 11: White Fleet, Courtesy of The Bancroft Library, University of California, Berkeley; USS California, National Archives and Records Administration; Planes, Courtesy Frasher's Fotos and Pomona Public Library; Cemetery, US Dept. of Veterans Affairs; Brochure, Special Collections, Honnold/Mudd Library of The Claremont Colleges; Gusher, Library of Congress, LC-USZ62-124337

Ch. 12: Watts Towers, Carol M. Highsmith, Library of Congress, LC-HS503-497; Orchard, Covina Valley Historical Society; Brown Derby, Photo by Chalmers Butterfield; Rappe, Library of Congress, LC-USZ62-13685; Semple McPherson, San Diego History Center ; Bungalow, Special Collections, Honnold/Mudd Library of The Claremont Colleges; Trolley, Whittier Public Library

Ch. 13: *All Races*, Library of Congress, LC-USZ62-137429; Migrants, Courtesy of the Franklin D. Roosevelt Presidential Library and Museum; Picker, Library of Congress, LC-USF34- 016642-E; Rolph, Library of Congress, LC-B2- 1232-13; Mural, Richard Thompson photo: Creative Commons; Striker & cop, Courtesy of the Franklin D. Roosevelt Presidential Library and Museum; Bridges, Courtesy of The Bancroft Library, University of California, Berkeley; Repatriation, *Los Angeles Times* Photographic Archive, Special Collections, Charles E. Young Research Library, UCLA; Strikers, Library of Congress, LC-USF344-007488-Z; Aerial, © Copyright California Department of Transportation; Buck & Playboys, Buck Owens American Music Foundation; Trailer park, Eastman Collection, Special Collections, University of California Library, Davis

Ch. 14: Bay Bridge, Doug Frost; Couple, National Archives and Records Administration; Santa Anita, Courtesy of The Bancroft Library, University of California, Berkeley; Manzanar, Courtesy of The Bancroft Library, University of California, Berkeley; Zoot Suit riot, *Los Angeles Times* Photographic Archive, Special Collections, Charles E. Young Research Library, UCLA; Sleepy Lagoon, *Los Angeles Times* Photographic Archive, Special Collections, Charles E. Young Research Library, UCLA; Poster, Courtesy GLBT Historical Society; Ferlinghetti, Courtesy of The Bancroft Library, University of California, Berkeley; Workers on ferry, Library of Congress, LC-USE6- D-009946

Ch. 15: Vandenberg Base, USAF/Master Sgt. Richard Freeland; Teller, Lawrence Livermore National Laboratory; Freeway, © Copyright California Department of Transportation; Tankster, American Hot Rod Foundation/Louis Senter Collection; Fremont High, *Los Angeles Times* Photographic Archive, Special Collections, Charles E. Young Research Library, UCLA; Disneyland, Special Collections, Honnold/Mudd Library of The Claremont Colleges; School bus, *Los Angeles Times* Photographic Archive, Special Collections, Charles E. Young Research Library, UCLA; Miners, Courtesy of The Bancroft Library, University of California, Berkeley

Ch. 16: Demolition, Library of Congress, HABS CAL, 19-LOSAN, 67-58; Tenney Cttee., *Los Angeles Times* Photographic Archive, Special Collections, Charles E. Young Research Library, UCLA; Movie stars, *Los Angeles Times* Photographic Archive, Special Collections, Charles E. Young Research Library, UCLA; Port, Port of Oakland; Design, Courtesy of the Southern California Library for Social Studies and Research; Eviction, *Los Angeles Times* Photographic Archive, Special Collections, Charles E. Young Research

Library, UCLA; Map, Courtesy Eric Fischer; Church, Robert J. Boser www.airlinesafety.com/editorials/AboutTheEditor

Ch. 17: Demonstration, Courtesy of The Bancroft Library, University of California, Berkeley; Reagan, *Los Angeles Times* Photographic Archive, Special Collections, Charles E. Young Research Library, UCLA; Savio, Courtesy of The Bancroft Library, University of California, Berkeley; Davis & Kalish, *Los Angeles Times* Photographic Archive, Special Collections, Charles E. Young Research Library, UCLA; Raid, *Los Angeles Times* Photographic Archive, Special Collections, Charles E. Young Research Library, UCLA; Chávez , *Los Angeles Times* Photographic Archive, Special Collections, Charles E. Young Research Library, UCLA; Moratorium, *Los Angeles Times* Photographic Archive, Special Collections, Charles E. Young Research Library, UCLA; Salazar, *Los Angeles Times* Photographic Archive, Special Collections, Charles E. Young Research Library, UCLA; Hippies , *Los Angeles Times* Photographic Archive, Special Collections, Charles E. Young Research Library, UCLA; *New Pioneer Family*, ©1972 Nicholas Wilson

Ch. 18: Jarvis, *Los Angeles Times* Photographic Archive, Special Collections, Charles E. Young Research Library, UCLA; Klansmen, Warren Leffler, Library of Congress, LC-U9- 12250M-13A; Queens, Henry LeLeu/GLBT Historical Society; Deukmejian et al., *Los Angeles Times* Photographic Archive, Special Collections, Charles E. Young Research Library, UCLA; Prison, California Department of Corrections; Train, Jim Husband

Ch. 19: Aqueduct, Victor Silverman; Dump, US EPA; Salty fields, USDA/Agricultural Research Service; Birds, Gary Cramer, NFWS; Refuge, Ian Parker, Evanescent Light Photography

Ch. 20: Moss Landing, Chad King, Monterey Bay National Marine Sanctuary; Homeless camp, Kelly Borkert; Villa family, *Los Angeles Times* Photographic Archive, Special Collections, Charles E. Young Research Library, UCLA; Webvan, Mark Coggins; Arrest, Courtesy of ICE; Pow Wow, UC Davis, Debbie Aldridge; McMansion, Brendel; Signs, photo: The Truth About; Arnold, Steven Hallon, Office of the Governor; Seals, Chad King, Monterey Bay National Marine Sanctuary

Ch. 21: March, Jonathan McIntosh; California, NASA www.visibleearth.nasa.gov

End matter: Mono Lake, Mono Lake Committee; Ranch hands, Special Collections, Honnold/Mudd Library of The Claremont Colleges; Bay schooner, Library of Congress, LOT 13923, no. 73 ; Death Valley, National Park Service; Palm Tree, Victor Silverman

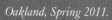
Oakland, Spring 2011.